The Governance of European Public Goods

"Stefan Collignon has put together an excellent set of essays around the theme of the desirability and legitimacy of public goods provision by the EU. This is an important contribution to the new debate about European integration, and more specifically the conditions under which the EU could take significant steps forward in deeper economic and political integration. The chapters combine new empirical insights, innovative theoretical ideas, and powerful analysis of the challenges and options for Europe."
—Professor Simon Hix, *Harold Laski Professor of Political Science, Department of Government, London School of Economics, UK*

"Is devising a new "Res Publica" the way forward for the European Union? This book analyses how rethinking the way in which public goods are supplied and administered by supranational institutions could reshape the future of European integration eventually leading to peace, prosperity and happiness."
—Professor Leila Simona Talani, *Professor of International Political Economy, King's College London, UK*

"There is a real need for a volume like this. As rational beings, we all crave a range of public goods. Where does Europe fit in to their most effective attainment? How can such an approach help to explain what has been achieved and what hasn't? Forget the talk of 'After Europe', this volume asks the basic questions afresh and offers greater clarity."
—Professor Kevin Featherstone, *Eleftherios Venizelos Professor of Contemporary Greek Studies and Director of the Hellenic Observatory, London School of Economics, UK*

Stefan Collignon
Editor

The Governance of European Public Goods

Towards a Republican Paradigm
of European Integration

Editor
Stefan Collignon
Scuola Superiore Sant'Anna
Pisa, Italy

and

London School of Economics
and Political Sciences
London, UK

ISBN 978-3-319-64011-2   ISBN 978-3-319-64012-9   (eBook)
DOI 10.1007/978-3-319-64012-9

Library of Congress Control Number: 2017950691

Cover credit: JOHN KELLERMAN/Alamy Stock Photo

Printed on acid-free paper

This Palgrave Macmillan imprint is published by Springer Nature
The registered company is Springer International Publishing AG
The registered company address is: Gewerbestrasse 11, 6330 Cham, Switzerland

List of Figures

List of Tables

1

Introduction

Stefan Collignon

The European Union stumbles from crisis to crisis. It is in need of a fundamental overhaul, while the geostrategic context is changing rapidly. Sixty year ago, the Treaty of Rome promised peace among European nations, freedom from Soviet domination and prosperity for citizens. While the promise was kept, it has become doubtful that it can be sustained.

From the beginning, the European integration process combined high hopes and pragmatism. Europe's Founding Fathers dreamt of the distant goal of creating a European federal state, but actual integration was based on practical steps of transnational cooperation between economic and political agents. The dream has inspired European federalists like Altiero Spinelli, but it was the realism of Jean Monnet's "community method", which has transformed Europe. It had the advantage of

S. Collignon (✉)
London School of Economics and Political Sciences, London, UK
e-mail: S.Collignon@lse.ac.uk

S. Collignon
Scuola Superior Sant'Anna, Pisa, Italy

© The Author(s) 2017
S. Collignon, *The Governance of European Public Goods*,
DOI 10.1007/978-3-319-64012-9_1

1

avoiding political obstacles by allowing governments to remain the ultimate decision makers, while agreeing to delegate some limited competences to Community institutions. Nevertheless, both visions shared the
idea that the "process of creating an ever closer union among the peoples of Europe" (Lisbon Treaty, Preamble) would create peace and lasting prosperity in Europe.

This process has now stopped. While peace still prevails and the
Soviet Union has disappeared, prosperity is under threat and social tensions fuel uncooperative nationalism again. The failure of controlling
external borders and migration flows supports those who are the enemies of open societies. Eurosceptics call for the re-nationalisation of a
growing list of policy responsibilities and suggest the exit from the euro
or even the European Union.

However, the problem is not the European Union; the problem is the
failing governance of the EU. The intergovernmental mode of governing Europe's public goods has become dysfunctional because national
governments take decisions, which reflect local policy consensus but
generate unwarranted external effects in other member states. For example, an irresponsible government in Greece triggered the Euro crisis
by not abiding with the rules of the Stability and Growth Pact, which
destabilised financial markets in the Euro Area. The subsequent lack of
solidarity in dealing with the Greek debt problems worsened the crisis
and then spilled over into Ireland, Spain, Portugal, Cyprus and Italy.[1]
For nearly a decade, excessive austerity under German leadership has
prevented Europe for from pulling out of the crisis and caused permanent high unemployment and a growing popular disenchantment with
the single currency. Even in the most harmonized policy area, foreign
trade, Europe has become paralysed: when Europe and Canada were
ready to sign a trade agreement, a Belgian province could hold up the
Union and undermine its credibility in the world. In the domain of
foreign policy, the shortcomings are even more apparent. The political
adventurism in Libya by the French President Sarkozy and the British

---

[1]See Stefan Collignon, Piero Esposito and Hanna Lierse: European Sovereign Bailouts, Political
Risk and the Economic Consequences of Mrs. Merkel, in: Journal of International Commerce,
Economics and Policy Vol. 4, No. 2 (2013).

Prime Minister Cameron has pushed North African regimes from authoritarianism into anarchy, while in the resulting refugee crisis each EU member state was left alone to deal with the consequences. Because the European Union has no effective border control, it is now forced to surrender to the demands and blackmail from the emerging dictatorship in Turkey. Even in the fight against terrorism on European territory, national administrations seem unable to identify and communicate the movements of undesirable persons.

As the capacity of the EU to solve its problems is diminishing, the legitimacy of the European integration project vanishes. It was built on the promise of peace, prosperity and democracy, but the governance of the Union seems to interfere with democracy, undermine prosperity and no longer guarantees peace. Democracy is the core problem, because Europe is not dealing with the contentious issue of sovereignty. Sovereignty refers to who has the *authority* to appoint a government. In modern democracies this authority belongs to the citizens who are affected by the policy decisions of such a government. But in the EU, sovereignty is "pooled", a euphemism that describes a system where national governments instead of citizens authorize policies. By definition, these governments will always represent the partial interests of their local constituencies and never the common interest of all Europeans. As a consequence, citizens perceive the Union as systematically preventing them from exercising their democratic rights of choosing the general orientations of the policies of their choice. The European Council says "We are Europe", like Louis XIV said "l'Etat, c'est moi". The Council decides and rules, but citizens cannot change the policies that it adopts. If proof was needed, the election of the Tsipras government in Greece made clear that it is impossible to change policies, which affect the whole of Europe and the Euro Area, by national elections. European public goods are indivisible. British voters drew the logical conclusion: if they wanted to have a say in public affairs, they needed to bring sovereignty back into the national fold and rid themselves of all European public goods.

But the British are not alone to contemplate leaving the European Union or the euro. In nearly all member states populist movements attack European integration. They claim that democracy is the power of the people, and that the people should *decide directly* what they want through referenda. Authoritarian governments in Eastern Europe believe that an elected government can do what it wants. They do not believe in the protection of equal individuals by laws and rights. Thus, populist governments in Poland and Hungary claim to implement "the will of the silent majority", which gives them the right to restrain the civic and constitutional rights enshrined in the European Treaties. This is not the philosophy on which the European Union was built.

Populist democracy ignores the danger of "the tyranny of the majority" which Tocqueville and John Stuart Mill saw in the excesses of French Jacobin democracy. Populists carry the flag of democracy, but they betray the values of modern democracies, which protect individuals. In modern liberal democracies, citizens have individual rights that protect them against the interference of the state and the conformism of community. Modern democracy is a deliberative and representative parliamentary democracy. Yet unfortunately, the conditions for a liberal democracy are hollowed out by intergovernmental cooperation between governments and do not exist at the level of the European Union, except in embryonic form.

Power is not the same as authority; authority invests power. In modern democratic constitutions, the people invest their parliament with the power to decide policies and to choose a government. Citizens are *represented* in the parliament that they elect, but given the enormous complexity of many issues they do not take policy decisions themselves. Nor are elected leaders authorized to impose their will on everyone.

How can the European Union overcome its crisis? One option is to dismantle and exit Europe. The British vote on Brexit has revealed the tensions, which had already accumulated for some time. No doubt, if Europe does not change track, such voices will find support in even more countries. But while Brexit stands in the British tradition of locating sovereignty in parliament, giving up the *acquis communautaire* is damaging the interests of many citizens inside and outside of Britain as the difficult Brexit negotiations reveal. Once the damage is done and Europe is broken up, it is hard to put the genie of destruction back into the bottle.

Second, the orthodox approach to the crisis is muddling through in the hope that the economy will improve because member states have done "the necessary reforms" and the rule-based system of governance will prevent further shocks. Maybe this will work. But this strategy does not address the democratic deficit which fuels the popular frustration with European integration. It does not solve the long run problems of Europe's governance, although it may give some short run reprieve. In fact, we witness more and more frequently that politics and not economics is causing shocks to the system.

Finally, a long run perspective is articulated by calls for "more Europe", although little is said what this means in practical terms. Protagonists of the orthodox approach believe more and better rules and surveillance will prevent crises and improve the efficiency of conventional policies. Their reforms create a more bureaucratic Europe, but do not deal with the democratic issue. Federalists look back to Spinelli and Monnet and hope to federate existing member states into a new state-like Union. But half a century of European integration has shown that nation states do not abolish themselves.

The European crisis challenges us to rethink the integration project. The great theories, which traced the path toward an "ever closer Union", were federalism, neofunctionalism and liberal intergovernmentalism. Each of these theories has contributed to the integration and study of Europe. Federalists have emphasized that the traditional European nation states were too small to be economically viable and therefore proposed the creation of a larger unit. Neofunctionalism took the debate away from nationalistic identity issues and focussed instead on state-transcending functions of public welfare. Liberal intergovernmentalism recognized that the common European interests of economic actors matter, even if they are articulated by member state governments. However, all of these approaches have avoided the issue of sovereignty rather than attempted to solve it.

In this book we have taken a fresh approach. We call it the republican paradigm. It is derived from the old Roman idea of *res publica*, of the public good. We define the European Union by the public goods it supplies to European citizens and ask how these public goods can best be administered. Rather than getting lost in peoples' problematic identities and cultures, we think it is more productive to focus on people's interests. This interest-focussed approach is a new form of functionalism insofar it takes the functions of public goods seriously.

Public goods provide benefits to a group of people who are their owners. Different public goods therefore affect individuals in different groups. European public goods affect all citizens in Europe; national public goods affect citizens in a given nation state; local public goods only concern those who live in proximity. Hence, individual citizens are simultaneously owners of local, national and European public goods. The question is then how do they authorize the governance of these public goods? By framing it in these terms, it becomes clear that belonging to a community or nation is not the right framework for controlling goods that reach a broader community. The nation state becomes dysfunctional for the decision of who ought to authorize policies that affect all citizens. The correct question would ask which goods affect all European citizens and, consequently, how should they authorize a common European government to administer them.

Republicanism is one of the oldest political philosophies in Europe and it has many articulations. The conservative version puts the accent on the communitarian sovereignist dimension, but our focus on public goods emphasizes liberal democratic values in a theory of individual responsibility for the collective good, i.e. participatory politics, constitutional government, and secure property (Connell 2000). The republican paradigm is therefore able to transcend the *aporia* of traditional integration theories. It shifts attention from identity to interests, it includes functionalism as the criterion for government competences, and it supports liberal democracy by acknowledging that individuals are the owners of public goods.

Economic theories of public goods are also complex as becomes apparent in the following chapters. The literature has classified defence and security as the classic examples for "pure public goods". They need to be provided by a government that has the power to do so. However, hybrid public goods, such as club goods and common resource goods, are more frequent. We have focussed in this book on such hybrid public goods, especially in the economic domain, because the creation of the euro has profoundly transformed the logic of governing European public goods.

The authors of the following chapters of this book have studied particular aspects of the role public goods play in the European integration process.

Robert Berith in Chap. 2 lays the ground by reviewing the basics of public goods theory and applies it to the neomedieval theory of governance in the European setting. He points out several inconsistencies, which render neo-medievalism as an unsuitable governance model for the EU.

Stefan Collignon in Chap. 3 develops the republican paradigm on the background of public goods theory and develops the need for a European government from the incentive structure of European externalities. He shows that policy centralization is necessary for exclusive common resource goods, but not all public goods.

Sebastian Diessner in Chap. 4 studies in greater detail the policy paradigm that governs Europe's monetary union, revealing its narrow focus on the public goods of 'sound' money and finances. He examines whether the euro crisis has undermined the paradigm and finds that, despite puzzling crisis responses, its prescriptions remain largely intact. This underlines the importance of advancing alternative approaches, such as the lens of European public goods championed in this book.

Benjamin Spoerer in Chap. 5 undertakes a thorough analysis of the implications of principal-agent relations which emerge from the existence of public goods. Referring to the debate about a democratic deficit in the EU, he shows that P-A theory reveals weaknesses within the different arguments used in the debate. It becomes clear that distinct arguments and assumptions lead to mutual incomprehension, and thus create the current deadlock in discussions.

Sebastian Salch in Chap. 6 asks the question why and how the governance changes in the European Union. The ever looming question of further and deeper integration gets a new answer with the help of public good studies, the distribution conflict and economic theories. He outlines a new approach and test it with the hiccup of European integration, the Empty Chair crisis, and the European Debt crisis.

Finally, Angela Han Shiyun in Chap. 7 applies the public goods paradigm to regional integration amongst the member states of the Association of Southeast Asian Nations (ASEAN). She uses the public goods paradigm to examine why ASEAN regional integration has been significantly slower than that of the European Union and examines how greater and deeper institutionalisation in ASEAN can address the governance of public goods in ASEAN. We have included her chapter because it shows that the logic of the republican paradigm of regional integration is not specific to Europe. It is a global challenge.

The world is changing rapidly. Europe is no longer challenged from within, but increasingly also threatened from outside. The capacity of absorbing and integrating refugees from the Middle East and North Africa has reached its limits. Having extended the EU's zone of influence far into the former Russian sphere, the backlash has taken violent turns in the Ukraine and may even threaten some new member states of the Union. The American retreat under Obama and Trump that is now doubled up by economic protectionism and anti-globalisation, leaves Europe alone in an increasingly hostile world. Europe would need efficient border controls at sea and military capacities in general. It would need a coherent common foreign policy not only with respect to the immediate crisis locations in its neighbourhood, but also to address the potential that can be mobilised in relation to the Far East. China and Europe seem to emerge as the two leading free-trade protagonists in the world. Responding to the Chinese government's Belt and Road Initiative offers new opportunities which ought to be shaped by the European Union as well.

All these are European public goods which potentially affect each citizen in the European Union. They deserve in-depth research and a separate volume. The European Commission has taken a first initiative to start the coordination of defence, although it is hardly more than creating a single market for weapons procurement. The foreign policy dimension is more elaborate, but the High Representative of the European Union for Foreign Affairs and Security Policy is hardly more than a coordinator of national policies. None of these initiatives can claim that it provides the European citizens with an efficient and democratically supported governance. The reason for this failure may well be the lack of a new paradigm to think Europe differently. This book proposes an alternative.

References

Collignon, S., Esposito, P., Lierse, H. (2013). European sovereign bailouts, political risk and the economic consequences of Mrs. Merkel. *Journal of International Commerce, Economics and Policy (JICEP)*, 4(2).

Connell, W. J. (2000). The republican idea. In J. Hankins (Ed.), *Renaissance Civic Humanism* (pp. 14–29). Cambridge: CUP.

2

European Public Goods in the Neo-Medieval Model of Governance

Robert Berith

What is the right dosage of market and state is the central question of the European Union governance. Does the EU need a government or could it be 'governed' by a market? Each time the EU is hit by a severe crisis, the state-market dilemma is reignited. Today, Europe is on fire! The word 'crisis' is repeated in European tabloids so often that it is more appropriate to speak of chronicle illness instead. That illness is the EU governance itself, since it has become unpopular, undemocratic but, worst of all, unresponsive to economic, security and social challenges of the post-Cold War era.

It was the fall of the Soviet empire and the economic power shift from the Atlantic to the Pacific Ocean that left Europe in permanent crisis of performance. The European elites, at first, responded with grandiose integration initiatives—'Project 1992', the Single Market and the Euro—to bring back much needed economic growth. The promised growth has never arrived, which gave rise to legitimacy crisis amplified by the elite-drive widening of the EU to include 12 new

R. Berith(✉)
University of Economics, Prague, Czech Republic
e-mail: rberith@gmail.com

© The Author(s) 2017
S. Collignon, *The Governance of European Public Goods*,
DOI 10.1007/978-3-319-64012-9_2

9

member states, largely ex-communist countries from Central and Eastern Europe. The popular unease with the sluggish growth and the Eastern enlargement was manifested in the Constitutional Treaty debacle. Astonished EU leaders called for a 'period of reflection' which concluded with the ratification of the Lisbon Treaty. Nevertheless, before the EU leaders could grandiosely celebrate the coming into the force of the Lisbon Treaty, a new economic hurricane was taking off in the US real-estate market, which would struck the EU with a devastating blow. The Global Financial Crisis revealed all flaws in the design of the Euro and the very existence of the Euro-area was threatened in the dire Euro crisis. Germany as a group leader of creditor countries took hardliner stance and imposed severe austerity measures on the European periphery. Grexit and the break-up of the Euro-zone have been on the table of countless European Council meetings ever since. However, in the 21st century globalised world, there is no time for endless EU-like intergovernmental summits and meetings. Notwithstanding that the EU had not yet solved its internal economic governance problems, Russian irredentism in the Eastern Ukraine, terrorists attacks inspired by the Islamic State and swarms of migrants put the union's both internal and external security under substantial stress. The migration crisis offered a unique opportunity for the austerity-afflicted periphery to strike back at Germany and other creditor states by free-riding on the migrant problem. The most recent episode in the "EU crisis" series is the Brexit. The UK's citizens have democratically decided to free-ride on the EU, by rejecting to bear the costs of maintaining European public goods but hoping to get free access to the single market. All these crisis in the past 25 years have been nurturing an extremely dangerous trend in European politics: the rise of both left-wing and right-wing populist and extremist political parties in every single EU member state.

When compared with global players USA, China, Japan or Russia, the political impotence of the EU is crystal clear. The EU governance model does not permit swift responsiveness to contemporary challenges. The EU is like one giant institutionalised talk-shop in which decision-making advances by the lowest common denominator. It is in this context that a new governance model is being debated. Federalists and supranationalists argue that the EU can surpass its imbroglio only by acquiring more state power. Euro-sceptics claim that the crisis is the product of too much control amassed by the EU and advocate for the re-nationalisation of the state control. Postmodernists defend that the best solution is more market, less state. The debate between market and state in the EU governance is served.

Since the end of traditional means of social organisation, markets and states acquired their modern meaning and have been co-evolving as two fundamental institutions of modernity. When modernity broke up traditions, it also 'emptied time' (Giddens 1990: 18) and disembedded private space from the holistic hierarchy. Therefore, markets could develop in abstract spaces where individuals exchange utilities through contracts. Money, as bridge in time, and private property became essential features of the market. However, the separation of time and space created uncertainty and the modern world came to be fundamentally insecure. States, as systems for interiorising the externalities of individualised and decentralised action, took the role of re-instating certainty and correcting market imperfections. States provide the general framework in which markets could efficiently operate. Given the association of power and state, the concept of state has been the subject of continuous contestation and debate (Skinner 2009).

Two theories of state emerged and competed with each other: one in which the authority of state power is located in the government which is separated from and controls the state's body, and the other where the people are the sovereign who authorise the government to act on their behalf. In the last two decades started to predominate what Skinner (2009: 361) calls reductionist view of the state. It indicates that the state is understood as a way of referring to an established apparatus of government, which could be argued to be of slight and diminishing significance in the globalised world. Numerous postmodern models of governance have made their appearances and their focal point has been the European Union, which constitutes market without state. To move to post-modernity means 'that the trajectory of social development is taking us away from the institutions of modernity towards a new and distinct type of social order' (Giddens 1990: 46). One of such postmodern approaches is the new medievalism, or neo-medievalism. This paper proposes to contemplate the neo-medieval paradigm as the model for

European governance. Concretely, this chapter will evaluate whether the neo-medieval model of governance is a viable solution for the provision of European public goods. This is an especially relevant inquiry given that Europe is looking for new and creative solutions to get out of its numerous crisis.

This chapter is divided into two parts. In the first part, I review the theoretical frameworks of public goods and collective action. Concretely, I will try to give answer to following questions: what are public goods?; which public goods do we have on the European level?; and what are the most crucial problems in their provision?. The second part explains the neo-medieval model of governance and then applies on it the theory of public goods to examine the implications in the European context. I argue that neo-medievalism, as a model of governance, is not suited for the provision of European common resource goods. Neo-medievalism implicitly assumes that all public goods are inclusive club goods which has a potential to lead to a greater number and scope of externalities. Lastly, I will conclude with a discussion of the applicability of neo-medievalism and the effectiveness of imaginative theorising.

Theory of Public Goods

It is generally assumed that markets are the most efficient way of providing private goods. But markets in order to function properly rely on a set of elements that they cannot provide or guarantee themselves, such as property rights, predictability, or safety. Mechanisms are needed to reduce uncertainty and transaction costs. Few of us are capable of imagining a world in which the rule of law is non-existent. In addition, there are goods such as highways and street lights that are of immense utility to all but nonetheless cannot be provided by a single individual or company either because the cost of provision is too high or the means to ensuring that the provider is compensated is inadequate. These goods differ from the private goods we buy in the market, like apples or television. They are called public goods. This section is focused on the concept of public goods. It will try to identify what are the different types of public goods, what problems occur in their provision and what public goods are European.

What Are Public Goods?

Firstly, it is important to explain the economic concept of good. An economic good provides a utility, that is to say, it is a thing that confers upon individuals certain effect (Collignon 2011: 44). When this effect is positive, we speak of economic goods. When it is negative, we use the term economic bad. The value of the good is its net benefit, that is the difference between costs of production and the conferred effect. Among goods, or bads, are included material objects such as cars, roads and schools as well as intangible things such as government policies, peace, price stability and law. Public goods are generally defined in contraposition to private goods. The key characteristic of private goods is that the property or possession of the good is transferred or denied depending on the payment of its price. Since the supply of private goods is limited, price acts as an exclusion instrument. When one individual consumes a private good, it cannot be consumed by others. You cannot have the same apple that I had just eaten. Private goods are excludable and rivalrous in consumption.

In contrast, public goods are non-excludable and non-rivalrous. After a public good is provided, it is impossible to exclude individuals from its benefits. Similarly, various individuals can consume a public good at the same time without any reduction of their marginal benefits. Public infrastructures such as traffic lights or lighthouses are typical examples of public goods. If one ship safely navigates to the dock thanks to a lighthouse, its utility for other ships is not reduced. There is no rivalry between consumers of public goods. Un-rivalrous goods have an unlimited supply. Everyone can consume them without limiting the consumption of others. Identically, to exclude the usage of the lighthouse would be economically and politically very costly, not to mention that it would be practically impossible. Its benefits are non-excludable. A peace treaty is another example of a public good. When a war is averted and a community is protected from external dangers, all members of the community profit. Similar illustrations can be made for law enforcement or price stability.

So far we have discussed only pure private and pure public goods, but theoretics of public goods (Collignon 2004, 2011; Desai 2003; Kaul et al. 1999) distinguish another two mixed categories of impure public goods. Impure public goods are either non-rivalrous or non-excludable

	Rivalrous	Non-rivalrous
Excludable	**private goods** *(apples, cars, private pool)*	**club goods** *(museum, tennis club, cable television network)*
Non-excludable	**common resource goods** *(fish stock, oil well, central bank liquidity)*	**pure public goods** *(judicial system, financial stability, public infrastructure)*

Fig. 2.1 Typology of public goods

but not both. Most public goods are of the impure type (Desai 2003). The first impure category, called "club goods", refers to goods that are non-rivalrous in consumption but excludable. For instance, the entrance to the museum is contingent upon payment of an entrance fee. Individuals who do not pay the fee cannot enter and are excluded from its benefits. When one person enters the museum, the museum is not closed down neither is there less of it for other visitors. In addition, club goods are inclusive in a sense that it is advantageous to include more members in the group provided that the maximum club capacity is not exceeded (Collignon 2004: 918). This is because members' net benefits increase as the group expands. With more visitors coming in, the art gallery is able to raise more funds to acquire new collections and all visitors benefit equally.

The second category of impure goods, called "common resource goods", represents goods that are non-excludable but rivalrous in consumption. Their total benefit is fixed and available to all. When one benefits, there will be less for others. Typical example are common resources that can't be replenished, such as common woods, mineral deposits, fish stocks or interconnected oil wells. Because a lake is common, everyone can come and catch a fish in it. Yet, the lake's total fish stock is limited and when one fisherman catches a fish, others will be getting less. There will be rivalry in consumption among fishermen. Common resource goods, as well as private goods, have an exclusive character (Collignon 2004: 918). When the size of a group that extracts common resources increases, average benefit of every group member falls. Consequently, individuals profiting from common resource goods try to exclude others. Figure 2.1 resumes all types of public goods.

Externalities and the Role of State

Closely linked to economic goods is the concept of 'externality'. Economic goods, both public and private, pose the problem of externalities. Kaul et al. (1999: xx) define externality as the difference between private and public benefit. Externalities arise when an individual takes an action but does not bear all the costs or benefits of his action. Depending whether these external effects increase or decrease the utility of the affected person, we speak of positive or negative externalities. When one person cleans the snow from the doorway of a communal building, all the occupants of that building stand to benefit. Similarly, if one country builds a dam on a higher part of a river, the countries on lower part are negatively affected by decreased water flow. Externalities are the major source of human conflict. If it was not for them, everyone's needs could be satisfied maximally by efficient markets. However, this is not possible and human societies need to employ mechanisms to internalise the externalities of human action. Governments have emerged as a central actor in providing collective goods and correcting market failures. Nevertheless, as pinpointed by Collignon (2004: 919), governments do not operate in the vacuum and governmental intervention produces its own externalities which are sometimes more a problem than a solution. This opens the discussion about the most efficient form of governance, which still has not been settled in the political and academic circles.

Historically, human societies have experienced multiple forms of governance with markets and states playing different and altering roles in the provision of public goods. When Samuelson (1954) set analytical foundations for what would become the theory of public goods in his seminal article, the state as an institution was at its highest point. Samuelson (1954) assumed that market and state overlap and he attributed to the state a greater role in the provision of public goods. The provision of public goods was one of the central justifications for the existence of the state (Desai 2003: 63). Nevertheless, Desai (2003) also demonstrated that public preferences for the provision of collective goods by the state have been changing according to socio-economical developments. Prior to the industrial revolution most of the things we now consider as public goods were provided by private actors or not provided at all. The traditional domain of the state was the provision of security and waging of war. The increased demand for the delivery of a vast array of public goods—sanitation, education, water or public infrastructures—by the state occurred only after the Europe's population quickly multiplied and concentrated in cities following the industrial revolution. The negative spillovers caused by crowded populations became too costly for private actors to bear. The 19th century western governments, now seen as agents of the people, gradually became more involved in public life. In the aftermath of the WWII, demands for public goods again increased, which fuelled the rise of European welfare states. However, the 'shaky' seventies, the rise of globalisation and neoliberal politics, undermined the trust in the state as the ultimate provider of public goods. This led to increased prominence of markets, public-private partnerships and club-based provision of collective goods.

In order to assess how markets and states fare in the effective delivery of public goods, it is necessary to look at the peculiarities and problems that affect their provision.

Problems in the Provision of Public Goods

Desai (2003: 64) described the process of provision of public goods in three steps, also known as the three Ps, as preference revelation, political bargaining, and production (Fig. 2.2). Firstly, a preference revelation mechanism is required through which the individuals can express what goods they prefer in the collective domain and how much they are willing to contribute. Secondly, as individual preferences may be incompatible between themselves, a form of political bargaining is necessary to decide and prioritise which goods and what quantity of those goods are going to be included in the public budget. The last step is the actual production and delivery of public goods realised either by public or private agents. Problems in the provision of collective goods occur especially in the first two phases. How do we collectively aggregate and prioritise conflicting individual preferences into a single public preference? This is the central problem in the theory of public goods (Desai 2003: 71). Every system of governance aspiring to efficiently provide public goods must have concrete mechanisms for revelation and prioritisation of public preference.

For private goods, price operates as an effective mechanism for the revelation of consumer preferences. Consumers react to different prices of various products by adjusting their levels of consumption. Each buyer must reveal his/her preferences by bidding. As a result, markets are able to supply every consumer who is willing to pay the marginal costs, and to exclude those who are not willing or not able to pay the price. However, market fails to disclose individual preferences for public

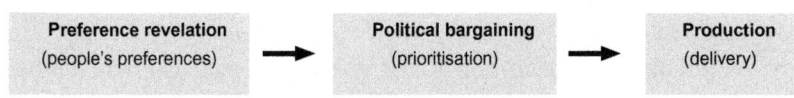

Fig. 2.2 The three steps in the provision of public goods

goods. Individuals have incentives not to reveal their preferences (Olson 1965) and, what's more, they derive interdependent utilities from public goods (Wicksell 1958). Samuelson (1954) assumed that individuals have independent utilities through which the aggregation of marginal utilities is realised. This allowed him to avoid the problems with revelation of preferences and prioritisation (Desai 2003). For Samuelson (1954: 388) collective preferences are knowable to a collective mind and constitute the 'ethical observer's optimum'. However, few of us pursue static set of needs without taking into account what others want. The opinion and behaviour of others is important to our decisions. Wicksell (1958) argued that individuals may have interdependent utilities, where each person's benefit depends on what everyone else does. As a consequence, a deliberation and public contestation between individuals or their representatives is needed to establish the balance between marginal utilities of public goods and their price (Wicksell 1958: 82). Collignon (2003, 2004, 2011) sustains that voting and democratic government are one type, however imperfect, of revelation and prioritisation of public preferences. In democratic states, political parties play essential roles in aggregating citizens' preferences and, consequently, in budget allocations (Desai 2003: 74). Every party (ideally) has its own political program which is different from the rest of parties, and citizens by voting for one party reveal their preferences for public goods. After that, it is in the legislative assemblies where elected representatives bargain and negotiate on behalf of their voters.

Mancur Olson and Garrett Hardin, two prominent scholars of the 20th century, showed that the provision of public goods requires also an efficient coercion mechanism to prevent free-riding and degradation of common resources. Olson (1965) proved that unless there exists some coercion device, public goods tend to be underproduced because rational self-interested individuals in large groups do not act to achieve their common interest. In sufficiently large groups where individual contribution makes no perceptible difference to the whole, rational individuals have incentive to act as free riders (Olson 1965: 44). That is to avoid contribution in hopes that others will pay and that the benefits of public good could be enjoyed for free. This decision is individually rational even if the public good is not provided since the free-rider will bear no costs and avoid the worst case scenario: contributing to something that might not be provided. However, if a large part of the group has the same attitude, the public good will not be delivered. In short, we can say that the larger the group, the bigger the incentive for individuals to free ride.

In a much cited article, Hardin (1968) explained another problem of collective action, 'the tragedy of commons'. This problem is characteristic of common resource goods, such as fish stocks or common pastures. In his (Hardin 1968: 1244) example of a pasture open to all, individual herdsman tries to increase his benefit by keeping as many cattle as possible on the commons. However, what improves his gain, decreases that of the other herdsmen. If multiple herdsmen have this attitude, the common pasture is quickly overgrazed and overall utility of all herdsmen is reduced given that the commons is now depleted and nobody benefits. Numerous tragedies of commons led quickly to privatisation of common resources (where it was possible) or to appearance of coercive bodies regulating access to them.

Despite the fact that a coercive device is required for the provision of pure public goods and common resource goods, it is not indispensable for club goods to be delivered. Collignon (2004) explained that whether cooperation happens or not in the absence of a coercion mechanism depends on the convergence or divergence of actors' preferences. In the case that actors have converging preferences, individual actions are complementary and actors cooperate in the interest of their common good. This is the situation of strategic complementarities and it is characteristic for inclusive club goods (Collignon 2004, 2011). In the other case of diverging preferences, voluntary cooperation does not occur for the simple reason that 'an individual can increase his/her own utility by doing the opposite of what everyone else would like to do' (Collignon 2011: 48). This is the situation of strategic substitutability and is typical for common resource goods and tragedy of commons.

Next, we must consider the provision of public goods in the international arena. The international system is characterised by the absence of coercive authority that could bide actors to cooperate. There is no global state and international organisations like the United Nations have little or no coercive power. Neither are there any international political parties that could aggregate citizens preferences for the international goods. As a result, public goods can be provided on the international level only through voluntary, non-binding cooperation either by governments or non-governmental actors. However, as was discussed above, the cooperation will only take place in the case of actors' strategic complementarities and stands to be more effective in smaller groups of states. Bilateral cooperation is more successful than multilateral. International clubs and regional integration proliferate, whereas international commons are characterised by long and thorny disputes.

Kaul et al. (1999) identified three key weaknesses in the current arrangement for providing global public goods. The first weakness, the jurisdictional gap, is the discrepancy between the national unit of policy making and the international scope of externalities. In integrated and interdependent markets, there is a growing number of situations where decisions made in one state have repercussions and spillovers in the jurisdictions of other states. This is especially true in the European Union where 'the set of those individuals who are affected by a policy decision and those who are involved in or legitimising these decisions do not coincide' (Collignon 2003: 30). To close the jurisdictional gap, Kaul et al. (1999: xxviii) proposes to strengthen regional and global governing bodies. The second weakness is the participation gap. All actors, including civil society and private sector must have a voice, an appropriate opportunity to contribute and have access to the produced goods (Kaul et al. 1999: xxix). The incentive gap is the last weakness. For a cooperation to be durable and efficient, it must offer appropriate incentives to individual actors. Nevertheless, we learned above that the incentive structure is different for club goods than for common resource goods.

European Public Goods

What are European public goods? For Collignon (2011: 45) public goods are European when they 'are available for all European residents and they exclude non-Europeans'. It is the scope of their externalities that makes them European. With advancement of the European integration, a large quantity of public goods now have wider and deeper impact on the continent. Especially since the establishment of the European Monetary Union (EMU), the growing interdependence between national economies within the same monetary framework has led to an increasing range of spillovers into other jurisdictions (Collignon 2003, 2011). The single market, fundamental rights of European citizens, price and exchange rate stability or freedom of movement are examples of European public goods. Collignon (2011) also includes policy areas such as monetary policy, Common Agricultural Policy (CAP), Common Foreign and Security Policy (CFSP), industrial policy, competition and antitrust policies, environment and energy policy. Responsible for a majority of these European goods are either supranational institutions, such as the Commission or the European Central Bank (ECB), and the intergovernmental Council. Nevertheless, there are goods that originate in member states and that have external effects on citizens elsewhere. Control of Union's external borders, training of human capital, national fiscal positions or dealing with cross-border crime are examples of goods that produce spillovers at the European level.

It is clear that the EU faces various, if not all, of the problems in provision of public goods discussed in the previous section. The EU lacks a proper coercive device and, instead, relies on the governmental apparatus of its member states. Its mechanism of preference revelation is ambivalent at least and not-functioning at most. Elections to the European Parliament (EP) are short of the public attention and their outcome has only a limited effect on the delivery of European public goods. Decision making in the Council does not reflect the collective European preference since the participating government officials represent only part of the electorate of their home country. On the other hand, independent technocratic institutions are efficient only in the delivery of public goods which have independent utilities, static public preference and which require a long term commitment. Even in spite of these setbacks, the European integration was able to proceed with voluntary cooperation and a number of European public goods linked to the single market have been delivered. This is because the creation of European communities, the common market, Schengen or the Euro-area can be contemplated as European club goods (Collignon 2004, 2011). We know that 'clubs' are inclusive and that club members' incentives are characterised by strategic complementarities.

Notwithstanding, as showed by Collignon (2011), with the creation of the Euro common resource goods have become dominant within the European Union. In his words (Collignon 2011: 50), 'the Euro introduces strategic substitutabilities into the interactions of member states and creates political incentives for governments to free ride on their partners'. In a market economy, money operates as the hard budget constraint. The scarcity of money is what ensures that buyer's market functions efficiently. In Europe the Euro is created by the independent ECB whose primary objective is the maintenance of price stability. Granted that the Euro supply is limited, it is rival in consumption in a sense that when liquidity concentrates in one member state, it is not available in others. The member state which benefits from large liquidity inflows has all the incentives to free-ride by letting its economy to boom while others suffer and by not adopting monetary and fiscal policies which would help to stabilise the Euro-area, the common public good. This has been the case in the painful Euro-crisis when money left the troubled European South (previously the most booming region) to the more secure Northern European countries such as Germany (the former laggard of Europe). All member states would have been worse off had the Euro failed and yet, the national governments were unwilling to cooperate and the collapse was only prevented at the last hour. The unwillingness to cooperate is explained as the product of strategic substitutability that governs the Euro, European common resource good par excellence (Collignon 2011).

Neo-Medieval Paradigm

One of the consequences of growing globalisation of markets has been the questioning of the state as an appropriate institution for governance in the 21st century. Simultaneously, the belief in complete and efficient markets has been on the rise and terms like transnational networks, self- and co-regulation, output legitimacy, or public-private partnerships have entered the vocabulary of scholars of political economy. Recently, various authors have been advocating "neo-medievalism" as a new form of European or global governance. Neo-medievalism has combined the belief in the power of market, the disregard of state and daydreaming reminiscence of the Middle Ages to provide an alternative for the future of the European Union. In this chapter I will look more closely at what is "neo-medieval" paradigm, what are its main features and what solutions does it offer for the provision of European public goods.

What Is the Neo-Medievalism?

Neo-medievalism is a postmodern political theory of modern International Relations. Its defenders argue that the modern world order, premised on the Westphalian nation state, is over and that we are living in a period of 'the second Renaissance' which will lead the humanity to a new postmodern world. This world in the eyes of neo-medievalists will be better suited to cope with the economic and political challenges of globalisation and digital revolution. The term 'neo-medieval' is used in this context as a metaphor which highlights the similarities between the new emergent order and the one that prevailed in Europe during the Middle Ages. This analogy is what unites and defines all neo-medievalists and distinguishes them from other postmodernists. What neo-medievalists and postmodernists share in common is the abhorrence of the modern state, the interstate world order, territorial sovereignty and central governments. Modernity in their eyes is either a relic of the past or an 'evil' which must be contested so that humanity could embrace a new form of (post-modern) governance. Amongst the most significant advocates of postmodern forms of governance are David Mitrany (1943), the father of functional theory of governance principled on independent technocratic institutions, James N. Rosenau (1992), a defender of 'governance without government', and Giandomenico Majone (1994), a proponent of 'regulatory state'.

Neo-medievalism, then 'new mediaevalism', got an important scholarly attention for the first time in the 70s when Hedley Bull (1977) discussed it in his classical work *The Anarchical Society* as one of the possible models for interstate order. At the time, for countless intellectuals the combined effect of contemporary features of world politics, such as the regional integration, the disintegration of states, the privatisation of international violence, the emergence of transnational organisations and the technological integration of the world, heralded a new age of neo-medieval order. Nevertheless, Bull (1977: 265) dismissed it saying that 'there is no clear evidence that in the next few decades the states system is likely to give place to any of the [proposed neo-medieval] alternatives'. The next hype of neo-medievalism came again in the 90s following the end of the Cold War, and the start of digital revolution driven by the success of the Internet. Stephen J. Kobrin (1999) believed that the world was living a systemic transformation from a modern political economy to a neo-medieval and postmodern digital world economy. Later in the 21st century the 5th enlargement of the EU and the global financial crisis sparked the current generation of neo-medievalists, represented most notably by Jan Zielonka (2006, 2014), a supporter of neo-medieval governance for the EU, and Parag Khanna (2008, 2011), a self-proclaimed global strategist, neo-medieval enthusiast and promoter of 'mega-diplomacy'.

Jan Zielonka (2006) in his book *Europe as Empire* accomplished the most precise up-to-date formulation of the neo-medieval governance for the EU, which he revamped in 2014 with the title *Is the EU Doomed?*. I will draw from his two books to evaluate the implications of neo-medieval governance for the provision of European public goods. Zielonka's (2006: 11) principal intention in his first book was to present 'a workable alternative to a Westphalian type of state in the contemporary European context'. He considers the neo-medieval alternative as better suited for dealing with the current cultural, economic and political pressures in Europe than any European super-state. What's more, for Zielonka the enlarged EU already resembles more a 'neo-medieval empire' than a Westphalian state. His 'neo-medieval European empire' is a type of postmodern non-aggressive entity exporting rules to its near abroad. To support his claims, he (Zielonka 2006: 2–3) wholeheartedly refutes the thought of the EU as a state:

> The Union is anything but a state. It has no effective monopoly over the legitimate means of coercion. It has no clearly defined centre of authority. Its territory is not fixed. Its geographical, administrative, economic, and cultural borders diverge. And the Union is a very different kind of international actor than any of the states we know from history.

Zielonka identifies three drivers of neo-medievalism in the EU. First, and most essential, is the 5th enlargement, which has fundamentally reshaped Europe. It 'has resulted in more layers of authority, more cultural, legal, and political pluralism, more diversified and cross-cutting institutional arrangements' (Zielonka 2006: 3). Enlargement has increased the diversity in the EU and practically has rendered the rise of the European state unattainable. Globalisation, the second driver, makes it difficult for any state to maintain a minimum degree of sovereignty, hierarchy, and order (Zielonka 2006: 15). Expansion of markets and subsequent privatisation of social activity means that a large part of the western public currently demands the reduction of taxes and provision of public goods by more efficient private actors. The last driver is the apparent rejection of the European super-state by European public, epitomised by the failure of the Constitutional Treaty in French and Dutch referendums. Zielonka believes that the idea of European super-state has never been popular among the European electorate. European citizens care less and less about the European institutions and the increases in the power of the European Parliament has been met by decreases of voter turnout.

Main Features of Neo-Medieval Paradigm

Zielonka (2006) divided the neo-medieval paradigm in three areas of governance: democratic, economic and governance beyond borders. Table 2.1 shows the essential features of these three areas. From the perspective of democratic governance, the enlargement reinforces its neo-medieval character. The power and authority in the EU is shared among various types of political units in a system with no clear hierarchy. This governance system is complex, heterogenous, flexible, multilevel and multi-centred in concentric circles. Jurisdictions and competences of governmental agencies are multiple and overlapping. There is not one Europe but "many Europes: a trading Europe, an energy Europe, an environmental Europe, and so forth" (Zielonka 2006: 138). Subnational actors, regions and cities, as well as supranational actors both increase their functional reach in the European governance. There

Table 2.1 Main features of neo-medieval governance

Democratic governance	Economic governance	Governance beyond borders
• Polycentric power system with no hierarchy • Flexibility and complexity • Non-majoritarian institutions dominant over weak parliaments • Output legitimacy • Multiplicity of identities and cultural heterogeneity • Multiplicity of political actors • No monopoly of law-making; multiple laws • Multiple and overlapping jurisdictions • Divided sovereignty	• Liberalisation, deregulation and devolution • State power increasingly 'privatised' by markets • Flexible rules and regulation • Creative implementation of laws • Autonomous regulating bodies • Spontaneous market adjustments • Voluntary redistribution based on the principle of solidarity • Economic divergence	• Non-aggressive imperialism • Stabilisation of the neighbourhood • Fuzzy borders • Legitimate interventions • Export of European laws and rules to its neighbours • Civilian means • Two power centres (the EU and the US)

is no monopoly of law-making, neither are all citizens subject to the single law. Non-majoritarian institutions proliferate and dominate the weak European Parliament, but also the increasingly weak national parliaments. Policy output rather than input is the standard of legitimacy. There is no pan-European identity and the European public space is segmented across various cultural and ethnic lines. Sovereignty is divided along different functional and territorial lines, it is neither unified nor exclusive.

With regards to economic governance, Zielonka (2006) asserts that the EU is facing three challenges: internal coherence; tough competition from the Pacific economies; and economic instability in the near abroad. The EU can cope with them in a neo-medieval way by 'stimulating interpenetration of various economic and administrative units through shared ownership and institutional differentiation' (Zielonka 2006: 92). Internal development gaps are tackled by 'spontaneous market adjustments' and redistribution (if any) is realised by different types of solidarity between various transnational networks. The assistance from central EU institutions is scarce and aimed at promoting efficiency rather than equality. As a result, European economies will diverge and socio-economic discrepancies are likely to increase. More importantly, the neo-medieval EU meets the challenge of global competition with increased liberalisation of markets, deregulation, flexibility and devolution. Rigid rules, such as fiscal constraints, are abandoned. The neo-medieval magic formulae is 'more market—less state'. The Union opts for decentralised and creative implementation of laws and regulations. EU institutions refocus to act as facilitators, mediators, and coordinators. The regulation is dominated by autonomous technocratic bodies carrying out collective tasks on behalf of the Union. The private actors, like municipalities, charitable institutions, and welfare associations extend their role in the provision of European public goods. For each specific class of public goods, economic actors are allowed to freely organise themselves into optimal clubs responsible for their provision. In addition, the EU's economic governance extends to its neighbourhood as the Union exports and imposes its laws and regulations on the unstable neighbours. Consequently, the European economic space expands as more countries participate (often voluntarily) in the common market without being EU members and without having a say in the EU decision making.

Lastly, the EU's governance beyond borders is dominated by non-aggressive imperial politics. The Union does not have an equivalent to a Westphalian *raison d'état* and its prime international objective is not to defend borders against foreign invasion. Its foreign policy aims are to diffuse internal conflicts and pacify the external environment, to which it uses more civilian than military means. The EU continuously exports its laws and rules to stabilise the unstable southern and eastern neighbours. Europe justifies its policies in terms of values and norms and not in terms of power calculations. Foreign and security policies remain largely in the hands of the individual member states, and the CFSP is just one of the many institutional frameworks (Council of Europe, NATO, UN, OSCE) employed by European states to pursue their national interests. Common foreign and security actions are carried out by coalitions of the willing. There exists the 'medieval' duality of competing universalistic claims with the US as the second power centre. External borders of the Union are soft, porous and in flux. Cross-border cooperation flourishes, and the difference between EU members and non-members is blurred. Intervention in 'domestic' state matters is seen as legitimate in support of certain moral norms or in order to enforce compliance with agreed.

Problems of Neo-Medievalism

Neo-medievalism, like any other model of governance, is not without its problems and disadvantages. Zielonka (2006) in his self-critique readily points to a number of deficiencies in democratic legitimacy, participation, accountability, social justice, or to a danger of the rising populism. He (Zielonka 2006: 22) affirms that 'the implications of neo-medievalism are anything but clear and it is highly uncertain whether a neo-medieval Europe will be a better place than the Europe of today'. Nevertheless, he is certain that the neo-medieval paradigm will fare better than any type of Westphalian state. I will briefly look at three problems mentioned by Zielonka and leave the issue of public goods, the main topic of this paper, for the next section.

Firstly, few people could imagine how democracy, participation and accountability could work in this complex, flexible and multi-layered system run by democratically unaccountable institutions and networks. Arguably, it is debatable whether neo-medieval governance can still be called 'democratic'. Zielonka (2006: 183), conscious of the fact that his model is undemocratic in the traditional sense of democracy, expects that in a polycentric system of governance with fuzzy borders, 'democracy assumes different meanings and features'. He (Zielonka 2006: 183) goes further by suggesting that democratic 'voice' in the political affairs could be substituted by the liberty of 'exit' as the ultimate source of legitimacy:

> Systems with soft borders and thus ample opportunities for exit may well have problems in developing structures of political negotiation, but there is also less need for such structures because individuals can seek fulfilment of their needs outside the borders of the system.

It is not necessary to state that his proposition goes exactly in contraposition to those (Dryzek 2000; Follesdal and Hix 2006) who see democratic legitimacy in terms of the opportunity to participate in effective deliberation for every one who is subject to collective decisions. European public deliberation in the neo-medieval model is an inexistent feature.

The second serious problem is associated with social justice and solidarity. Zielonka (2006: 99) admits that greater devolution, flexibility, and deregulation will leave some people disadvantaged and that differentiation may imply discrimination against some actors. Redistribution of wealth is supposed to happen only by spontaneous market adjustments. Zielonka dedicates little attention to social justice, does not present any workable alternative, and rather disregards it completely. Therefore, it could be implied that in a neo-medieval world social justice imposed by state is no longer necessary as efficient markets and networks self-adjust and self-regulate themselves to cover all social needs. However, economists still have not proved that markets and networks are efficient, which justifies the existence of the state and its interventions in the market.

Ultimately, neo-medievalism may endanger the internal stability of the Union and give a rise to widespread populism. Zielonka's (2006: 171) most stressing point is that the EU will continuously enlarge for strategic reasons to stabilise its southern and eastern neighbours and to maintain a zone of prosperity and peace in Europe. In short, the EU's overarching objective is the endless stabilisation of neighbourhood by means of enlargement. For Zielonka the 5th enlargement has further opened the doors to the EU rather than closing them. Countries such as Turkey, Russia, Georgia, Israel, Morocco, Lebanon, or Jordan are all conceivable future members of the EU (for strategic reasons). Zielonka (2006: 165) confesses that 'this will stir up public resistance … and give populist politicians an opportunity to exploit protectionist and xenophobic sentiments across Europe'. However, by him proposed remedy comprised of longer admission process and stricter EU conditionality for new prospective members can be questioned on several grounds. Is it proofed that it will have the same stabilising effect? (think about the stability in Bosnia). Why will it calm down the populism? Will the EU public accept further enlargement to countries whose European credentials are doubted? Without answering these questions, it may be too soon to conclude that neo-medievalism is bound to arrive due to strategic reasons of peace and stability.

Neo-Medieval Provision of European Public Goods?

What implications has the neo-medieval paradigm for the delivery of public goods and more precisely of European public goods? Zielonka (2006: 18) mentions that it would be difficult to distribute public goods in any organised manner and that flexibility may encourage free riding. However, he does not offer any concrete answers and presumes that flexible networks and self-regulating agencies will take care of provision of public goods. We have learned in the first section of this chapter that any governance system has to deal with two fundamental problems: one associated with preference revelation and prioritisation, and the other with collective action. How does the neo-medieval paradigm deal with these issues? Now, let us apply the developed theoretical framework of public goods.

Firstly, there is the eternal issue of preference revelation for public goods and their prioritisation. How are preferences for public goods revealed in neo-medieval model? Zielonka (2006) circumvents the topic by suggesting that 'exit' could be employed as a mechanism by which individuals could reveal their preferences. Here, the market analogy with 'clubs' and club goods is evident. If an individual is not satisfied with common goods in one club, he/she can freely leave and join other club that will better satisfy his/her preferences, on the assumption that complete markets will provide clubs for every existing set of preferences. Notice that efficiency of the 'exit' option depends upon the completeness of the market. It will work better when there is a club for every possible preference than when there is not. The Brexit example clearly shows that the market of European clubs is incomplete, since there is no "Single Market without free movement of people" which the UK could readily join. Moreover, the logic of 'exit' could hardly work with common pool resources. How many rational herdsmen will choose to leave the common pasture, before it is depleted, and search for another if they are not pleased with how this common resource good is being provided? Not to say that common resource goods are mostly limited goods that can't be provided by the market. People in Greece are highly dissatisfied with how the Euro (European common resource good) is managed. Nevertheless, they have preferred to stay in the Euro-zone and to suffer painful austerity measures, since no better option is available. There are also those pure public goods, such as peace or financial stability, whose scope includes everyone and 'exit' is not possible. If financial chaos or war were to return to Europe, could any EU member state reasonably hope to isolate itself from negative effects by exiting the EU club? Zielonka dedicates no attention to these drawbacks. It seems that he assumed that there exist only club goods or that other public goods could be converted into them.

Another important source of difficulty with the 'exit' logic is that it assumes that every actor has only independent and functionally separable preferences which do not depend on what other actors do or want. Therefore, Zielonka (2006) attributes no value to public deliberation and inclines towards weak parliaments losing power to non-majoritarian institutions and private actors. This is the weakest point of neo-medieval provision of public goods inasmuch that without public deliberation and contestation, priorities and marginal utilities of public goods (which do have interdependent utilities) could be put in balance only by chance. And from the statistical point of view, that chance is rather low. Similarly, as the Brexit shows, 'exit' is not going to work for interdependent and linked European public goods. Brits decided to exit the EU, nevertheless they expressed their wishes to maintain the access to the Single Market for goods and services while limiting the movement of people from the EU to the UK.

Secondly, how are the problems of collective action overcome in the neo-medieval paradigm? We learned that incentives to cooperate decrease as the the number of actors rises and that they are different in situations of strategic substitutability than in situations of strategic complementarity. Neo-medievalism promotes the multiplicity of actors and Collignon (2004, 2011) proved that since the establishment of the Euro, there is a thick layer of European public goods characterised by strategic substitutabilities. Through subsequent enlargements, the Union now has 28 member states and other actors in the form of regions, cities, transnational group or supranational non-majoritarian institutions have increased their participation in the provision of European public goods. We have learned that larger the group, bigger the propensity to free ride. It is to be expected that without central coordination and coercion mechanism, free riding will be a frequent practice and common resource goods such as the Euro would be a source of constant friction. The recent events confirm this and free-riding has become an existential issue for the EU. Greece, Spain, Italy, Portugal and Ireland free-rode on the common currency by increasing their borrowing during the boom-times. Poland, Hungary, the Czech Republic and Slovakia openly defied the migrant resettlement program and left the burden of migrant resettlement on other member states.

For Zielonka, who disregards the hierarchical coordination by central institutions, the best option on how to cope with this multiplicity of actors is to completely curtail central coordination and foster a flexible implementation of rules. In neo-medieval paradigm, effective provision of public goods is dependent on the organisation of member states in overlapping jurisdictions. 'Optimal "club size" for individual public goods differs and so does the optimal membership for individual jurisdictions' (Zielonka 2006: 94). Now it is clear that when he speaks of public goods, Zielonka only focuses on 'club goods' and thus is able to avoid the intrinsic problems involved with common resource goods. He either assumes that European public goods have only independent utilities, thus allowing the creation of optimal clubs or independent regulatory agencies, or that European cooperation should occur only in the fields of strategic complementarities. However, we know that at present the majority of European public goods have interdependent utilities and thus independent clubs with overlapping members would only produce conflicts of interests. Even the seemingly independent ECB is dependent on coordination of fiscal policies and wage settlement of member states to prevent destabilising outcomes. Consequently, in an environment dominated by strategic substitutability, more flexibility will only aggravate the tendency of free riding as individual actors would have even greater incentives to bypass the rules. The repercussions of such flexibility or creativity in implementation could be illustrated with the break of the Stability and Growth Pact celebrated by Zielonka (2006: 103) as 'the triumph of flexibility' and now regarded as one of the main causes of the dire Euro-crisis.

Source of additional tensions in the neo-medieval EU will be public policies originated in one club or one EU member but with European-wide externalities. There is no explanation nor a reason to believe why the multitude of European actors will be willing to minimise and to take responsibility for externalities (the difference between private and public benefit) of their actions. Contemporary situation suggests that in a flexible setting individuals will seek to maximise private benefit at the expense of others and externalities will increase. A number of examples can be given. Germany has imposed the policy of austerity in the Euro-area, which saves the money of German taxpayers but at the same time asphyxiates the Mediterranean economies. Greece and Italy are letting through their 'soft' and porous borders a constant flow of migrants from the Middle East and North Africa, thus putting pressure on countries in Central and Western Europe. Poland and Baltic states are supporting American foreign policy and democratisation of former Soviet republics, which brings the EU on the collision course with Russia. What is clear from these illustrations is that if externalities are not reduced, neither are conflicts. With conflicts there is no stability and no peace.

Finally, in the theory of clubs, every club has a maximum member capacity, which when overreached, the club will start to provide diminishing returns. So do the European clubs, such as the EU, the Schengen zone or the Euro-area, have their capacity limits beyond which the individual members will be worse off since the cons of admitting new members will outweigh the pros. At present, it seems that the capacity has been reached and that it will take a long time to extend it so that new members could come in. This contradicts Zielonka's premise that the EU will be become gradually more neo-medieval by enlarging and admitting more members. Rational self-interested actors will oppose the enlargement of clubs beyond the maximum capacity on grounds that it will reduce their individual club benefits.

Conclusion

This chapter has inquired into the theory of public goods and the neo-medieval model of governance. It tried to show the implications of neo-medievalism on the provision of European public goods. The process of European integration and successive enlargements have increased the number and scope of public goods that affect all Europeans. In addition to pure public goods, which are non-excludable and non-rivalrous in consumption, it is important to differentiate two more groups of public goods: club goods and common resource goods. The former are inclusive goods characterised by strategic complementarities, what facilitates voluntary cooperation. The latter, on the other hand, are exclusive goods distinguished by strategic substitutabilities, what requires central coordination and a coercion device for cooperation to take place. The principal problem intrinsic to all public goods is the issue of preference revelation. Without a mechanism for preference revelation, public goods can't be delivered efficiently. For public goods with independent utilities, voting can function as a preference revelation device. However, when public goods have interdependent utilities, public deliberation is required to establish the balance between their marginal costs and benefits.

Neo-medievalism is a model of governance built upon multiplicity of actors and power centres, overlapping jurisdictions, flexible implementation of laws, self-regulation and soft borders. It has been shown that neo-medieval paradigm would be inadequate and inefficient solution for the provision of European public goods for at least two reasons. The first reason is that the model lacks a proper mechanism for preference revelation. Neo-medieval model, essentially undemocratic, tries to substitute voting for the possibility of exit even though it is not only ineffective but also impractical in many instances. The second reason is that the flexible nature of neo-medievalism, based on voluntary cooperation, can only operate with inclusive club goods and is therefore unsuitable for exclusive public goods with strategic substitutabilities. Neo-medievalism assumes that public goods have independent utilities that would allow the creation of independent non-majoritarian institutions for their delivery. Notwithstanding, this is not the case in the contemporary Europe and even the seemingly independent public goods such as price stability have interdependent utilities. Similarly, neo-medievalism assumes that all public goods could be delivered by flexible and overlapping networks and clubs through voluntary cooperation. However, this assumption has been refuted by the theory of collective action.

Another possibility can be that neo-medievalism implicitly proposes that exclusive public goods should not be in the domain of European integration. As such, it would be necessary to reduce the number of European common resource goods and decrease the scope of externalities. It would be necessary to abolish the Euro and curtail the effects of national policies on other member states. This practically equals disintegration, and the desirability of such a scenario is questionable. Not to mention that the neo-medieval model would result in an extension of externalities given that the number of actors increase and the borders become more loose. The model is thus not coherent and we may conclude that it is not an efficient alternative for the governance of European public goods. This conclusion is strengthened by the fact that up-to-date not a single society could successfully implement postmodern system of governance where the state, as a modern institution, is no longer necessary and markets are capable of delivering all goods which the public requires. Attempts to cut down the state and to completely liberalise markets, such as those in Chile or Argentina during the Cold War, gave rise to severe crisis and chaos that ultimately led to the reimposition of the state.

To conclude, envisioning and speculating on how the EU could be or would be is a cost-free human activity in which the author can afford to leave blank spots in his blueprint and state that there are some details that must be still thought about. Putting together a working governance system is a completely different undertaking where author has to execute with precision and perfection taking care of every aspect and detail. A model of governance, whatever noble its goals, is of no value if it is not internally consistent, coherent with reality and executable. If any of the aforementioned characteristics are not met, the expected results will greatly diverge from the real outcome. For neo-medievalism to become more than just a utopian blueprint, it must define carefully its working mechanisms and prove that they are functioning and that the intended results will equal the real ones. Until then it will remain in the realm of theorising and does not deserve any attention in the realm of political practice.

References

Bull, H. (1977). *The anarchical society: A study of order in world politics.* Basingstoke: Palgrave.

Collignon, S. (2003). *The European: Reflections on the political economy of a future constitution.* London: Federal Trust for Education and Research.

Collignon S. (2004). Is Europe going far enough? Reflections on the EU's economic governance. *Journal of European Public Policy, 11*(5), 909–925.

Collignon, S. (2011). The governance of European public goods. In D. Tarschys (Ed.), *The EU budget: What should go in? what should go out?* (pp. 42–57). Stockholm: SIEPS.

Desai, M. (2003). Public goods: A historical perspective. In I. Kaul, P. Conceição, K. L. Goulven, & R. U. Mendoza (Eds.), Providing public goods. Managing globalization (pp. 63–77). New York: Oxford University Press.

Dryzek, J. S. (2000). *Deliberative democracy and beyond. Liberals, critics, contestations.* New York: Oxford University Press.

Follesdal, A., & Hix, S. (2006). Why there is a democratic deficit in the EU: A response to Majone and Moravcsik. *Journal of Common Market Studies, 44*(3), 533–562.

Giddens, A. (1990). *The consequences of modernity.* Cambridge, UK: Polity Press.

Hardin, G. (1968). The tragedy of the commons. *Science, 162*(3859), 1243–1248.

Kaul, I., Grunberg, I., & Stern, M. A. (1999). Defining global public goods. In I. Kaul, I. Grunberg, & M. A. Stern (Eds.), Global public goods: International cooperation in the 21st century (pp. 2–19). New York: Oxford University Press.

Khanna, P. (2008). *The second World: Empires and influence in the new global order.* New York: Random House.

Khanna, P. (2011). *How to run the World: Charting a course to the next.* New York: Random House.

Kobrin, S. J. (1999). Back to the future: Neomedievalism and the postmodern digital world economy. In A. Prakash, & J. F. Hart (Eds.), *Globalization and governance* (pp. 165–187). London: Routledge.

Majone, G. (1994). The rise of the regulatory state in Europe. In M. Eilstrup-Sangiovanni (Ed.), *Debates on: A reader* (pp. 378–390). Basingstoke: Palgrave Macmillan.

Mitrany, D. (1943). A working peace system: An argument for the functional development of international organization. In M. Eilstrup-Sangiovanni (Ed.), *Debates on: A reader* (pp. 43–67). Basingstoke: Palgrave Macmillan.

Olson, M. (1965). *The logic of collective actions: Public goods and the theory of groups.* London: Oxford University Press.

Rosenau, J. N. (1992). Governance, order, and change in World politics. In J. N. Rosenau., & E. -O. Czempiel (Eds.), *governance without government* (pp. 1–29). Cambridge, UK: Cambridge University Press.

Samuelson, P. A. (1954). The pure theory of public expenditure. *Review of Economics and Statistics, 36*(4), 89–387.

Skinner, Q. (2009). A genealogy of the modern state. *Proceedings of the Academy, 162,* 325–370.

Wicksell, K. (1958). A new principle of just taxation. In R. A. Musgrave & A. T. Peacock (Eds.), *Classics in the theory of public finance.* London: Macmillan.

Zielonka, J. (2006). *Europe as Empire: The nature of the enlarged.* New York: Oxford University Press.

Zielonka, J. (2014). *Is the EU doomed?* Cambridge, UK: Polity Press.

3

The European Union as a Republic

Stefan Collignon

In this chapter, I suggest that European integration theory would benefit from reconsidering the republican paradigm, which provided one of the foundations of political philosophy since the Renaissance.[1] European integration drew its inspiration from federalism (Spinelli et al. 2016) and neofunctionalism (Haas 1964), but in the end it has become nothing else but a very advanced form of intergovernmentalism. This does not work. The cooperation between nation states has generated an impressive amount of Europe public goods, but the Union and especially the Euro Area lack an efficient and democratic government to

---

[1]For my previous work see: (Collignon 2003); (Collignon 2004); (Collignon, Bundesrepublik Europa? Die demokratische Herausforderung und Europas Krise, 2007); (Collignon, Three Sources of Legitimacy for European Fiscal Policy, 2007); (Collignon 2008); (Collignon and paul 2008). See also: (Bogdandy, Die europäische Republik, ApuZ 36/2005, pp. 21–27, 2005); (Bogdandy, Konstitutionalisierung des europäischen öffentlichen Rechts in der europäischen Republik, 2005)); (Bogdandy 2004)).

S. Collignon (✉)
Scuola Superiore Sant'Anna, Pisa, Italy
e-mail: S.Collignon@lse.ac.uk

S. Collignon
London School of Economics and Political Sciences, London, UK

© The Author(s) 2017   **39**
S. Collignon, *The Governance of European Public Goods*,
DOI 10.1007/978-3-319-64012-9_3

administer these goods. Without a proper European government, the European Union will disintegrate and the euro will disappear.

However, arguing in favour of a European government does not necessarily mean going down the federalist route. Federalism bundles different political communities into a larger and hierarchically structured whole. It thereby preserves cultural identities and the feeling of "belonging", but it also generates resistance to the cultural domination by "others". This is why federalism never took off in Europe and often looks messy when it is built on principles of decentralizing "subsidiarity".

By contrast, I propose a republican paradigm that offers a different perspective. While some ancient articulations of republicanism have also emphasised the identitarian and "patriotic" characteristics of republics (and even the undemocratic hierarchies of the early Italian republics), see (Bobbio and Viroli 2003), I propose a modern version of the republican paradigm that is derived from the existence of European public goods (I), which allows re-interpreting the traditional concept of the Republic (II). I propose then a new synthesis between European public goods theory and traditional republicanism (III). Finally, the republican principal-agent relationship between citizens and governments grounds a European government in representative democracy (IV). My objective is to reconsider the basic principles on which Europe's governance is built, not to propose detailed institutional changes.

Public Goods in the European Context

For the last 50 years, the European integration process was driven by the so-called Monnet Method, the neo-functionalist premise that the partial integration of specific and strategic sectors in the economy creates incentives for further integration because it would unlock, capture, preserve and generate additional benefits for all citizens. The method has been successful in creating an ever larger supply of European public goods: from the Coal and Steel Union to the internal market and single currency; from the Common Agricultural Policy to regional policy and structural funds; from competition policy to market regulation; from the four economic freedoms in the domestic market and the creation of Schengen to the legal framework of Europol and Eurojust; from common foreign trade policies to the nucleus of a common security and defence policy. These policies have provided public goods which are used and shared by all Europeans. They define a joint interest for those who use them and are affected by them.

Yet, who takes care of these goods? Who governs them? Modern democracies live by the principle that citizens are the owners of public goods and as such they control governments as their agents who administer these goods. But that is not how it works in Europe. The realism of Monnet's method has kept national governments in control of managing Europe's public goods—with a few exceptions like competition and trade policy, for which the European Commission is responsible, and monetary policy for which the European Central Bank has exclusive authority. Thus, the administration of most of these public goods remains in the hands of a consortium of governments that escapes the collective control by European citizens. This contradiction between the common interests, which European citizens derive from their public goods, and the absence of a government, which they would authorize to manage them, is at the core of the much-bemoaned 'democratic deficit'[2]; it has significantly contributed to the European crisis, to growing Euroscepticism and, indeed, to the British vote on Brexit.

Governing Externalities

The problem is the internalisation of political externalities. An externality is the effect that the decisions of one agent may impact upon other actors who are not able to influence the decision maker. Internalizing such effects means including the excluded actors into the decision-making set. Policy externalities occur when the democratically legitimised preferences of one government are superimposed on citizens in other countries which have no say in this decision. This generates only partially legitimized policy decisions which cause so-called deadweight

---

[2]According to Eurobarometer 73 (August 2010), 23% of European citizens consider the EU to be a waste of money, 21% associate the EU with bureaucracy, and only 19% associate the EU with democracy, see http://ec.europa.eu/public_opinion/archives/eb/eb73/eb73_first_en.pdf (22.10.2011).

losses of welfare. Welfare is understood as the satisfaction of preferences and if the preferences of some people do not count for the decision-making, welfare is necessarily suboptimal.

One may argue that even within nation states such losses are inevitable. For, by their very nature public preferences may diverge from individual preferences. In fact, Arrow (1963) has argued that welfare economics is incompatible with democracy. However, this is only true if we assume fixed and given preferences. If preferences change, welfare may improve. Yet, preference change is what democracy is all about, because the collective deliberation in democracies transforms individual desires into collective preference. The right to participate in the collective deliberation and the confidence that each political argument receives a fair hearing are necessary (and often sufficient) conditions for the acceptance of collective decisions, although individuals may disagree with the concrete solution that will come out of the deliberation process. Even if no policy consensus is possible at a given time, democracies are built on a constitutional consensus by which individual and minority rights are protected. Hence, collective welfare must be measured not just by whether the allocation of resources satisfies the preferences of individual users of public goods, but also by the fact that *users have a right to determine their* collective preferences. This democratic right of jointly appointing an agent for administrating their shared interests is a necessary condition for generating the solidarity whereby minorities accept the preferences of the majority.

However, this condition is not satisfied in the European Union. Member state governments take policy decisions in the European Council that concern all European citizens, but the Council is not the agent of all Europeans; it is the agent of governments. National governments represent only the voters in their national constituencies. This is no problem when the majorities in all member states agree on the same policy, but if the majority in one state is different from the Council majority, the democratic majority in that country is overruled. If the policy concerns a matter where qualified majority voting is the rule, the "will of the nation" is ignored; if Council unanimity is required, like in tax and budget affairs, vetoes can paralyze the decision making process. Because governments are elected in their home constituencies, they must resist or refuse policies which do not represent the preferences of the majority of their electorates, even if they would reflect the majority among all European citizens. Not refusing such policies would appear as a betrayal of democratic principles of nation states. For example, when the Greek citizens elected Prime Minister Tsipras to finish austerity, his new government was forced to choose between staying in and exiting from the euro. He chose Europe, which probably reflected the "basic constitutional consensus" in Greece, but the concrete policy preferences of the Greek people were ignored. Similarly, when the German Chancellor Merkel proposed to resettle refugees in other member states, most other governments refused because there was no majority for her immigration policy in Europe.

As a consequence, policy making in the European Union is either seen as hollowing out of democracy, or it is confined to a small domain of policy solutions for which governments find an overlapping consensus although the overall efficiency of governing Europe remains low. Thus, to sum up, in the intergovernmental system of policy making, national governments represent a small subset of voters from local jurisdictions, while all other citizens are by definition excluded from the democratic process by which policies are decided. This "democratic deficit" generates welfare losses and undermines the legitimacy of the European integration project.

For a long time European integration seemed to generate benefits for all with no one being made worse off. "More Europe" was seen as a Pareto-improvement where distributive justice is of no concern. National governments could agree on policies that were supported in all member states. But this is no longer true. With the creation of the single market and the euro, distributive justice has become a major problem for policy making in the European Union.

Nation states can impose the redistribution of welfare, because they are authorized to do so by the democratic consensus. In fact, ideas of social justice and the purpose of democratic government are inseparable. "One man, one vote" is a principle of political equality that translates into economic fairness when a broad policy debate settles on principles of justice. However, in the European Union policies are decided by national governments which only reflect the partial interests of their constituencies. The problem is not only the political inequality between governments representing large and small populations, but even more importantly, the fact that citizens cannot jointly deliberate and decide how to govern the public goods they all share. Bargaining compromises between national governments cannot resolve problems of social justice.[3] As long as preferences are exogenously given by the national constituencies, negotiations on how the winners of European integration should compensate potential losers can only shift welfare gains and losses from one member state to another. This has two consequences: on the one hand, European integration generates problems for social justice; on the other hand, it opposes nations as policy units rather than individual winners and losers for which distributive solutions could be found. This generates absurd situations, for example, when a poor single mother in a rich member state has to pay taxes that are then transferred to a low-income region where the subsidy allows a millionaire to receive public goods for free.

The described welfare losses do not just result from transgressions by self-seeking ("corrupt") politicians or from the imposition of ideological principles (neoliberalism)[4]; they are caused by institutional shortcomings. It is the intergovernmental structure of the European Union that deprives citizens from clarifying different realisations of social justice and then correcting the injustice. Hence, given that the intergovernmental system has few if any tools to deal with concerns of social justice, governments give priority to minimizing welfare losses by blocking more integration rather than maximising welfare by the right policies. Instead of considering how the largest possible gains from integration can be achieved, governments refuse to "pay for others" and to compensate potential losers from integration. Thus, the democratic deficit creates a second deficit of social justice and both undermine the acceptability and efficiency of the European Union.

---

[3]See (Joerges 2005). In a Rawlsian perspective of justice as fairness, one would model this by saying different nations are presented with different choice sets, and individuals would have to choose from these choice sets behind the veil of ignorance. The unfairness is then a consequence that they do not have access to the same choice sets.

[4]I owe the distinction between behavioural transgressions and the basic institutional system in theories of justice to (Sen 2009) and (Rawls 1999).

Some observers, especially among populist politicians, have drawn the conclusion that only the nation state is and remains the appropriate tool for pursuing social justice and it is, therefore, also the only place from which political legitimacy emerges.[5] It is of course true that if we assume that all public goods are national goods and all state authority emanates from its citizens, the nation state has solved admirably the problem of internalising externalities. The political decisions of the state are then naturally legitimised by those who are affected by these decisions. However, the increasing range of European public goods has blurred the traditional congruence between the regulatory *power* of governments and the democratic *authority* of citizens. Eurosceptics seek to restore this coherence by reversing integration, and even leaving the Union, but they can do this only at the price of lower welfare. Thus, while the democratic deficit has been widely discussed, the issue of social justice has remained in the shadow. And yet, it is probably the main driver behind populist-Eurosceptic movements.

Unfortunately, the problems of social justice have become even sharper with the creation of the single currency, because money is the hard budget constraint. A hard budget constraint is a functional requirement for a market economy. It means that in aggregate one cannot spend more money than is available. In monetary union, the European Central Bank determines the budget constraint for the Euro Area as a whole by issuing currency, although all banks, and ultimately to all citizens, have the equal right to access this limited resource. This defines the euro as a public good. In fact, it is a clear case of a common resource good, which is limited in supply but accessible for all. The constraint ensures that the decentralised decisions by private and public entities remain mutually coherent because relative prices reflect the intensity of relative preferences and relative costs. With national currencies, by contrast, different economies face different budget constraints and the resulting exchange rate variations reflect varying degrees of budget softness. The institutional coherence of the single market is the reason why the euro is necessary as a complement for the single market.

---

[5]For the general philosophical argument see (Nagel 2005). For a critique: (Cohen and Sabel 2006); For the European debate see (Moravcsik 2008); (Majone 1998).

However, with a hard budget constraint it becomes inevitable that one has to make tough choices about how to allocate money and resources. Policy areas which are subject to the hard budget constraint are working like zero-sum games, where the gain of one is the loss of another. As a consequence, the political incentives have shifted for member state governments. If money is tight, either I have it or you have it, but we cannot have it both. I may be willing to lend you my money, provided you pay it back and compensate me for my loss of convenience and the risk of losing it. As a lender, I therefore insist on imposing conditions which assure me that I will be reimbursed by my debtors. This logic reduces the spaces for overlapping policy consensus between national governments, because if one government makes a concession to another, the net welfare of its own constituency is reduced. Gridlock and policy paralysis will follow.

This strategic substitutability can only be overcome by a single decision maker, a government that imposes the general welfare solution.[6] Hence, intergovernmentalism cannot offer a solution to this dilemma. The old neofunctionalist Monnet model relied on so-called output legitimacy because the efficiency gains from integration were increasing welfare. But under conditions of a hard budget constraint the net benefits from integration no longer satisfy the standards of social justice without some form of redistribution, so that Europe's output legitimacy is diminishing.[7] Thus, we find ourselves in a vicious circle: the output legitimacy of European integration requires higher economic efficiency and therefore deeper market integration; deeper markets require coherent price mechanisms by setting up a hard budget constraint and a single currency. But with a single currency distributional conflicts increase, which undermines output legitimacy.

However, federalism, at least in the German decentralising form which is often proposed as a model for Europe, offers no way out of the dilemma,[8] because it preserves national governments' involvement

---

[6]For the formal model see (Cooper and John 1988).

[7]This distinction was made by (Scharpf 1999).

[8]For a discussion of the fallacies of the (Pocock 1975) German federal system, see (Scharpf 1985).

with European policy issues. It leads to political gridlock and restricts democratic participation rights. On the other hand, centralizing Eurofederalists also fail because they are blocked by communitarian concerns of national identity.

One way out of this dilemma is to complement output legitimacy with input legitimacy. Input legitimacy, i.e. the democratic participation in decision making, addresses the social justice gap because the collective deliberation about European public goods will generate standards of shared judgement. In other words, if the congruence between the regulatory *power* of governments and the democratic *authority* of citizens has worked in the traditional nation state for national public goods, a similar congruence must now be established at the level of the Euro Area where the budget constraint is binding.

The untenable stalemate between intergovernmentalism and federalism requires a new perspective and this is where the republican paradigm offers a new solution. I suggest that by looking at the functions of public goods, we may slice the competences for political decisions not vertically in terms of member states, but horizontally in terms of the reach of externalities.

The Concept of the Republic

Historic Roots

The Republic is one of the oldest political concepts. Its roots lie in *Plato*'s and *Aristotle*'s Politeia and in the Roman Republic, which served as a model for the Renaissance city states in Italy and the German Hanseatic states. From there, republican ideas travelled west. Pocock (1975) has described how the concept of republican liberty went from *Machiavelli* in Florence to *Harrington* and the English Commonwealth, finally reaching the Founding Fathers of the United States. On the other hand, Israel (2004) has investigated how the republican ideal of equality in the Dutch Republic has influenced the egalitarian ideas of the French Republic. In Germany, the term is rather underdeveloped and is mainly used as a contrast to the idea of a monarchy.

Republicans have always sought to unite the people against domination and the subjection under the autocratic rule (*sub potestate*) of kings and despots.[9] This, too, has a long tradition: during the Renaissance, the Republic of free and equal citizens became the counter-concept to the "*regnum*" of the Emperor, claiming that the community of citizens retained the final sovereignty over their governments which they charged with the administration of public goods.[10] Thus, the freedom and equality of citizens is the common core of all concepts of the Republic.

The republican tradition has also been shaped by ideas of community and individualism.[11] Conservative-holistic[12] interpretations of the Republic, which start with Plato, emphasise common culture and habits to which people belong (the *demos*) and to which individuals must submit. However, in the original Latin tradition of the Republic, the people are defined as the set of all citizens who share common interests rather than feelings of belonging. Even today the concept of the Republic[13] still invokes *Cicero*'s definition: "*res publica res populi*", which one

---

[9]See (Isensee, Republik - Sinnpotential eines Begriffs, 1981); (Henke 1981); (Anderheiden 2006).

[10](Skinner, From the State of Princes to the Person of the State, 2002, p. 38ß): "The community must retain ultimate sovereignty, assigning its rulers and magistrates a status no higher than that of elected functionaries. These officials must in turn recognize that they are mere agents or *ministeri* of justice, charged with the duty of ensuring that the laws established by the community for the promotion of its own good are equitably enforced.".

[11]See (Collignon 2003) for a full discussion.

[12]I use the concept of *holism* in the sense of (Popper 1995).

[13](Gröschner 2004), § 23, endeavours to show a continuity of republicanism from Aristotle to Cicero. However, (Wesel 2010, p. 99) stresses that the similarity between Athens and Rome is purely extrinsic: "[T]he Greeks gave us the scientific philosophers that established the basis for European humanities and natural sciences. The Romans gave us the lawyers that developed their legal system in a way that the Greeks could never do due to the collective decision-making of their citizens in their courts." The difference between Aristotle and Cicero is important for another reason related to *B. Constant's* distinction between ancient and modern forms of freedom in his famous discourse of 1819 (Constant 1816). Modern freedom based on individual rights is a renaissance development, invoked by Cicero but not by Aristotle; see (Tuck 2003). A. *von* Bogdandy (2005, p. 26) refers to the modern conception of the republic when he writes that "a republican understanding of the European Union cannot be built on republican theories that follow the conception of a 'stronger' and 'narrower' community. The European Republic can form a liberal democratic community, but certainly not a communitarian community".

may translate as "public goods are the goods of the people".[14] Cicero explained that "a people (*populus*) is not any collection of human beings brought together in any sort of way, but an assemblage of many, associated in an agreement with respect to law and the utility of a mutual partnership."[15] Thus, people's interests derive from public goods and, from the outset, the Republic was conceived as a community based on law, i.e. legal rights and obligations by individuals seeking joint welfare. *Cicero*'s "*res publica res populi*" translates therefore as a modern community of free and equal citizens who jointly determine the laws by which they manage the public goods that they own jointly and that affect their common welfare.[16] The modern Republic is a democracy.

The Republic and the State

The republican concept of laws and legal rights also distinguishes republicanism from liberalism. Pettit (1997) has argued that republican rights-based liberty is a form of "non-domination", while the liberal concept means "non-interference". A slave may be free from interference of a benevolent owner, but he is not free by law; he has no rights. Liberals seek to protect individuals from arbitrary interference; republicans see the need of a legal framework that citizens jointly establish and voluntarily accept.

Yet, with freedom comes conflict. The Republics of the Italian Renaissance were characterised by tough factional conflicts, which carried the risk of civil war. The liberty of the Republic therefore had to be supported by "*civitas*", i.e. active citizenship, and republican virtues. As

---

[14]For reasons which will become clear soon, my translation varies from the conventional "a commonwealth is the property of a people". The Latin *res* stands first of all for items, things, goods, affairs.

[15]"Est igitur, …, res publica res populi, populus autem non omnis hominum coetus quomodo congregatus, sed coetus multitudinis iuris consensu et utilitatis communione sociatus", (Cicero 2006, p. 64); my translation is slightly at variance with Keyes. *Utilitatis communione sociatus* may also be translated as Welfare.

[16]Already *Machiavelli* stressed that "cities have never managed to increase their acquired rights or prosperity unless they were in a state of liberty" (perché si vede per esperienza le cittadi non avere mai ampliato né di dominio né di ricchezza, se non mentre sono state in libertá) (Machiavelli 2000, p. 139).

Machiavelli already observed, this orientation towards public morality was the reason for welfare gains. In a similar vein, Isensee (1981, p. 3) has argued that in a Republic, it does not matter "who is governing, but rather which objective is guiding the government". Thus, the Republic generates its own civic morality inspired by principles of social justice when citizens collectively agree on which policies support collective welfare. The concept of the Republic is therefore founded on the voluntary agreement among citizens living in a just society.

A Republic is not the same as a state. The notion of a state "relates to the impersonal rule of men over men. It emerged in opposition to the idea of an association founded on ties of personal loyalty" (von Münch, Ingo and Ute Mager 2009, p. Rn 3). Traditionally, absolute sovereigns could do as they pleased,[17] and their subjects owed them fidelity and obedience. By contrast, the modern state is an instrument for objectified and value-neutral rule. It can be liberal-democratic, social-democratic, communist or fascist. It exercises power in the name of an authority without questioning who the authority is. Max Weber defined the state as an "apparatus of power whose existence is unaffected by whoever is controlling it at any given time" (Skinner 2002 p. 378), or as an "institutional operation" (*Anstaltsbetrieb*), in which "administrative staff successfully make use of the monopoly of legitimate physical coercion for enforcing order" (Weber 1972, p. 29). Thus, even in democratic constitutional states, the concept of the state emphasises the power and holistic-hierarchical authority of the sovereign over his subjects.[18]

---

[17]As Hobbes (1996, pp. 139, Chap. XX) so elegantly put it: "He cannot be Accused by any of his subjects, of Injury: He cannot be punished by them: He is Judge of what is necessary for Peace; and Judge of Doctrines: He is Sole Legislator; and Supreme Judge of Controversies; and of the times and Occasions of Warre and Peace: to Him belongeth to choose Magistrates, Councellors, Commanders, and all other officers, and Ministers; and to determine of Rewards, and Punishments, Honour and Order." Hobbes would have felt at home in the European Council!

[18]For a discussion of holism, hierarchies and individualism, see (Popper 1995); (Dumont 1986). Concerning state authority, (Isensee 2004) says they have "two faces: inwardly facing—effective and organised sovereign authority, internal sovereignty; outwardly facing—legal independence, external sovereignty". According to this interpretation, states are sovereign rather than their citizens. See also (Grimm 2009). I will discuss the inconsistency of the principle of state sovereignty with the Republic later.

The early concept of *Res publica* did not have these connotations. It referred to the liberty and equality of citizens. Hence, republican theory proclaims citizens, rather than the state, to be the bearers of sovereignty.[19] It is only when the concepts of state and Republic merge, as they did after the French Revolution, that the Republic is simply reduced to a particular form of state.

This reduction has caused a dual impoverishment. First, if the Republic is only an abstract form of state, the sense that the Republic is a way of collectively owning and managing public goods disappears. Second, the concept of the state is focused on the *possession* of power and the control of resources,[20] whereas the republican concept highlights the idea that public goods are the *property* of the citizens from which citizens derive the *claim-right* to control common resources.[21] To use the concept of the Republic effectively for the governance of the European Union, it is necessary to restore the original Roman meaning based on the *res publica* that is owned by all citizens. This requires linking it to the insights of Principal-*Agent* theory.

---

[19]Republican writers "make no ... distinction between the powers of states and the powers of communities over which they rule. On the contrary, the whole thrust of republican theory is towards an ultimate equation between the two. This undoubtedly yields a recognizable concept of the state, one that many Marxists and exponents of direct democracy continue to espouse. But it involves a repudiation of the most distinctive element in the mainstream theory of the modern state: the claim that it is the state itself, rather than the community over which it holds sway, that constitutes the seat of sovereignty." Skinner (FN 10), p. 386.

[20]Q. Skinner (2009) shows that the concept of "state "derived from the concept of vested rights in the Renaissance.

[21]Hobbes makes this clear in his distinction between 'right' and 'law': "RIGHT consiteth in liberty to do, or to forbare; whereas LAW, determineth, and bindeth to one of them: to that Law, and Right, differ as much, as Obligation and Liberty; which in one and the same matter are inconsistent" (Hobbes 1996, pp. 91, Chap. 14).

The Logic of Public Goods

Public Goods, Republics and Citizenship

Public goods define the *res publica*. However, there are two interpretations of republicanism. Plato (2003, p. 6.505) has derived public goods from the idea of the common good: goods are things that serve what is commonly considered as good and just. This led to the idea of the Republic as a "unity of sameness", which became the leitmotiv for the French Jacobins (Urbinati 2003). The other tradition had its origin in the Republic of Rome. Roman law was less concerned with ethics than with the formalities of law. It established the principle of property as a *claim* for control over resources (*dominium*) rather than considering the *possession* of the resources themselves (Eckl und Ludwig 2005). Of course, the possession of goods and land implied enjoyment of utilities, but property was the right of the *dominus*. Rome's aristocrats were the owners of land, although they granted user rights to the *plebs* and the provinces. Chiusi (2005) therefore concludes that there was no property without sovereignty. This concept of property allowed the distinction between *res publica*, which was ruled by user rights (*ususfructus*) for the many, and *res privata*, which was defined by the freedom of *dominium*. It continues to be influential in modern economic theory which distinguishes private from public goods.

Yet, Roman property laws were ignorant of the concept of externalities, which only emerged with modern economics. Samuelson (1938, p. 387) defined a public good as something that can be used by everyone, so that "each individual's consumption of such a good leads to no subtraction from any other individual's consumption of that good". For example, if two people cross a street during the night, the streetlight provides visibility for both of them; the light will not become weaker for each because it is providing utility to more than one person. The collective benefits and costs of public goods constitute *externalities*, which structure the incentives for their provision. As explained in Chap. 1 of this book, the "consumption" of public goods is joint and collective in the sense that each individual in a given user group is able to draw utility from its existence. We may also say that the groups of users are defined by being affected by the good's existence. By contrast, the consumption of private goods is rivalrous and competitive in the sense that usage by one makes usage by another impossible: if one person eats an apple, no one else can eat it. Thus, private goods are rivalrous, while public goods are non-rivalrous. It follows that the public character of a good depends on who is affected by the good. It is private when only one person, its owner, is affected; it is public when many are affected. In this case, the good has many owners. While it is possible to establish property rights that bar access to some goods for consumers who are unwilling to pay the price, and thereby turn them into private goods or at least into club goods, John Stuart Mills (1909, pp. Bk V, §15) has shown that this is not always the case. In his famous example one cannot exclude ships from enjoying the benefit of a lighthouse.

The link between public goods and property rights defines the status of citizens. If property is the right to utilise goods, then private property is the exclusive *entitlement* to usage of a good, and common property is the entitlement to use public goods. The republican concept of *civitas* derives from the idea that citizens are the collective owners of public goods, and that they are jointly responsible for how the group may use the public goods. Implicit in the notion of *civitas* is the fact that public goods require rules and regulations for their collective use. From the republican point of view, all affected individuals must therefore have equal rights to determine the common usage. Thus, the legal community of republican citizens emerges from their status as common property owners rather than from the "shared cultural, historical or linguistic understanding" of a people that is implied by the holistic concept of nation-state citizens (Grawert 2004). In *Cicero*'s conception it is the *utilitas* of the *res publica* that determines what the *populus* is.

This republican theory allows addressing European democracy in new terms. Critics have often claimed that there can be no democracy because no European *demos* exists. In the holistic-communitarian tradition, which goes back to ancient Greek democracy, the *demos* or pre-political nation reflects the "unity of sameness". By contrast in the Roman tradition of the Republic, it is the common ownership of public goods that defines what is a *people*, the *populus*. Because *European* public goods are goods that are the property of all citizens of the European Union, the property rights in European public goods define citizens as the European *demos* in the sense of *populus*. The Treaty of Lisbon recognises this indirectly by stating that the citizenship in the European Union results in a catalogue of "rights and duties".[22] It therefore places citizens of the Union into the "consensus of the law" (*Cicero*), so that the *populus* of the European Republic is the collective of citizens of the Union who share equal rights, including the right of jointly managing their public goods.

Incentive Structures for the Provision of Public Goods

The founders of the European Union focused on market integration, because larger markets are generating economies of scale and therefore net benefits for the Union. The First Fundamental Theorem of Welfare Economics states that competitive markets for private goods generate a Pareto optimal allocation of resources. It implies that the acceptance of the market outcome, manifested in the market price which represents a negotiated equilibrium of acceptance between all parties of the deal. Such an outcome supports the political integration project because it hinges on the acceptance of the distribution of costs and benefits from integration, and markets generate a culture of negotiated agreements. Yet, as markets have become more integrated, private decisions by market participants have also generated increasingly more far-reaching externalities; European public goods have therefore become more prominent.

This poses the question of their governance, i.e. how to deal with externalities emerging from private transactions. A notorious problem, which dominates the economic literature on the efficient provision of public goods, is *free-riding*. If a good is not rivalrous and it is not possible to exclude others from its usage,[23] its supply depends on how much

---

[22]Art. 20 TFEU; see also (Haratsch et al. 2010, S. RN 725).

[23]In microeconomical theory, this means that in a two-dimensional world of price and quantity, the demand curve for private goods will horizontally intersect the quantity axis, whereas public goods will vertically intersect the price axis. See (Samuelson 1938).

a group of consumers is willing to pay for its provision. The sum of all individual contributions must cover the marginal cost of production of the public goods. If individual consumers believe that the contributions of others are adequate to guarantee the supply of the good and that their own contribution is not needed, they may attempt to "free-ride" at the cost of others. Thus, because those who are unwilling to pay cannot be excluded, the provision of public goods will remain *suboptimal* (Musgrave 1996) unless there is a mechanism that forces them to reveal their preferences sincerely and to contribute to their provision fairly. This dilemma between public welfare and self-interest is referred to as the *collective action problem*.[24]

However, in the European Union we observe also the opposite of free riding: because the Treaty obligations are strict and cannot be avoided, the high costs of public goods generate the demand to exit the system that generates the public goods. The tedious negotiations about Brexit are in effect about a deal that would allow the UK to keep some of the benefits from the single market without having to pay the price of complying with other rules and regulations such as immigration. The same logic applies to the demands of many Eurosceptics in Central and Eastern Europe.

In principle, there are two approaches to solve the collective action problems, namely by voluntary cooperation or by centralised decision making, i.e. by a government.[25] However, which of the two methods yields the best solution depends on the incentives which public goods provide for individuals to cooperate. Two groups of goods must be distinguished; *club goods* and *common resource goods*. The former are public goods whose usage can be restricted to the particular group of individuals that is willing to contribute towards the production of these goods.

---

[24]See (Olson 1965); (Cooper and John 1988); (Collignon 2003).

[25]See (Hobbes 1996) and also (Hume 1978 [1740], pp. 534–539) who derives government from externalities: "Two neighbours may agree to drain a meadow, which they possess in common; because it is easy for them to know each other's mind; and each must perceive, that the immediate consequence of his failing in his part, is, the abandoning the whole project. But it is very difficult, and indeed impossible, that a thousand persons should agree in any such action; it being difficult for them to concert so complicated a design, and still more difficult for them to execute it.".

By contrast, common resources are limited in quantity and individual consumers seeking to get larger shares can only get them at the expense of others. This is the same mechanism that we have seen in the case of hard budget constraints.

In the first case, members of the group owning the club goods have clear incentives to cooperate as they would otherwise not be able to benefit from these public goods. It is, however, possible that informational asymmetries may hinder or prevent cooperation, if actors are uncertain that their partners will stick to their agreements. In that case, a common institution, such as the European Commission that is committed to the overall maximisation of societal wellbeing, must ensure that the level of informational asymmetries are minimized, so that all actors know and recognise their own best interest. Such an institution is therefore welfare augmenting, but it is not a government.

In the second group of public goods, namely common resource goods, the incentive structure is different. Here, it is not possible to exclude individuals from accessing the benefits derived from these goods, even though the goods themselves are limited resources. The limited amount of resources coupled with the unlimited access and usage by consumers creates the incentive for each actor to acquire as much of these resources as possible before the supply is exhausted, and to exclude others from access. However, that will generate skewed distributions of benefits for other consumers, or the excessive consumption by a large number of consumers will reduce the quantity of the resources. In the literature this is called the "tragedy of the commons" (Hardin 1968): each individual actor is tempted to act in a way that is directly opposed to the overall collective interests. Voluntary cooperation between individual actors is therefore doomed to fail.

To overcome such coordination failure, strict regulations are required. There are two ways for doing this. On the one hand, binding rules with sharp sanctions may prevent individuals from acting contrary to the collective interest. This is the logic behind the strict fiscal rules in the Euro Area. But, as Hume (1978 [1740]) already remarked, if the number of potential free-riders is large, the monitoring costs of compliance with the rule become too high. Only a government that takes decisions as the representative agent on behalf of the whole group can regulate and police individual actions. Citizens as the "owners" of the public good must then set up a government with the intent of preserving their common interests. The common property title gives them the right and the authority to use, if necessary, legitimate violence (the power of government) to prevent individuals from increasing their personal benefit at the cost of the common interest.

Hence, the two different classes of public goods, namely club goods and common resource goods, reflect diametrically opposed incentives for collective action and require different mechanisms for their efficient management. Because voluntary cooperation between individuals and national governments is possible for club goods, decentralised forms of governance would be sufficient to manage these goods. Hence, intergovernmentalism and subsidiarity are methods for successfully governing European club goods. However, these methods no longer work in the European internal market with a single currency, because money is the hard budget constraint. Given that the access to the limited resources is free, the administration of *common resource goods* has to be centralised in a government that is capable of regulating access and solving collective action problems.[26] It follows that the Eurozone must be governed by such a representative agent, i.e. by a proper government.

The Euro and the European Republic

Thus, with the creation of the euro, the dynamics of European integration have changed. The hard budget constraint has created a new logic for governing European public goods. In its early stages, the EU was characterised by the creation of European club goods and the benefits from being part of the club made the EU attractive for new members. Thus, for half a century, this integration strategy has been successful as the gains achieved through cooperation have outweighed coordination

---

[26](Ostrom 1990) has claimed that "an external actor", i.e. a government is not the only solution governing the commons, provided insiders can make binding commitments. However, the point of what I call common resource goods is precisely that such commitments cannot be made because of strategic substitutabilities as described by (Cooper and John 1988).

costs considerably. The Commission, as a custodian of common interests, has reduced informational asymmetries and ensured that member states clearly have recognised their shared interests and cooperated with each other.

However, whilst intergovernmental cooperation has expanded the range and number of public goods,[27] the spillover effects described by neo-functionalists has now also spilled over from club goods to common resource goods. This necessitates the centralisation of decision making. New institutions like the ECB and new policies like the fiscal pact have been set up. As mentioned above, the introduction of the single currency was inevitable after the creation of the European internal market. For without the stability of a single currency, the cost competitiveness of firms and the benefits for consumers would have been constantly distorted by foreign exchange markets.[28] However, the euro has transformed the incentives for policy makers. Because money is the most important *common resource good* of a market economy, it generates distributional gains and losses in a zero-sum game.[29] This has generated new spillover effects into fiscal policy, which is at the core of national sovereignty. For example, interest rates indicate the scarcity of money, so that if a member state government becomes an important net borrower, it pushes up interest rates for all others. This makes borrowing in the Euro Area more expensive for everyone and slows down economic growth for all. It is, therefore, in the common interest of all member states to constrain public borrowing and the Stability and Growth Pact was created for this purpose. However, for individual states the incentives are different: each government could borrow cheaply as long as the partners adhere to the Stability and Growth Pact. In this case, every government would prefer to borrow and spend rather than tax their constituency. National governments have therefore reasons for constraining their partners while they are tempted to free-ride at the expense of their partners. Hence, the interests of each individual

---

[27]This was envisaged and even desired by neofunctionalists from the very beginning, see (Haas 2004).

[28]See (Collignon and Schwarzer 2003) for further details.

[29]See (Collignon 2003) for a full development of this argument.

member state are directly opposed to the collective welfare, and this will generate cooperation failure.

Thomas Hobbes and David Hume have pointed out long ago that such cooperation failure requires a unified government that represents the common interests of all citizens to improve welfare. This argument now also applies to the European Union. The logic of our fiscal policy example can be applied to many other political fields such as structural reforms, competition policy, the completion of full market integration, uniform financial supervision, etc. The most striking example in recent times is migration policy. We may call peace and prosperity the club good which attracts many migrants. In order to avoid overcrowding, Europeans would have to control their borders and exclude undesirable immigrants. However, the costs of border control are unequally distributed with Greece and Italy bearing the heaviest burden. But if these member states are not securing the borders, the cost of dealing with overcrowding immigration will fall on all countries. It is then less surprising that the UK has opted out of this system. The efficient management of the common European interest, however, would consist in a centralized immigration authority with the power of granting asylum and residences to refugees and migrants. But that means giving up the pretence of national sovereignty.

As we saw, common resource goods generate new problems of distribution and social justice. The exclusion principle is at the very core of private property rights and market efficiency, for only those with money can consume private goods. But when market dynamics cause distributional outcomes, which are considered as unfair, losers make moral claims to be compensated. Because inclusive club goods generate positive sum games, compensation is easily justified as no one is made worse off. But for exclusive resource goods, the game is zero-sum and compensation of loser reduces the gains of winners. This redistribution must therefore command the legitimacy and acceptance by all group members concerned. This does not mean that in a Republic every distributional solution is without objection, but that those whose preferences are overruled will still accept the solution at least on procedural grounds. This is the fundamental principle of democracy. Yet, the considerations of fairness and social justice go further; they touch the core of the republican principle. Democratic nation-states have developed the modern welfare state as a redistributive instrument, but this poses a problem for European integration. The EU does not have the legitimacy-generating process of a genuine democracy that justifies the imposition of fairness and social justice.[30] The deeper integration becomes, the larger will be the issues of social justice. Of course, one may stop the integration process itself, but this means abandoning all the benefits derived from public goods. To deal with the issues of social justice would require democracy at the European level. How can a European democracy be legitimized?

Democracy and the Principal-Agent Relationship

State and Republic

For some readers our republican paradigm may sound like a call for setting up a European super-state. This is wrong. The European Union is not a state. Even if it has acquired some traits of statehood and even if more and more areas of life are being touched upon by European decisions, the Union lacks the "monopoly of legitimate physical coercion for enforcing order" (Weber 1972, p. 29). But even if the EU is not a state, it is governed by a statist ideology that positions the Member states as the "masters of the treaties" and "puts European conciliation on the basis of a contractual union of sovereign states".[31] This interpretation has put the clock back in history: in a modern state, governments are agents for the people who are their principals. But if states are the "masters" of the treatise, the agent has usurped the position of the principal. Hence, it is the concept of an absolutist state rather than the concept of a Republic that has become the normative anchor for European law. As "masters" states make sovereign decisions for Europe as a whole, while

---

[30]Rawls has argued that principles of justice should be universally acceptable, but this requires still some form of deliberation for their practical implementation. The European Union is institutionally deprived of such deliberation process.

[31](Bundesverfassungsgericht 2009, S. § 249).

European citizens have no authority to legitimate power. European policies are imposed, but not "owned" by citizens. Such a weak normative foundation of the EU can only lead into an impasse. By contrast, the republican paradigm offers an alternative.

Statism explains how sovereign rule can be legitimate, i.e. under which "circumstances an order of particular content will be obeyed by specific persons".[32] By contrast, the concept of the Republic is related to freedom rather than sovereign rule. It is not value-neutral. The Republic protects the liberty of its citizens against the *domination* of lords and masters by assigning individual *rights* to all citizens.[33] Republican *self-government* is the freedom of citizens to determine the administration of the common public goods that they own. This freedom renders all citizens equal. The republican paradigm must, therefore, explain how to safeguard the ownership rights in public goods and liberties for equal citizens.[34] The Republic is not the objectified exercise of power, but the intentional control of common affairs.[35]

Within the republican tradition different approaches for this control can be identified. The first approach extends from Florence and Venice, through *Montesquieu* and *Rousseau* up to modern-day Switzerland and calls for "small Republics" where direct democracy by all citizens is easily-manageable. This model inspires "populist" interpretations of republicanism. The second tradition began with David Hume and James Madison's *Federalist Paper No. 10* and sees the advantage of a "large Republic" in the fact that in large units the common interest is less likely be blocked by particular interests, so that minorities are less prone to be tyrannized.[36] In a large Republic, the common good can, however,

---

[32]According to Weber's (1972, p. 28) definition of sovereign rule.

[33]For a discussion of Republicanism as non-domination (contrary to liberalism as non-interference) see (Pettit 1997); see also (Kant 1977) for a contrast of the republican constitutional state with the arbitrariness of despotic rule.

[34]For further information about the revival of this republican principle in the American constitutional debate, see (Michelman 1986); (Michelman 1988).

[35]This focus gives republicanism a weak voice in international relations, see: (Onuf 1998).

[36]See (Hume 1978 [1740]); (Hamilton et al.1788) and also (Wood 2003). In modern political economic theory, the problem of small Republics is referred to as *agency capture*.

only be managed through *representative democracy*.[37] The citizens, as the owners of public goods, appoint a government as their agent and custodian. Because the agent is controlled by the principal, the *principal-agent* relationship is the key issue in this Republic.[38] This view links the Republic to modern democracy theories.

Since *John Locke*'s Two Treaties on Government and the Glorious Revolution in 1688, the theories of republicanism and liberal democracy have converged to the core principles that governments are appointed as the agent of the citizens *for a limited time* only, and remain accountable to the principal.[39] *Citizens have the authority* to elect a government as well as the right to dismiss an administration and name a new one.[40] Measured by these standards, the EU is still far from being a democratic Republic. The intergovernmental principle of statehood, which declares that states are sovereign rather than citizens, has deprived Union citizens from exercising their rights as owners of the European *res publica*. How one should set up a constitution for European citizens to appoint an agent for the administration of their European public goods is beyond the scope of this chapter.[41] However, the republican paradigm

---

[37]"A true Republic ... is, and cannot be anything else but, a *representative system* of the people whereby the people's rights are looked after on their behalf by deputies who represent the united will of the citizens." *I.* (Kant 1996 [1785]) § 52, III. (Urbinati 2012) has shown that for early republicans representation was a tool to prevent the populist corruption of democracy and allowed correcting policy mistakes.

[38]As (Price 1991), a radical English Republican and supporter of American independence wrote: If governments "are subject to no control from their constituents, the very idea of liberty will be lost and the power of choosing representatives becomes nothing but a power, lodged in a few, to choose at certain periods a body of masters for themselves and for the rest of the community".

[39]This convergence became possible, because accountability for a limited mandate reduced the danger of populist corruption.

[40](Locke 1988, p. 367): "yet, the Legislative being only a Fiduciary Power to act for certain ends, there remains still in the People a Supreme Power to remove or alter the Legislative, when they find the Legislative to act contrary to the trust reposed in them.".

[41]For a discussion of how the European Republic could be better structured, see (Collignon and Paul 2008). (Besson and Martí 2009, S. 28) distinguish between Republican legal theory and jurisprudence and Republican law, which they continue to divide into substantive and procedural Legal Republicanism. In this paper, I focus on the normative basis of a substantive form of Legal Republicanism although I agree with the authors when they write: "Constitutional provisions are crucial from a republican point of view. ... A republican lawyer is expected to endorse a strongly democratic theory of legal authority" (pp. 29–31).

can re-articulate the principal-agent relationship in ways that are different from federalist statism, which often serves as the benchmark for European integration.

The Sovereignty of the Citizens Against the Power of the State?

In contrast to statism, the republican paradigm differentiates between authority and power. We have argued that the efficient administration of European common resource goods requires a government with centralised power in order to overcome collective action problems. If it is properly authorised by the principal, a government has the power to act in the name and mandate of citizens. Authorised power is right; unauthorised power is tyranny. Bodin (1993) was the first to recognize sovereignty as the authority that is the ultimate source of legislative power.[42] Hence, governments are merely authorised agents, and this implies that states are instruments for the exertion of power. This power must be authorized by someone and this implies that sovereignty can never lie with those *who exercise power*. Since the American and French Revolutions, the people—in the sense of *populus*—have seized this ultimate authority; they are the collective sovereign. The differentiation between authority and power, between citizens as principals and governments as agents, explains the key contribution that the republican tradition can offer towards the institutional reform of the European Union's governance.

Almost all debates concerning the European Union's powers and rights, or its responsibilities and competences, are limited to the question who controls whom, how and why. European Treaties, just as state constitutions, are essentially a set of rules articulating the distribution of power. However, at the European level, the authority of the principal that legitimates the exercise of power is weaker than in nation states, because the power of European institutions is based on the fact that "Member States confer competences to attain objectives they have

---

[42]See (Collignon 2003) and (Grimm 2009, p. 18).

in common"[43] and not on an authoritative act of citizens. Ratifying treaty changes by national referenda does not remedy this weakness, for the vote reflects the opinion of nation state aggregates, not European citizens.[44] European citizens are unable to exercise their sovereignty, because the states consider themselves the "masters of the treaties" and perceive EU citizens merely as "belonging" to nation-states. The division of citizens into nations, which alone have democratically legitimising authority, is the *divide et impera* strategy by which nation-states maintain their monopoly of power. In other words, governments claim an authority, which the republican paradigm would only recognise as coming from all citizens collectively as the unified sovereign.

This dilemma has become particularly clear with the election of the Syriza government in Greece, which promised to change macroeconomic policies, but was unable to convince other member states. The sovereignty of a small subset of European citizens cannot count for the will of all citizens. Only a European government that draws its legitimacy from the universal suffrage of all citizens could claim to be authorized to change policies.

For these reasons, European debates concerning competences, subsidiarity, and loss of sovereignty are rather arbitrary; without the higher authority of the European *populus* the reach of power, which states can confer to the European level, remains normatively undetermined. In the 18th century, this arbitrariness would have been called "tyranny"; nowadays we speak politely of a "democratic deficit". The German Federal Constitutional Court has recognised this problem, but its solution remains within the context of state power. By referring power back to the authority of *Staatsvolk (demos* and not *populus)*, i.e. to the fusion of the state and people in their "unity of sameness", the German court has adopted the communitarian-holistic interpretation of pre-political nationhood as the source of democratic legitimacy. This interpretation

---

[43]Art. 1 Para. 1 TEU.

[44]To give an example: the Constitutional Treaty was submitted to ratification by national referenda in Spain, the Netherlands, France and Luxemburg. Out of the total 49 329 676 votes, 26 661 082 were in favour of the Treaty and 22 668 594 were opposed. Despite this solid majority of 8.1% in favour of ratification, the Treaty was rejected because in France and the Netherlands local majorities were against.

is shared with French sovereignists, who see it as their Jacobinist inheritance.[45] It has become the default mode for discussing the governance of the EU. However, this sovereignism intensifies the European legitimacy problems. The violations of the Stability and Growth Pact, the difficulties of setting up a European bailout fund and concluding the fiscal compact, not to speak of the complete breakdown of cooperation in the refugee crisis, they all show how nation-states are generating negative externalities for the Euro Area, because their governments are defending the interests of partial electorates and not the European sovereign. These policy externalities would be overcome by a European government with a unified constituency able to authorize European policies.

Hence, the European Republic paradigm avoids the externality dilemma for three reasons. First, all European citizens are defined as the owners of those and only those public goods by which they are all affected. This definition establishes a clear norm for delineating the competences of a European government. The reach of usage defines the public good. A person can be an owner of private, local, national and European public goods and is, therefore, simultaneously a member of multiple communities. For each class of public goods, the owners can appoint different agents to take care of their specific common properties. The government of the European Republic can therefore concentrate on the efficient administration of European public goods instead of being gridlocked by communitarian-holistic claims from other policy constituencies. By focussing on European public goods and the interests citizens have with respect to their administration, the European Republic stops short of being a superstate, which assimilates different cultures and communities into a hierarchically structured whole. It, therefore, preserves the freedom of diversity.

Second, as the owners of public goods, all European citizens are the principal with the authority to bestow power on a government. For this reason, citizens must have the right to choose and control their agents through general elections. This right constitutes their *republican*

---

[45](Sieyès 1789) proclaimed: « *La nation existe avant tout, elle est l'origine de tout.* » and *J.-P. Chevènement* (La faute de M. Monnet; Paris, 2006, p. 65) explained: "*Avec la Révolution naissent ensemble le 'Peuple français' et la République 'une et indivisible'*". The paradigm of the

freedom. As owners of European public goods, all citizens are also equal in their rights and duties, and this means that the asymmetry of power between large and small member states is counterbalanced by the democratic principles of One man, one vote. Presently, Europe's governance does not give citizens this right, because national governments control the policy-making process and its institutions (Commission, Parliament, Council, etc.). No doubt, the EU is formally a legitimate institution, because democratic states have conferred competences to the European level (Bogdandy and Jürgen 2009), but this fact does not satisfy the radicalism of the republican paradigm, because the recourse to citizens' authority, by which that transfer of power is authorised, is fragmented and incomplete.

To avoid misunderstandings: the authority of the owners of public goods is not only manifested in a one-off constitutional act, i.e. in their *pouvoir constituant;* it reappears every time the republican government is up for election. It allows citizens to choose policies consistent with their preferences for social justice and European public goods. National elections cannot fulfil this task, because they are only offering choices between national policy bundles which contain, at best, a few low-salience European components but no coherent European policy designs. The Europe of nation-states prevents citizens systematically from participating in the important collective deliberation and will formation, through which all citizens constitute themselves as free and equal individuals. Only this broad deliberation will gradually generate the epistemic transformation which, in turn, will widen the boundaries of trust and solidarity.[46]

Third, as the sovereign who owns European public goods, all citizens are equally affected by the externalities of public goods and this fact constitutes their *civic equality*, which gives them a right to participate in the political process and public deliberation of collective choice. This

---

European Republic proposed here would require German communitarians to understand that the *Bundesrepublik* is first of all a republic, and the French souverainists to understand that the Republic can be « *une et divisible* » . See also (Chopin 2002).

[46](Eriksen 2009) especially Chap. 3.

equality requires, of course, fair procedures for decision-making, such as "One man, one vote" in general elections; but, in addition, the republican paradigm asserts that through their participation in public deliberation, people find solutions and form opinions about how to administer public goods.[47] Public deliberation takes place in the form of political campaigns focussed on choosing a government. The indirect choice through national governments is not democracy, but only its derivative. With the present governance of the EU, democracy is impossible. The Council operates like an "eternal parliament", which renews itself only through by-elections. From a republican perspective, political decisions about the orientations of the administration of European public goods must be authorised by *all* European citizens *together*, as they are all collective owners of these goods.

The Federal Order of the Republic

With the republican *principal-agent* approach we can now derive normatively the competences of a European government from public goods and define sovereignty as ownership rights in these public goods. By contrast, intergovernmentalism and federalism are statist theories based on power relations (Schönberger 2004). Intergovernmentalism identifies sovereignty with states. Thus, in its ruling on the Lisbon Treaty, the German Constitutional Court has viewed the European Union as "an association of sovereign states (*Staatenverbund*). The concept of *Verbund* covers a long-term close association of states which remain sovereign, a treaty-based association which exercises public authority, but whose fundamental order is subject to the decision-making power of the member states and in which the peoples, in the form of cultural groups and not as owners of public goods, remain the property of the states."[48] Hence, citizens are *subjects*, not sovereign.

---

[47]For a discussion see: (Habermas 1996); (Habermas 1997); (Collignon 2003); (Eriksen 2009).
[48]Quote from (Bundesverfassungsgericht, 2 BvR 2/08 from 30.6.2009, 2009, p. §1).

The point of being dominated by foreign states was one of the most convincing arguments made by Eurosceptics in the British Brexit debate. But the desire "to take back sovereignty" implies logically the dissolution of collective property rights for goods shared with other Europeans. Preserving the benefits of integration requires "taking sovereignty forward" into a European democratic republic.

However, the European Republic is not a federal state. European federalists interpret the European Union as a state in-the-making. Citizens are the sovereign, but they are assimilated by a European state, to which local interests are subordinated. They assume the federation to be founded on an identity of interests (say because everyone wants peace), and this justifies conferring power to a federal government. This government then has the power to interfere with local public goods, even if they do not concern *all* European citizens. The Euro-federalist approach remains indifferent to the diversity and heterogeneity of cultures, values, preferences that characterises the European Union.

Neither intergovernmentalism nor Euro-federalism are able to define coherently which competences ought to be delegated to a local and which to a European government. By contrast, the republican approach calls for a government at the European level that is founded on the communality of particular interests with respect to specific public goods. Such government is *solely* responsible for the administration of European public goods and must be legitimised through pan-European elections. National governments are responsible for the administration of national public goods, which affect citizens exclusively in their respective states and for this reason they are appointed by national elections.

A European government would logically arise from redefining the competences of the current European Commission, as the Commission already possesses the requisite administrative and technical infrastructure necessary for a government. The European Parliament would have to provide the democratic legitimacy, as it is the only institution which is grounded in universal suffrage. There is an important difference between the present day Commission and a democratic government because governments are agents that are politically responsible for and accountable to their citizens who are sovereign, while the European

Commission is responsible to member states—even if its president is elected by the European parliament. This dependency on member states follows from the idea that states are sovereign and not citizens, so that member states keep political competences for European public goods under their control and the European Parliament's legislative competences are severely constrained. The republican approach to Europe's governance would broaden its competences to cover the full range of European public goods and establish stronger institutional links between the Commission and the Parliament.

The European Republic will politicise the Commission through the Parliament. If the President of the Commission (functioning as the government of the European Republic) is elected by the Parliament, political parties have to present alternative candidates prior to EP elections. In order to win a majority, candidates must present alternative programmes, which seek cross-border support and would thereby become integrative. Given their right to choose, citizens would deliberate about policies that serve their interests as owners of European public goods. The interests of the citizens would then be articulated on a left-right political spectrum rather than according to national identities and reflect ideas of social justice for the EU rather than nation states (Hix 2008). This politization will generate the public sphere for European-wide debates, deliberation and policy consensus. Hence, republican participation is dependent on institutions, which encourage it and not on pre-existing demos-identities.

However, if European public goods *define* the European Republic, the *need* to create European government arises only from the existence of common resource goods, which are generated by the hard budget constraint. Hence, common resource goods are the hard core of the European Republic. A republican government must have clear competences for these common resource goods, because this is where voluntary cooperation between member states will not produce optimal results. In the case of club goods, where national governments have an incentive to cooperate with each other, the European government would mainly fulfil a supportive role by overcoming information asymmetries. However, the differentiated incentive structure for decision making means that the federal order of the European Republic is complex. The Treaty of Lisbon has already divided the Union's competences into *exclusive, shared, coordinated,* and *supporting* competences.[49] From a republican perspective, exclusive goods should be administered through the exclusive competences assigned to a European government. Shared competitive and coordinated competences are sufficient for inclusive goods.[50]

Hence, if the European Union is to survive, policy competences, must be re-allocated. Fiscal and related tax policies are a good example. It was argued above that a large number of common resource goods have come into existence because of the hard budget constraint of money. The euro crisis has shown that the stability of the Euro is a European public good which is threatened by the actions of single member states. The same problem has appeared as a threat to the liberty of free movement of people during the refugee crisis. While the proper solution is to appoint a European government with the power to enforce coherent policies after being authorized by all European citizens, the European *governance* must also take into consideration that there are public goods that do not affect all, but only a subset of citizens in different member states. For example, common monetary and financial policies currently affect only 65.8% of the population of the EU (before Brexit), although all member states, with the exception of Denmark and previously the UK, are obliged to adopt the Euro. Also, there are public goods that exhibit only mild external effects in other member states. For example, the Mediterranean Cooperation and Baltic Sea Cooperation affect neighbouring states far more than those on the other side of Europe. Hence, not every public good with transnational externalities should be administered by a single government. However, it would defeat the principles of representative democracy, if every configuration of public goods had its own government and parliament. This is why proposals for multispeed Europe cannot solve the externality problems. In a Republic, public goods are therefore bundled to serve the common interest of all concerned, and in the European Republic all

---

[49]Art. 3–6 TFEU.

[50]For a classification, see also (Haratsch et al. 2010, S. Rn 149–155).

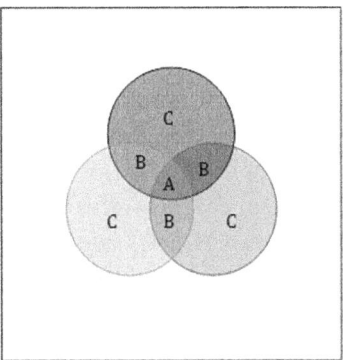

Fig. 3.1 Overlapping externalities

European public goods would have to be bundled together, so that they could be administered efficiently. The key to deciding how this is done lies with the principle of *minimisation* of negative externalities (rather than their elimination).

This complex allocation of competences is demonstrated in a simplified way in the Venn diagram in Fig. 3.1. Each circle represents the set of citizens of a member state that are affected by a certain policy decision. In section A where all circles overlap, we find European public goods that affect all citizens; these goods define the European Republic and require a European government. In section B, the externalities of some subgroups of European citizens overlap. There is a large potential for intergovernmental policy in this section, although the European government may play a supportive role in such intergovernmental cooperation. In section C, member states are largely autonomous and national parliaments must be able to represent the sovereign rights of their citizens. This shows how the republican paradigm can provide clear criteria for structuring the competences of a European government.

Conclusion

The Euro crisis, the refugee crisis and Brexit have clearly exposed the limits of the traditional European model of integration. Sovereign member states are not capable of administrating the common goods of European citizens efficiently. The fractioned sovereignty of nation states cannot change European policies because partial legitimacy cannot be generalized into full legitimacy. After some hesitation, the Euro Area Member states have finally agreed in the Euro crisis to increase cooperation and control mechanisms through the Commission and the Council. Yet, the policies imposed on some Member states have widened the democratic deficit and deepened concerns with social (in) justice because they were not chosen by citizens after European-wide deliberation. These reforms are inconsistent with republican principles of freedom, equality, democracy and the self-determination of citizens. They have tempted voters to support sovereignist parties who challenge the mainstream consensus between member state governments.

The alternative is exit. The British voters have made a decision that was consistent with the traditions of Westminster's parliamentary democracy, but the price of this coherence was giving up the benefits of European public goods.

The republican paradigm allows a new perspective, not only in relation to politics, but perhaps more importantly in relation to European law. It focuses on social justice and European public welfare as the property rights of free citizens define who has the right to appoint and control a government that administrates their public goods. With the large range of European public goods already in existence, the European Republic is not a utopia but rather a daily reality for all citizens. Citizens, as the owners of European goods, must therefore have effective control rights that they could exercise through elections. The precise details of how a republican practice could be put into place must still be decided upon. Working this out is the challenge of our time.

References

Anderheiden, M. (2006). *Gemeinwohl in Republik und union.* Tübingen: Mohr Siebeck.

Arrow, K. J. (1963). *Social choice and individual values* (2nd ed.). New Haven and London: Yale University Press.

Besson, S., & Martí, J. L. (2009). *Legal republicanism. National and international perspectives.* Oxford: Oxford University Press.

Bobbio, N., & Viroli, M. (2003). *The idea of the republic.* Cambridge: Polity Press.

Bodin, J. (1993). Les six livres de la République. Paris: Librairie Générale de France.

Bundesverfassungsgericht (BVerfG). (2009). 2 BvR 2/08 from 30.6.2009.

Chevènement, J. (2006). La faute de M. Monnet. Paris: Fayard.

Chiusi, T. (2005). Strukturen des römischen Eigentums im Spiegel rhetorisch-philosophischer Texte Ciceros. In A. Eckl & B. Ludwig (Eds.), *Was ist Eigentum? Philosophische Positionen von Platon bis Habermas, München* (pp. 59–72). München: C. H. Beck.

Chopin, T. (2002). *La République une et divisible: Les Fondements de la Fédération Américaine.* Paris: Plon.

Cicero. (2006). *De re publica.* (1. Keyes, Trans.) Cambridge, MA: Harvard University Press.

Cohen, J., & Sabel, C. (2006). Extra Rempublicam Nulla Justitia? *Philosophy & Public Affairs, 34*(2), 147–175.

Collignon, S. (2003). *The European republic: Reflections on the political economy of a future constitution.* London: Federal Trust for Education and Research.

Collignon, S. (2007a). *Bundesrepublik Europa? Die demokratische Herausforderung und Europas Krise.* Berlin: Vorwärts Verlag.

Collignon, S. (2007b). Three sources of legitimacy for European fiscal policy. *International Political Science Review, 28*(2), 155–184. Sage Publications.

Collignon, S., & Schwarzer, D. (2003). *Private sector involvement in the Euro: The power of ideas.* London: Routledge.

Collignon, S. (2004). Vive la République européenne. Paris: Ed. La Martinière.

Collignon, S. (2008). Viva la Repubblica Europea!. Venezia: Marsilio editore.

Collignon, S., & Paul, C. (2008). Pour la République européenne. Paris: Éditions Odile Jacob.

Constant, B. (1816). The Liberty of Ancients Compared with that of Moderns. In B. Constant (Ed.). Liberty Fund. Retrieved from http://oll.libertyfund.org/title/2251.

Cooper, R., & John, A. (1988). Coordinating coordination failures in a keynesian model. *The Quarterly Journal of Economics, 103*(3), 441–463.

Dumont, L. (1986). *Essays on individualism*. Chicago: Chicago University Press.

Eckl, A., & Ludwig, B. (Eds.). (2005). *Was ist Eigentum? Philosophische Positionen von Platon bis Habermas*. München: C.H. Beck.

Eriksen, E. O. (2009). *The unfinished democratization of Europe*. Oxford: Oxford University Press.

Eurobarometer. (2010). Standard Eurobarometer 73. Public Opinion in the European Union, First Results.

Grawert, R. (2004). Staatsvolk und Staatsangehörigkeit. In Isensee & Kirchhof (Eds.). Handbuch des Staatsrechts, Bd. (II, 3. ed). § 16.

Grimm, D. (2009). *Souveränität. Herkunft und Zukunft eines Schlüsselbegriffs*. Berlin: Berlin University Press.

Gröschner, R. (2004). Die Republik. In Isensee & Kirchhof (Eds.). Handbuch des Staatsrechts, Bd. (II, 3. ed.). Heidelberg: C.F. Müller.

Haas, E. B. (1964). *Beyond the nation state: Functionalist and international organization*. Stanford: Stanford University Press.

Haas, E. B. (2004). The Uniting of Europe. Political, Social and Economic Forces 1950–1957. Indiana, USA: Notre Dame Press.

Habermas, J. (1997). *Between facts and norms; Polity Press, Cambridge UK*. Cambridge, UK: Polity Press.

Habermas, J. (1996). *Die Einbeziehung des Anderen. Studien zur politischen Theorie*. Frankfurt A. M.: Suhrkamp.

Hamilton, A., Madison, J., & Jay, J. (1788). The federalist papers. New York.

Haratsch, A., Koenig, C., & Pechstein, M. (2010). Europarecht (7th ed.). Tübingen: Mohr Siebeck.

Hardin, G. (1968). The tragedy of the commons. *Science, 162*(3859), 1243–1248.

Henke, W. (1981). Zum Verfassungsprinzip der Republik. *JuristenZeitung (JZ), 36*, 249–251.

Hix, S. (2008). *What's wrong with the Europe union and how to fix it*. Oxford: Polity Press.

Hobbes, T. (1996). Hobbes, Thomas. (R. Tuck, Ed.). Cambridge: Cambridge University Press.

Hume, D. (1740). *A treatise of human nature: Being an attempt to introduce the experimental method of reasoning into moral subjects.* London: Oxford University Press.

Isensee, J. (1981). Republik—Sinnpotential eines Begriffs. *JuristenZeitung (JZ), 36,* 1–8.

Isensee, J. (2004). Staat und Verfassung. In J. Isensee & P. Kirchhof (Eds.). *Handbuch des Staatsrechts,* Bd. (II, 3. ed.). Heidelberg: C.F. Müller.

Israel, J. (2004). The intellectual origins of modern democratic republicanism (1660–1720). *European Journal of Political Theory, 3*(1), 7–36.

Joerges, C. (2005). What is left of the European Economic Constitution?A melancholic eulogy. *European Law Review, 30,* 461–489.

Kant, I. (1977). Über den Gemeinspruch: Das mag in der Theorie richtig sein, taugt aber nicht für die Praxis. In I. Kant (Ed.), Werke in zwölf Bänden (Vol. 11, pp. 143–165). Frankfurt A. M.: Suhrkamp.

Kant, I. (1996 [1785]). Groundwork of the metaphysics of morals. In I. Kant, & A. W. Wood (Ed.), Practical Philosophy. Cambridge: CUP.

Locke, J. (1988). Two treaties of government. (P. Laslett, Ed.) Cambridge: CUP.

Machiavelli, N. (2000). Discorsi sopra la prima deca di Tito Livio, Torino: ed. Einaudi.

Majone, G. (1998). Europe's 'democratic deficit': The question of standards. *European Law Journal, 4*(1), 5–28.

Michelman, F. I. (1986). Foreword: Traces of Self-government. *Harvard Law Review, 100,* 4–77.

Michelman, F. I. (1988). Law's republic. *The Yale Law Journal, 97*(8), 1493–1537. Symposium: The Republican Civic Tradition.

Mill, J. S. (1909). *Principles of political economy.* London: Longman, Green & Co., London.

Moravcsik, A. (2008). The myth of europe's 'democratic deficit'. *Intereconomics: Journal of European Public Policy (November–December 2008),* pp. 331–340.

Musgrave, R. A. (1996). The role of the state in Fiscal Theory. *International Tax and Public Finance, 3,* 247–258.

Nagel, T. (2005). The problem of global justice. *Philosophy & Public Affairs, 33*(2), 113–147.

Olson, M. (1965). *The logic of collective actions: Public goods and the theory of groups.* London: Oxford University Press.

Onuf, N. G. (1998). *The republican legacy in international thought*. Cambridge: Cambridge University Press.

Ostrom, E. (1990). *Governing the commons: The evolution of institutions for collective action*. Cambridge: Cambridge University Press.

Pettit, P. (1997). *Republicanism. A theory of freedom and government*. Oxford: Oxford University Press.

Plato, (2003). *Republic (Politeia)*. Cambridge, MA: LCL, Harvard University Press.

Pocock, J. G. A. (1975). *The machiavellian moment: florentine political thought and the atlantic republican tradition*. Princeton: Princeton University Press.

Popper, K. (1995). *The open society and its enemies*. London: Routledge.

Price, R. (1991). *Political writings*. Cambridge: Cambridge University Press.

Rawls, J. (1999). *A theory of justice*. Cambridge: Harvard University Press.

Samuelson, P. A. (1938). A note on the pure theory of consumers' behaviour. *Economica, 5*(17), 61–71.

Scharpf, F. W. (1985). Die Politikverflechtungs-Falle: Europäische Integration und deutscher Föderalismus im Vergleich. *Politische Vierteljahresschrift (PVS), 26*(4), 323–356.

Scharpf, F. W. (1999). *Governing in Europe: Effective and Democratic?* Oxford: OUP.

Schönberger, C. (2004). Die Europäische Union als Bund. Zugleich ein Beitrag zur Verabschiedung des Staatenbund-Bundesstaat-Schemas. *AöR, 129*, 81–120.

Sen, A. (2009). *The idea of justice*. London: Penguin Books.

Sieyès, E. J. (1789). *Qu'est-ce que le Tiers Etat*. Paris: Presses Universitaires de France.

Skinner, Q. (2009). A genealogy of the modern state. *Proceedings of the British Academy, 162*, 325–370.

Skinner, Q. (2002). From the state of princes to the person of the state. In Q. Skinner (Ed.), *Visions of politics* (Vol. II). Cambridge: Cambridge University Press.

Spinelli, A., & Rossi, E. (2016). 1 Manifesto di Ventotene / The Ventotene Manifesto, Altiero Spinelli e Ernesto Rossi. Editrice Ultima spiaggia. Camogli: Editrice Ultima spiaggia.

Tuck, R. (2003). *Philosophy and government 1572–1651*. Cambridge: Cambridge University Press.

Urbinati, N. (2003). *Mill on democracy. From the athenian polis to representative government*. Chicago: The University of Chicago Press.

Urbinati, N. (2012). Competing for liberty: The republican critique of democracy. *American Political Science Review, 106,* 607–621.

von Bogdandy, A. (2004). Europäische Verfassung und europäische Identität. Juristenzeitung. 53–56.

von Bogdandy, A. (2005). Die europäische Republik, ApuZ 36/2005, pp. 21–27. ApuZ(36), 21–27.

von Bogdandy, A. (2005). Konstitutionalisierung des europäischen öffentlichen Rechts in der europäischen Republik. *Juristenzeitung.* 529–534.

von Bogdandy, A., & Jürgen Bast., (2009). The federal order of competences. In A. V. Bogdandy (Ed.), *Principles of European constitutional law* (2nd ed., pp. 275–307). Oxford: OUP.

von Münch, I., & Mager, U. (2009). Staatsrecht I. Staatsorganisationsrecht unter Berücksichtigung der europarechtlichen Bezüge (7th. ed.). Stuttgart: Kohlhammer.

Weber, M. (1972). Wirtschaft und Gesellschaft. Tübingen: Mohr Siebeck.

Wesel, U. (2010). Geschichte des Rechts in Europa. Munich: C.H. Beck.

Wood, G. S. (2003). The American revolution. *A history.* New York: Modern Library.

4

On Paradigms and Public Goods: Has the Eurozone Crisis Changed the Economic Paradigm of EMU?

Sebastian Diessner

A first glimpse at the policy responses to the Euro Area crisis leaves us puzzled. We observe that the policy paradigm of 'sound money, sound public finances' that has dominated the construction of monetary union has been both confirmed *and* undermined. Some scholars speak of 'lock-in to' (Featherstone 2012) as well as 'collapse of' (Jones 2013) the policy prescriptions of the Brussels-Frankfurt consensus. But while these observations can hardly be true at the same time, the empirical evidence seems to support both positions: an ostentatious toughening of EMU fiscal surveillance underlines the notion of 'sound public finance' (Boyer 2013; Woodruff 2014), while unconventional monetary policy decisions by the ECB have called into question the hard-nosed stance of 'sound money' (Stark 2013; Sinn 2014). We have lost track of how the European macroeconomic policy consensus has developed and changed throughout the existence of EMU and in particular during the Euro Area crisis. In other words: What currency does the Euro Area's policy paradigm of 'stable money and sound finances' still have today?

S. Diessner(✉)
London School of Economics and Political Science, London, UK
e-mail: s.diessner@lse.ac.uk

© The Author(s) 2017
S. Collignon, *The Governance of European Public Goods*,
DOI 10.1007/978-3-319-64012-9_4

Despite puzzling signals, I argue that the empirical evidence of early crisis responses does not support the view of a paradigm shift in EMU; the stable-money-sound-finances paradigm continues to be of heightened significance for the governance of the Euro Area. In the remainder of the chapter, I will first provide a brief review of the relevant literature dealing with ideas and paradigms in Euro Area policy-making. Second, I will elaborate on how to theorize paradigm shifts in the context of policy change (Hall 1993). Third, I will spell out the major elements of the Euro Area's policy paradigm of stable money and sound finances as a basis for my subsequent empirical case studies. Fourth, I will analyse two key policy responses to the Euro Area crisis employing the theoretical framework. Finally, I will discuss the implications of this analysis in relation to the other chapters of this book.

The Crisis and the Euro Area's Dominant Paradigm

What cues can we take from the academic literature with regard to paradigms and the Euro Area crisis? Generally speaking, the literature has two foci: some deal with responses to the 'first' or 'second' crisis in the Euro Area (i.e. the financial crisis of 2008/2009 or the sovereign debt crisis that erupted in late 2009/early 2010) (cf. Schelkle 2011) and others analyse national or EU responses to these crises.[1] I will briefly discuss the major arguments of these contributions.

We find a growing number of analyses of policy-makers' reactions to the fallouts of both the financial and debt crises, spanning different disciplines and often bundled to include European cases under the

---

[1]For the sake of brevity, the focus of this section is on the expanding body of literature dealing with responses to the financial and economic crisis, while, needless to say, the study of ideas and politics in European economic and monetary cooperation can be traced back much further. Early intriguing accounts include, for instance, Ludlow's (1982) longue durée view of the politics behind the establishment of the European Monetary System and Garrett and Weingast's (1993) construction of the EU's Internal Market. A concise summary of different works is also provided by McNamara (1998, Chap. 3).

tagline of the global 'Great Recession' (Bermeo and Pontusson 2012; Kahler and Lake 2013; Grant and Wilson 2012). While basically all countries and regions of the European Union are covered,[2] the studies dealing specifically with the role of ideas in policy reactions have centred conspicuously around government responses in France and Germany, sometimes also including Italy or Spain (Schmidt 2012), be it in the form of stand-alone case studies or in comparative perspective. Representative for the argument of a strong ideational influence are the accounts of Clift (2012), Vail (2014) and Schmidt (2012) who elaborate on the tenets of 'post-dirigisme' in France (i.e. the notion of an activist state, intervening in markets but also facilitating the market position of multinational French firms) and of Vail (2014), Schmidt (2014) and Siems and Schnyder (2014) who trace German crisis responses to the origins of ordoliberal thinking (i.e. the idea of an 'enabling' state whose principal role is to create a rule-based framework that enables market competition, mainly by preventing cartels and monopolies). Scholars like Young (2014), Dullien and Guérot (2012) and Schäfer (2016) take this argument further and suggest that Germany's national policy responses and German preferences for EU-level crisis management are heavily influenced by ordoliberal philosophy.

An opposing view to most of these arguments is provided by Schelkle (2012b), who contends that German and French reactions to the crisis have been in contradiction with the notions of (post-)dirigisme and ordoliberalism, although governments have guised them in the rhetoric of these traditions in order to uphold the appearance of continuity. Her argument, however, is more convincing with regard to the financial crisis than regarding the Euro Area sovereign debt crisis, where she sees French and German executives as acting indeed according to their 'political visions for a united Europe' which she perceives to be 'long-standing' (whether these are congruent with dirigisme or ordoliberalism as is claimed by other authors can, of course, still be debated) (Schelkle 2012b: 144).

---

[2]See, amongst others, the works on policy responses in Southern Europe (Armingeon and Baccaro 2012), the Nordic countries (Lindvall 2012; Martin 2012), France and Germany (Schelkle 2012b), Central and Eastern Europe (Darvas 2010) and Great Britain and Ireland (Barnes and Wren 2012).

A notable non-Euro Area country case study is that of Hodson and Mabbett (2009) who analyse crisis responses in the UK relying on the same analytical framework as I do in this chapter (i.e. the analysis of policy paradigms). The authors' findings are analogous to mine since they claim that, despite puzzling signs, a paradigm shift has not occurred in UK policy-making. Hodson and Mabbett (2009) focus, is however, on the attempts of a nation-state to contain the financial crisis while mine is on the Euro Area as a monetary union battling through the sovereign debt crisis, which has profound additional implications.

When looking at EU-level responses to the debt crisis, many scholars have critically examined the policy consensus that guides Euro Area governance and policy-making in 'normal' as well as in crisis times.[3] Two opposing lines of argument can be detected in this debate and this is where my chapter aims to make a contribution. On the one side, authors like Featherstone (2012), De Grauwe (2013) and Boyer (2013) argue that EMU crisis management is *locked in*—and thus hampered by—the policy paradigm that was dominant at its creation, ultimately leading policy-makers to misdiagnose both the causes and the severity of the crisis. In this view, the founding consensus of EMU continues to be of marked significance.[4] On the other side, Jones (2013) and Stark (2013) hold that this founding consensus has collapsed, thereby causing a paradigm shift in EMU policymaking. The clearest manifestation of this collapse, they argue, is the European Central Bank's intervention in sovereign bond markets. On the whole, the signals we can extract from the Euro Area's response to its prolonged crisis are indeed mixed and thus nurture both positions. I will now assess each side's views in light of empirical evidence and show how they may even be reconcilable.

---

[3]Studies on EU-level responses to the *financial* crisis, by contrast, tend to be merely collections of different national crisis responses, for the notable reason that responsibility for emergency measures such as fiscal stimuli 'was left almost entirely in the hands of the member states' (Cameron 2012, as quoted in Schelkle 2012b: 146). EU-level action in the form of the so-called European Economic Recovery Plan was, on the whole, far from coordinated and constituted little more than a smaller top-up to what member states had already decided to be their fiscal stimuli (ibid.).

[4]A variant of this argument is offered by Schelkle and Hassel (2012) who assert that while EMU's policy consensus is indeed persistent, it is not limited to Euro Area policy-making and rather forms part of the mainstream macroeconomic consensus known as the 'new neoclassical synthesis' (Woodford 2009).

Studying Policy Paradigms

In order to make sense of the Euro Area's policy paradigm and its evolution, I first introduce the necessary theoretical foundations regarding the study of ideas and paradigms in the process of policy-making. Based on these considerations, I will explain and justify the methodological framework and empirical material employed in this chapter.

Ideas and Paradigms in the Study of Policy-making

Most likely to some disdain of the distinguished Thomas Kuhn (2012[1962]), the concept of ideational paradigms has travelled from its original sphere of application, the natural sciences, to inform a significant body of research within the social sciences as well.[5] This includes the study of politics as the process of policy-making. Ideas, best defined as shared causal beliefs, can be deemed central to policy-making in the very general sense that all policies 'are made within some system of ideas and standards which is comprehensible and plausible to the actors involved' (Anderson 1978: 23; Hall 1993: 279). If such a system of ideas induces broad consensus about the appropriateness of policy-makers' responses to the policy challenges they face, we may speak of a paradigm (Béland and Cox 2011, 2013: 193). In his 1993 classic paper about macroeconomic policy-making in Britain, Peter Hall has further advanced and clarified this concept of paradigms in policy-making: We can conceive of a policy paradigm as a 'framework of ideas [...] that specifies not only the goals of policy and the kind of instruments that can be used to attain them, but also the very nature of the problems they are meant to be addressing'[6] (Hall 1993: 279).

---

[5]Indeed, Kuhn's seminal work on *The Structure of Scientific Revolution*s was written precisely as an attempt to distinguish the natural from the social sciences (2012[1962]: *x*).

[6]Note that this type of paradigm is distinct from the notion of an overarching paradigm that 'usher[s] in a new era' of approaching policy problems (such as, for example, the common perception of Keynesianism or neoliberalism): A policy paradigm typically dominates a specific policy field, while an overarching paradigm may prove broad enough to encompass a number of different policy fields (Hall 2013b: 191; Béland and Cox 2013: 193).

For scholars of European politics and beyond, Hall's article laid the foundations for an ideational research agenda which has evolved ever since. Many of these variants aim at integrating the study of ideas with other objects of study in the social sciences, such as the role of institutions or (material) interests as explanatory variables (Schmidt 2011; Hay 2011). Most notably, the years following the publication of Hall's seminal piece have seen the rise of the 'new institutionalisms' whose number typically ranges from three to four, all of which have come to rely increasingly on incorporating ideas into their frameworks of analysis[7] (Hall and Taylor 1996; Schmidt 2010). However, a key problem in ideational scholarship remains. Most scholars would agree that the nature of ideas, in contrast to other objects of study, can be seen as particularly elusive. In simple terms: Ideas, it seems, may just be too fuzzy and impalpable to get a proper hold on. It thus appears all the more relevant to devise and employ a framework of analysis that relies on clearly defined variables, allowing ideas to be subjected to rigorous scientific scrutiny.

How are we then supposed to make the impact of ideas apparent, by means of clearly defined and testable variables? To begin with, the concept of social learning expressed through 'three orders of policy change' that Hall (1993) delineated in his original article can guide us particularly well in that respect (building on Heclo (1975) and Kuhn (1962)). The argument, in short, is that if policy responses change alongside three major variables (policy goals, instruments and instrument settings) as a reflection of past experience and new information, then learning on behalf of the involved policy-makers has taken place (Hall 1993: 278). Hence, social learning emphasises the impact of ideas on policy-making in the form of policy-makers' interpretation of—and dissatisfaction

---

[7]As Berman (2013: 217) notes succinctly, we can indeed say that the ideational research agenda has expanded 'to the point where it now includes everyone from constructivists to rational choice theorists'.

with—past events and policies as well as their screening and incorporation of new policy-relevant knowledge, both of which inform their attempts to adjust policy outcomes (Berman 2013: 219–220).

The policy fields most amenable to studies of social learning are, according to Hall, those that are particularly technical and knowledge-intensive in nature, such as macroeconomic policy[8] (cf. Heclo 1975: 312), and that are thus often under the control of hierarchical and somewhat closed agencies and bureaucracies (Hall 1993: 277). Both of these properties are clear from our study of Euro Area policy responses: The macroeconomic policy fields that I examine are monetary policy (conducted by the politically independent European Central Bank) and fiscal surveillance (lying within the shared sphere of responsibility of the Economic and Financial Affairs Council, short ECOFIN, and, albeit to a lesser extent, the bureaucratic administration of the European Commission). Beyond this, the need and willingness of policy-makers to adjust policy responses due to dissatisfaction with past experiences is particularly pronounced during the 'hard times' that crisis situations typically entail (cf. Gourevitch 1986; Hall 2013a).

The Three Orders of Policy Change

This chapter focuses on the policy-making process as typically involving three central variables: the overall goals that policy in a specific field is geared to, the policy instruments that are devised and employed to achieve these goals, and the specific levels or settings of the instruments (Hall 1993: 278). Depending on which of these variables are modified and how, the process of policy change may take one of three different forms or 'orders'. First, if policy-makers adjust only the settings

---

[8]We can understand why ideas are central to macroeconomic policy-making if we bear in mind the fundamental uncertainty about the workings of the macroeconomy: As policy-makers face difficulties to collect and properly interpret macroeconomic data as well as to find an agreement over what constitutes the 'correct' macroeconomic policy path for an uncertain future, their shared beliefs indeed become a guiding principle for policy (McNamara 1998: 57). Issing (2006: 3), for instance, recalls that the creation of the ECB's monetary policy strategy at the outset of EMU was perceived by officials as occurring in 'a situation of extreme uncertainty'.

of policy instruments without changing the instruments themselves, nor the goals they are meant to attain, we may speak of first order change. Second, if both instruments and their settings are altered, but the overall goals of policy remain unchanged, we call this second order change. Third, in cases where all three variables of the policy-making process are deliberately modified in response to past experience (hence, including changes in the hierarchy of goals that are to be achieved in the respective policy field) we speak of third order change (ibid., 278–279).

How can we utilize this basic model to understand the movement of ideas and policy outcomes in the Euro Area crisis? Here, the insights and propositions of social learning (Heclo 1975) come to our aid, as they enable us to establish measurable criteria. Borrowing from Kuhn's (1962) observations about 'normal science' and paradigmatic movements, we can give meaning to the three orders of policy change in relation to one another and flesh out some of their specific characteristics. In general, first and second order change can be associated with 'normal policy-making', broadly preserving the patterns and continuities of policy within an overarching policy paradigm, while third order change plays out as a more profound shift in the terms of policy discourse with far reaching changes in policy goals (Hall 1993: 279).

More specifically, these three different orders of shift entail several key features relevant to the subsequent analysis. First order change, for instance, typically shows signs of incrementalism, routinized decision-making and a politics of satisficing (i.e. discarding an optimal solution in favour of a merely satisfactory one for its being more familiar, attainable and thus incurring lower perceived costs).[9] The single major orientation for a new policy (or a policy at 'time 1') is, hence, an already existing policy (at 'time 0'). While second order change may often bear resemblance to these characteristics, it is more likely to move one step beyond the routine of everyday policy-making, displaying more strategic considerations in the development of new policy instruments. Both first and second order policy change are further demarcated by the fact that officials rather than politicians are central to the process, acting

---

[9]These properties correspond to the ones Charles Lindblom (1968) has championed in his influential account of the policy-making process (Hall 1993: 280).

with a significant degree of discretion and autonomy from the pluralist pressures commonly attributed to the political system (ibid., 280–283).

Third order change, in contrast, demonstrates a couple of fundamentally different properties. Typically, the decline of a pervasive paradigm will be initiated by a series of disruptive events that are not fully comprehensible within the terms of the paradigm, not even as puzzles (the prime example being the stagflation of the 1970s and the failure of the Keynesian paradigm to account for these). Policy-makers facing these developments are likely to try and 'stretch' the terms of the paradigm to accommodate for the disruptions. They might also engage in ad hoc policy experimentation. Both of these, however, will eventually result in policy failure, which further undermines the authority of the policy paradigm and its proponents. The rise of a new paradigm gaining authority will, in contrast to what we have claimed about first and second order change, be a contest of competing views in the broader political arena (ibid., 280–281, 289). A key insight about the shift of policy paradigms is thus that it results from an evolving societal debate instead of autonomous actions by a set of policy-makers. In the end, it is not only theoretical soundness but also political attractiveness that tips the balance in favour of a new paradigm (Hodson and Mabbett 2009: 1054; Schelkle and Hassel 2012). Its instalment ultimately manifests itself in pronounced discontinuities in policy responses compared to the policies devised under the old prevailing paradigm.

We now have at our disposal a set of concise criteria against which we can examine the policy changes undertaken in response to the Euro Area crisis. These are, on the one hand, the three central variables of policy-making (goals, instruments, settings) as well as, on the other hand, the key characteristics of social learning associated with changes in these variables (routinized politics of satisficing versus pronounced discontinuities in policy; autonomy and discretion in policy-making versus marked influence of pluralist pressures; officials versus politicians as the key actors). While this set provides a useful framework for the analysis of policy change, I am aware that it may also face limitations. For the most part, it lacks a more detailed account of how to examine the 'political attractiveness' and more generally the influence of 'pluralist pressures' on policy outcomes that are perceived to be of central importance in the process of third order policy change.

Such an account was provided, amongst others, by Hall's (1989) study of the political power of the encompassing paradigm of Keynesian economics. However, I am, not relying on this framework,[10] for it seems to me more sensible to regard the policy paradigm that governs EMU as dominating only one policy field, namely EMU macroeconomic policy, and not as an overarching 'era-defining' idea that encompasses many policy fields[11] (Béland and Cox 2013: 193; Hall 2013b: 191). This has the advantage that, given the current scenario where most observers would agree that we have not (or not yet) witnessed a pronounced shift in the overarching paradigm away from neoliberalism (Blyth 2013; Schmidt and Thatcher 2013; Quiggin 2012), employing a framework that accommodates for more nuanced types of policy change is more fruitful and illuminating. It allows me to study and understand the policy changes that *have* actually taken placed in response to recent policy challenges, instead of those that have not (or not yet) been realized.

Which policy responses are these and what empirical material do we have at our disposal to analyse them? The next section will work out the precise elements of EMU's original policy paradigm of 'stable money and sound finances', focusing on our key variables of goals, instruments and instrument settings. I will then conduct two concise case studies involving major policy responses by the European Union to the sovereign debt crisis that erupted in late 2009/early 2010, testing the changes that these responses have introduced in terms of the framework of three orders of policy change. The two cases are the reform of EMU fiscal surveillance (namely the 'Fiscal Compact' and the 'six pack' and 'two pack' legislations) enacted between November 2011 and May 2013 and two of the European Central Bank's 'non-standard monetary policy measures' (namely its two 3-year long-term refinancing operations (LTRO) and the outright monetary transactions (OMT) programme) pursued

---

[10]For an insightful application to the Eurpean case, however, see Schelkle and Hassel (2012).

[11]This does not rule out that it may be embedded in and display traits of a more encompassing ideational framework such as neoliberalism, ordoliberalism or monetarism (Schmidt and Thatcher 2013; Fitoussi and Saraceno 2004, 2013). Note also that Jones (2013) arrives at a similar conclusion regarding EMU's policy paradigm, but he draws the distinction between encompassing policy paradigms and a 'more partial framework of ideas', which I consider less pronounced and intelligible than the notion of a specific policy paradigm (Jones 2013: 149).

since December 2011. I argue that neither of these instances can be seen as constituting third order policy change—although this has been argued particularly with regard to LTRO and OMT (Jones 2013; Stark 2013)—and that both cases thus represent instances of either first or second order change.[12] To illustrate this claim, I will study the official announcements of the two policy responses in question and, in particular, the legal and accompanying documents specifying their details.

The Policy Paradigm of 'Stable Money and Sound Finances'

Why 15 member states of the then European Community came to agree on the adoption of a single currency in Maastricht in February 1992 is a matter of debate to this very day.[13] There is, however, notably less dispute about what facilitated this agreement, compared to earlier attempts at creating a monetary union in Europe. Monetary integration, in short, is seen to be founded on a convergence of beliefs about the merits of monetary stability and fiscal consolidation—a broad consensus that has come to be termed the paradigm of 'stable money and sound finances' or the 'Brussels-Frankfurt consensus' (with a view to the location of the principal actors upholding the consensus, namely the Brussels-based EU Council and Commission responsible for fiscal surveillance and the Frankfurt-based ECB guaranteeing price stability)

---

[12]In this context, my case selection is consistent with general principles of 'critical case study' design with regard to hypothesis-testing (Gerring 2007; Rohlfing 2012). The case of fiscal surveillance reform represents a 'most likely' case due to its relatively high probability of confirming the hypothesis, in contrast to the non-standard monetary policy case whose probability is comparatively low, thus constituting a 'tough test' for my hypothesis of non-third order change (Eckstein 1975; Rohlfing 2012: 84; Levy 2008). In analogous terms, we could also speak of an 'easy' and a 'hard' case for my proposition (cf. McKeown 1999; Van Evera 1996).

[13]Noticeable justifications range from functional-economic pressures to complete the single market in the face of increased capital mobility (Padoa-Schioppa et al. 1987; Eichengreen and Frieden 1998; Moravcsik 1998; Collignon and Schwarzer 2003) to the ideational hegemony of monetarism and neo-liberalism (Moss 2004) to combinations of both (McNamara 1998; 1999). Others invoke reasons beyond the macroeconomic realm, such as geo-strategic considerations of tying a recently reunified Germany to the West Katzenstein (1997) (Jones 2013: 145).

(Sandholtz 1993; McNamara 1998; Dyson and Featherstone 1999; Marcussen 1999; Collignon and Schwarzer 2003; Sapir et al. 2004; Torres 2008; Jones 2013: 145; Schelkle 2013: 41). In terms of this chapter, this set of beliefs represents a policy paradigm insomuch as it makes clear prescriptions for policy-makers in an otherwise markedly uncertain policy realm: it specifies what problems are of relevance in the macroeconomic sphere, what goals are attainable through macroeconomic policy, and what instruments can be used to attain them.[14]

Stable Money

The first of the two pillars of the policy consensus is the notion of monetary stability. The strong commitment to monetary stability in EMU is derived from shared beliefs about the nature of monetary policy that can broadly be associated with the demise of Keynesianism and the ascent of monetarism in Europe and beyond between the late 1970s and early 1980s, as is well understood and documented in the literature (cf. McNamara 2006: 808). In short, these beliefs hold that the reform of creating the single market was necessary to reinvigorate European economic growth and that this improved 'efficiency' needed to be counterbalanced by macroeconomic 'stability' (Padoa-Schioppa et al. 1987; Collignon and Schwarzer 2003). In this vein, expansionary monetary and fiscal policies aimed at stimulating demand would merely result in inflation and were therefore seen as highly inefficient. Moreover, high and varying inflation rates were perceived to generate uncertainty with regard to future prices (including interest rates and financial asset values), thus impairing business and spending activity even further. In consequence, inflation was to be seen as incompatible with employment and growth, in contrast to the assumptions of the Phillips curve. Hence, governments should commit to abjuring from expansionary policies and

---

[14]An exhaustive review of the elaboration and adoption of this policy paradigm—including the role played by the 'epistemic community' of central bankers, business people and politicians in facilitating both—will have to give way to a more focused description of the paradigm's major elements here, due to delimitations in size. For illuminating sources, nonetheless, see Verdun (1999) and especially Collignon and Schwarzer (2003).

shall place monetary policy in the hands of independent central banks which, by focusing on price stability, do all they can possibly do to stabilize the economy (ibid., Barro and Gordon 1983; De Grauwe 2006).

These prescriptions can be found in the following policy outcomes of the Maastricht process, reflecting our three key variables of the policy-making process. First and foremost, the European Central Bank, entrusted with the centralized monetary decision-making power for the Euro Area, was created as an ostensibly independent central bank whose mandate gives overriding priority to the goal of monetary stability. Both these aspects were made explicit in the mandate of the ECB enshrined in the Maastricht Treaty (now consolidated in the Treaty on the Functioning of the European Union, TFEU). Article 127(1) attests to the 'primary objective' of price stability which is hierarchically superior to the decidedly vaguer notion of 'support[ing] the general economic policies in the Union with a view to contributing to the achievement of the objectives of the Union'. Political independence is mandated in Article 130 which states that the central bank shall not 'seek or take instructions from Union institutions, bodies, offices or agencies, from any government of a Member State or from any other body'.[15] Moreover, the mandate's vagueness about which other objectives are to be pursued leaves the ECB with the autonomy not merely to choose the appropriate instruments to achieve its objectives, but also to choose the objectives themselves as long as these do not violate the hierarchical order in favour of price stability or constitute outright debt monetization (De Grauwe 2012: 151–153, 159–162). In this context, the ECB has defined for itself what constitutes the goal of price stability, namely 'a year-on-year increase in the Harmonised Index of Consumer Prices (HICP) for the Euro Area of below 2%' (ECB 1999), which was later somewhat clarified as meaning 'below, but close to, 2%' (ECB 2003). On the whole, we can see that the interpretation of these statutes

---

[15]Despite the frequent claim that the European Central Bank was modelled after the German Bundesbank, the ECB arguably displays a higher degree of independence due to the fact that revising its statutes requires difficult revisions of the European Treaties (while changing the Bundesbank mandate merely requires a legal act passed by simple majority in the German Bundestag) (De Grauwe 2012).

by successive ECB presidents is consistent with the aforementioned beliefs about the nature of monetary policy: Although the ECB could have legally pursued other economic objectives in the pre-crisis years, it independently decided not to, since keeping prices stable was already seen to be the best contribution that can possibly be made to furthering other objectives (De Grauwe 2006: 725; Jones 2013: 148).

The types of instruments the ECB employs to achieve its goals are threefold: In descending order of importance, the central bank makes use of open market operations (i.e. buying and selling securities in order to increase or reduce liquidity in the money market), standing facilities (i.e. lending to commercial banks as a means to provide or absorb overnight liquidity) and minimum reserve requirements for credit institutions (mainly used to smooth short term interest rates) (De Grauwe 2012: 198–202). With regards to its most important policy instrument, the open market operations, the ECB has throughout most of its existence not relied on outright purchases and sales of securities in the 'open market' (which is the typical form of use for other major central banks), but has rather made use of so-called refinancing operations in which it merely acquires a collateral in return for the liquidity it provides in the market, typically for a period of three months (ibid.). It is of interest to note however, that outright transactions are generally allowed for within the central bank's mandate, as long as these do not constitute a direct provision of credit to (or a direct purchase of debt instruments from) public entities such as governments (Protocol No 4 on ECB statute, Articles 18 and 21; Art. 123 TFEU).[16]

Sound Finances

I now turn to the second pillar of the policy paradigm in question, namely that of sound public finances. In short, this dimension of EMU's policy paradigm is guided by the principal belief that a monetary union changes the incentive structure of governments in so far as

---

[16]Beyond this, a more thorough discussion of the technical functioning of all three instruments (including the precise settings determined for each) is omitted here, since it would neither particularly further my argument nor sensibly fit the limited size of this chapter.

the lower risk premia and interest rates that governments have to pay for issuing debt (due to the elimination of the devaluation risk) (De Grauwe 2012: 220–222) could induce over-borrowing and ultimately lead to unsustainable public finances. This is most frequently framed as the risk of 'moral hazard'. To prevent a member state's unsustainable budgetary policies from jeopardizing the stability of the monetary union as whole, governments are to benevolently 'tie their hands' (Giavazzi and Pagano 1988) by means of adhering to strict budgetary rules rather than enjoying unrestricted discretion (Kydland and Prescott 1977).

The dimension of disciplinarian, rule-based fiscal surveillance is often thought of as one of the most characteristic of EMU's framework of governance (Mabbett and Schelkle 2014). One can easily identify the line of reasoning depicted above in the policy goal to prevent 'excesses' in government finances, for which the policy instrument of the Stability and Growth Pact (SGP) and its two 'arms' were devised shortly before EMU was put into place (in July 1998 and January 1999, respectively). On the one hand, the 'preventive arm' of the SGP sets out that national budgetary indicators be monitored by the Commission and the EU Council on the basis of annual compliance reports ('stability programmes') and that the Commission issue a warning if these are not met by the respective member state (Art. 121 TFEU). More crucially, on the other hand, the 'dissuasive' (nowadays 'corrective') arm entails the Excessive Deficit Procedure (EDP) under which the EU Council can mandate a member state to correct its deficit within a given period of time, including the possibility of sanctions. These sanctions are named as 'fines' and 'interest-bearing deposits' that shall be 'of an appropriate size', but they have not been specified in quantitative terms (Art. 126 TFEU). An important instrument setting here is that the Council can only initiate an EDP by qualified majority. The other settings of the SGP include the well-known thresholds of a 60% debt-to-GDP ratio and a 3% deficit-to-GDP ratio (Protocol No 12 on EDP; TFEU). Since the reform of the SGP in 2005, the settings also include country-specific medium term objectives (MTO) that take business cycle-related fluctuations and one-off and temporary measures into account, constituting the so-called 'structural deficits'. These shall not exceed 1% of GDP (amended Council Regulations 1466/97 and 1467/97).

The Separation of Monetary and Fiscal Policy

We now have a clearer picture of the two major elements of EMU's dominant policy paradigm in terms of their main goals, instruments and relevant instrument settings.[17] This two-fold ideational construct, and the way it has informed the institutions of EMU, highlights an important aspect for the public goods approach of this book, namely the crucial interaction between monetary and fiscal policies. The design of EMU prescribes that monetary and fiscal policy concerns are to be kept strictly separate,[18] as enshrined in our two key principles of stable money (to be achieved by the ECB) and sound public finances (to be achieved by national governments and monitored by the EU Council as well as the EU Commission). There is, however, strong reason to question the logic of this separation if we take a public goods approach to the Euro Area. Crucially, the introduction of the euro has meant that the common currency serves as the *hard budget constraint*[19] for all economic agents, i.e. households, firms and governments alike (Collignon 2003: 49, 127). This entails that the euro can effectively be understood as a scarce resource, a *common resource good*, commanded by the independent monetary policy-maker that is the ECB. In consequence, the

---

[17]One could add to the two key tenets presented here a number of auxiliary ideas and assumptions, which are not treated in more detail precisely due to their auxiliary nature. These are, for instance, the idea of efficient financial and local-factor markets (following from the role that is ascribed to financial markets in assessing governments' budgetary positions) (Schelkle 2013; Jones 2013) as well as the shared belief in the necessity of structural reforms to be implemented by national governments (due to the fact that the rule-based agreement on EMU did not identify a role for aggregate demand management in the case of economic shocks, thus leaving the burden of adjustment to be borne by governments via supply side oriented measures) (Dyson and Featherstone 1999: 784–785; Sapir et al. 2004; De Grauwe 2006). The latter aspect raises additional questions about whether the terms of the consensus are in themselves logically consistent, i.e. whether both fiscal consolidation and entrenching reforms can sensibly be pursued at the same time. Compare, for example, Mabbett and Schelkle (2007) with Buti, Röger and Turrini (2009).

[18]Charles Goodhart (1998: 410) aptly referred to this strict separation as an 'unprecedented divorce between the main monetary and fiscal authorities'.

[19]For a discussion of 'hard' and 'soft' budget constraints, see Maskin (1999) who reviews Kornai's (1980) seminal work on the economics of shortage in the former communist states of the Eastern bloc, as well as later contributions.

ECB's primary function of providing monetary stability, by means of keeping money scarce, does interfere with the public financing needs of Euro Area governments. The implications of this tension are further discussed below.[20]

A number of studies reviewing the Euro Area's paradigm have found these macroeconomic prescriptions to have persisted during the first years of EMU. This goes for the monetarist focus of a highly independent ECB pursuing the foremost goal of preserving price stability as much as it goes for a continued commitment to coordinating national fiscal policies as the only tools of macroeconomic stabilization, even despite substantial frictions that led to the 2005 reform of the SGP (Fitoussi and Saraceno 2004; De Grauwe 2006; McNamara 2006; Howarth 2012)[21] . Do we arrive at a similar judgement about the persistence of EMU's policy paradigm if we now take policy responses to the Euro Area sovereign debt crisis into account?

Major Responses to the Euro Area Crisis: Within or Beyond EMU's Paradigm?

The Case of EMU Fiscal Surveillance Reform

To provide a firm response to the Euro Area crisis, policy-makers in Europe revised the EMU's framework of fiscal surveillance by negotiating the Treaty on Stability, Coordination and Governance[22] (TSCG) in March 2012 as well as a set of legislations that became known as the 'six pack' and 'two pack', enacted between November 2011 and May 2013. A notable peculiarity is that the TSCG was created as an intergovernmental treaty outside of the EU's legal framework (and signed by all of the then 27 member state governments except the UK and the Czech Republic).

---

[20]See also Collignon's contribution in this book.

[21]For qualifying views, see Chang (2006) and Jabko (2010).

[22]Although the TSCG consists of a total of six titles, its integral third title, the 'Fiscal Compact', commonly serves as *pars pro toto* for the entire treaty. References to the TSCG in this chapter therefore specifically mean title III.

In contrast, the 'pack' legislations—albeit stemming from the propositions of Council President Herman Van Rompuy's 'task force' of EU finance ministers (EU Council 2010)—are eight initiatives of the European Commission that were, for the most part, adopted in co-decision between the EU Council and European Parliament (six co-decision regulations, one Council regulation and one Council directive[23]). This emphasises neatly the conspicuous consensus on rule-based fiscal surveillance as a pivotal mode of EMU governance nurtured by both national and supranational authorities.

Let us now analyse the major innovations of these responses in terms of our conception of three orders of policy change. First, while the instrument settings for debt and deficit ratios were left unchanged, the maximum permissible structural deficit was changed to 0.5% for those countries that do not fulfil the debt requirement (Art. 3(b) and (d), TSCG). In addition, the scope of permissible sanctions was specified as comprising fines with 'a fixed component equal to 0,2% of GDP' or interest-bearing deposits 'amounting to 0,2% of GDP'.[24] Sanctions can be levied either if a country is perceived to make too little progress in averting an excessive deficit or if the implementation of an already ongoing EDP is deemed unsatisfactory (i.e. they operate under both the preventive and the corrective arm). Moreover, the decision rule for launching an excessive deficit procedure was changed to the mere requirement of a reversed qualified majority (same for the imposition of fines) and provisions for the monitoring of government budgets were adjusted to the extent that not only the overall budget but also its components are to be scrutinized.[25] Remarkably, a 'debt brake' rule was introduced bearing the logical implication that, in the long term, countries' debt to GDP ratios are to converge asymptotically towards zero. Together with other provisions of the TSCG, this rule further has to be incorporated into national, 'preferably constitutional' law (TSCG Art. 3(2)). Lastly, the scope of goals to be achieved was extended to not only

---

[23]For an overview, see European Commission (2017).

[24]See Council Regulation 1177/2011; Regulation 1173/2011.

[25]See Regulation 473/2013; Council Directive 2011/85.

comprise excessive debts and deficits, but also macroeconomic imbalances such as current account imbalances and nominal unit labour cost deterioration,[26] which are to be governed under the same principles of monitoring and sanctioning as the budgetary requirements (Eurostat 2013).[27] On the whole, this set of measures constitutes an ostentatious toughening of fiscal surveillance rules and some parts of it, such as the debt brake requirement and the compulsion to transpose the Fiscal Compact into national law, have been perceived as 'astoundingly radical' policy measures (Schelkle 2012b: 139–141).

Yet, how can we assess these changes in the wider context of EMU's policy paradigm and the three orders of policy change? To begin with, it is clear that a number of instrument *settings* have been altered, mostly in the sense that existing arrangements have been reinforced: in addition to the lowering of the permissible structural deficit, sanctions have finally been quantified and the decision rule under which they operate has been amended. What is more telling than these alterations, however, is that all of the endeavours outlined above rely on already existing policy *instruments*, namely the preventive and corrective arms of the SGP, with their reporting and monitoring principles on the basis of Eurostat-approved data and the same processes of proposing and deciding upon excessive deficit procedures. In addition, although the focus of attention was broadened to include macroeconomic imbalances, this is far from a subversion of the hierarchy of policy *goals*: If anything, the emphasis on tackling allegedly unsustainable debt and deficit positions was strengthened by recent reforms, instead of being dampened or undermined altogether. The given policy responses are therefore merely instances of first-order change, since the only substantial adjustments made are the ones concerning instrument settings.

---

[26]In this vein, the Commission has defined a scoreboard of various statistical indicators with upper and lower alert thresholds. These indicators range from current account balances, total private and public sector indebtedness, to real effective exchange rates, house prices, and unemployment rates.

[27]See Regulation 1174/2011; Regulation 1176/2011.

With a view to our understanding of social learning and policy change, we can make further observations that strengthen this notion. On the one hand, the principal orientation for new proposals (the policies at time 1) was the already existing Stability and Growth Pact (the policy at time 0) which was merely complemented. In this respect, the policy process at hand resembles the notion of satisficing, as only the most familiar and attainable policy changes were undertaken. On the other hand, however, these changes were initiated by politicians instead of bureaucrats, namely the heads of state and government devising the TSCG as well as the EU finance ministers in Herman van Rompuy's task force working out the proposals that ended up in the 'pack' legislations. At first sight, this is at odds with the theoretical notion of first and second order policy change, which are typically brought about by autonomous officials rather than elected politicians. Yet, it is a particularly intriguing question to consider whether the concerned (national) politicians might nonetheless have acted with a significant degree of autonomy on the European level. Indeed, accounts of the remarkable executive discretion that policy-makers enjoyed in the context of the Euro Area crisis as a 'state of emergency' abound: Executives in the European Council and the Council of the EU, convening in countless extraordinary summit meetings, have been described as effectively having seized control over an insulated policy process that sidelines both the European and national parliaments, taking fast-paced decisions that hardly allow for scrutiny and opposition on behalf of the representatives of European citizens (Puetter 2012; Puntscher Riekmann and Wydra 2013; White 2014).

On the whole, the policy changes introduced in terms of fiscal surveillance do not deviate from the prescriptions that EMU's policy paradigm makes with regard to the centrality of sound finances. The rules governing debt and deficit levels in EMU member states have been reinforced by means of altering instrument settings (but not instruments themselves or even policy goals), at the hands of policy-makers who acted with some degree of autonomy and who did not transgress the routine of calling for fiscal consolidation. Fiscal surveillance reform during the Euro Area crisis therefore constitutes an instance of first order policy change, thereby validating the hypothesis of non-third order change. For proponents and critics of the 'disciplinarian' approach to monetary integration alike, the reform outcomes described in this section were expectable given EMU's policy paradigm—and policy-makers did not belie the expectations.

The Case of the ECB's Non-Standard Monetary Policy Measures

The European Central Bank has in several instances enacted policies that have played a decisive part in responding to the challenges of the Euro Area crisis, such as its non-standard policies of two 3-year long-term commercial bank refinancing operations (LTROs) (in December 2011 and March 2012, respectively) and the launch of its outright monetary transactions programme (OMT) (announced in July 2012 and specified in September of the same year) (ECB 2011a, 2012a, 2012b). Both of these policies fall within the set of instruments of open market operations.[28]

The formal changes brought about by these measures can be summarized as follows. In effect, the two liquidity-providing LTROs work like the refinancing measures that the ECB typically undertakes, albeit with a significant change in *settings*[29] from the usual 3-month maturity period (which had already been increased to including 6-month and then 12-month maturities since March 2008 and June 2009, respectively) to an unprecedented 36 months, with an interest requirement at the same low level as the Bank's main short-term refinancing operations (at the time at 1%) (ECB 2011a. As regards OMT, the ECB specified that it would undertake 'outright transactions in secondary sovereign bond markets' with a particular focus on 'sovereign bonds

---

[28]It is acknowledged that the ECB deployed a number of other significant policies throughout the crisis, not least the frequently discussed Securities Markets Programme (SMP) (Schelkle 2014). The latter is not covered explicitly here since OMT constitutes, in effect, an unlimited version of SMP and can thus be seen as both fully implying and moving beyond it, which ultimately makes for a stronger case.

[29]For a recent publication that focuses entirely on the policy settings of ECB bond-buying programmes, see Lombardi and Moschella (2015).

with a maturity of between one and three years' (ECB 2012a, 2012b). Although the Bank had already done likewise in the course of its securities markets programme (initiated in May 2010), the fundamental difference is that '[n]o ex ante quantitative limits' were set with regard to the size of OMT (ibid.). With the introduction of SMP and OMT, the ECB has effectively added previously unexploited *instruments* to its repertoire of open market operations, in the form of outright purchases of sovereign bonds. The stated aim of such instruments was to safeguard the singleness of monetary policy as well as its appropriate transmission to businesses and households, which was severely threatened by the divergence in sovereign borrowing costs throughout the Euro Area (not least since local financial institutions are often the major owners of their governments' bonds). Lastly, it is notable that any liquidity to be released by potential bond purchases would be absorbed by means of 'sterilization' (i.e. issuing bills in exchange for banks' cash or incentivising banks to hold reserves at the ECB) and that the decision on performing outright monetary transactions in favour of any country was made conditional on that country's enrolment in a European Stability Mechanism (ESM) programme (ibid.).

While the two long-term refinancing operations were readily harnessed by Euro Area banks—at times making up a remarkable 80% of the assets in the Eurosystem balance sheet (Claeys 2014)—the OMT programme has not been activated to date. The impact and merits of both measures can, nonetheless, hardly be overstated: The LTROs have contributed substantially to alleviating banks' liquidity constraints in the 2011–2012 period,[30] and the mere announcement and specification of outright monetary transactions is frequently credited with ending the acute phase of the Euro Area crisis by significantly calming sovereign bond markets (Wolff 2013; Altavilla et al. 2014).

---

[30]See Claeys (2014: 6–8) for a review of empirical evidence.

In how far have these unconventional tools challenged or even subverted the terms of EMU's policy paradigm of 'stable money and sound finances', as has been claimed repeatedly? We can shed light on this question by resorting to the three orders of policy change. It is evident that the ECB has changed some of its instruments' *settings* (such as the length of maturity of its LTROs) and that it has even enlarged the range of available *instruments* (in the case of SMP and OMT as novel types of open market operations) in response to the challenges arising from the Euro Area crisis. Whether it has also subverted the hierarchy of policy *goals*, however, is less obvious. One of the strongest allegations voiced against OMT is that the programme shifts the ECB's focus from monetary policy to fiscal policy goals, such as the monetary financing of governments (which would be in breach of its mandate; Art. 123 TFEU; Council Regulation 3603/93). A more muted form of this argument maintains that even if the ECB only purchased bonds in secondary markets (as it has announced) this would still have significant fiscal implications[31] (Stark 2013; Sinn 2014). These implications supposedly materialise if the ECB holds bonds of a sovereign that subsequently defaults, making the recapitalization of the central bank necessary. Since the European governments are the shareholders of their national central banks which, in turn, are the shareholders of the ECB, this recapitalization would have to be paid out of governments' budgets. There is a striking parallel to the question of how to govern European public goods here: If the ECB's market operations provide for much-needed financial stability in the Euro Area, and if individual member states refuse to guarantee fiscal backing for these operations, then the public good of financial stability may ultimately be undersupplied.

For the sake of argument, let us assume that the recapitalization of a central bank would indeed be necessary in such a scenario, although this continues to be a matter of debate.[32] The problem with this argumentation, more generally, is that any of the main open market

---

[31]Concerning the now discontinued securities markets programme (in combination with LTRO), commentators have also spoken of a 'quasi-fiscal' role for the ECB (Schelkle 2014).

[32]The counter-argument is that a central bank cannot 'default' as long as it has the monopoly to issue money and as long as additional issuances do not impinge on its promise to preserve price stability (see, inter alia, De Grauwe and Ji 2013).

operations a central bank undertakes may entail a risk of loss – asking a central bank to avoid this risk altogether would amount to asking it to go out of business. Unsurprisingly, there is no provision whatsoever in the ECB statutes that prevents, let alone formally prohibits, the central bank from making losses (cf. Protocol No 4 on ECB statute, Articles 32 and 33, TFEU). Additional points can be raised with regard to the ECB's non-standard policies in relation to its policy goals, which go beyond merely refuting that the Bank has started to embrace fiscal policy objectives. On the one side, it must be stressed that if OMT were ever activated, this would only proceed under the condition of an ongoing or imminent ESM programme for the member state(s) in question (ECB 2012a). In turn, the launch of such a programme is conditional on the ratification (and transposition into national law) of the TSCG (cf. Art. 3 ESM Treaty). Consequently, the goal of fiscal consolidation would not be undermined by the launch of OMT, but rather amplified.[33] On the other side, there is little reason to assume that the ECB is anywhere close to overthrowing its preference for 'stable money', since its major non-standard open market operations have been sterilized to minimize excess liquidity in the monetary system (as with SMP, until mid-2014), or have been announced to be subjected to sterilization if implemented (as with OMT). As regards the policy paradigm in question, all signs thus point to continuity in the hierarchy of policy goals of the ECB.

Does our understanding of social learning confirm this finding? To begin with, it is acknowledged that the ECB's unconventional monetary policies are, indeed, rather unconventional (at least for its own standards). They bear little resemblance to the routinized policy-making the central bank pursues in 'normal times' (mainly consisting of short-term to medium-term refinancing operations) and can rather be understood as policy experiments intended to cope with the anomalies of the Euro

---

[33]An indication of just how central the requirements of the TSCG were in the view of the ECB may be president Draghi's postulation of a 'new fiscal compact' in his very first hearing in front of the European Parliament (ECB 2011b) and on a number of other occasions at the very beginning of his tenure (Schelkle 2014).

Area crisis. It must be noted, however, that these changes only came about incrementally, instead of manifesting themselves as unprecedented discontinuities: only when 6-month and 12-month refinancing operations did not attenuate banks' liquidity shortages, were 36-month offers placed; and only when the limited SMP was found to do too little to calm financial markets, was the unlimited OMT programme announced and devised. For now, the facts therefore point neither to routinized policy-making nor to an instance of radical third order change, leaving the option of strategic second order change.

To gain additional clarity on this, another characteristic of the social learning process is of help, namely that of autonomous officials being in charge of policy (as in first and second order change) versus politicians driving the policy-making process (being more typical in third order change). There should be little doubt that the ECB's policies are developed and executed by officials rather than politicians. Likewise, with regards to autonomy, we may be tempted to view the overtly independent ECB as an autonomous decision-maker *par excellence*. And yet again, just as in the first case, it is worth taking a second look, as one can possibly see some of the Bank's autonomy being eroded 'through the backdoor' (Schelkle 2012a, 2014). In essence, it can be argued that the ECB was under pressure to do what national political authorities could not get around to, namely stabilizing financial markets by means of decisive and reassuring policy reactions. Thus, it was compelled to intervene in inter-bank lending markets and to display a readiness to do likewise in sovereign bond markets. This speaks to the problem of an exclusive public good once again: Member states' refusal to contribute to the good of stabilization ultimately resulted in a coordination failure (cf. Cooper and John 1988), leaving it to the ECB to step in and stabilize.

It is important to note, nonetheless, that the ECB's apparent loss of autonomy has come about creepingly, playing itself out in the sidelines rather than the limelight of the political arena. After all, decisions were taken at the discretion of the supranational ECB governing council and its president, instead of resulting from an openly contested societal and partisan-political debate. In accordance with our conception of policy change, it is this creeping nature that marks the difference between larger-scale, paradigmatic transitions and more nuanced types of policy shift: In the case of the Euro Area, change has manifested itself not in the form of publicly debated and encompassing institutional adjustments, but rather as short-dated, executive and not rarely minimalist policy reactions. What lends further support to this conclusion is the remarkable uncertainty that has surrounded the ECB's non-standard policies and especially the OMT programme, on two different counts. First, there is uncertainty about whether OMT could be realized technically, due to significant dilemmas of 'monetary policy under conditionality' (Darvas and Merler 2013). Second, it has proven far from certain whether the promise to buy unlimited sovereign bonds can actually be upheld, let alone ever be activated (highlighted not least by the challenge brought forward by the German Constitutional Court) (White 2014). Under these circumstances, it becomes evident that the ECB's policies, despite being impactful, are not the result of a durable shift in the public debate that resulted in an institutionalized change in the hierarchy of policy goals. They are much rather strategic, incrementally achieved reactions to a policy problem that politicians eschewed to address on the 'open stage', involving the creation and announcement of new policy instruments. In terms of the theoretical framework of this chapter, they thus best qualify as instances of second order change, validating the hypothesis of a non-paradigmatic policy shift.

Conclusion

What have we learnt from the preceding analysis? First of all, we are now better equipped to explain the puzzling signals of early Euro Area crisis responses and their implications for EMU's dominant policy paradigm: On the whole, the prescriptions of stable money and sound finances still have significant currency in guiding Euro Area policy-making, as reflected in key initiatives enacted in the fields of fiscal surveillance and monetary policy. Moreover, we are now able to make sense of interpretations which, at first, appeared starkly contrasting or even irreconcilable: scholars arguing for a '*lock-in*' of policy-making into EMU's paradigm, as well as those attesting a *breakdown* of the same, are right only to the extent that they describe policy changes of a different *order* – namely those differing between first and second order change, but not between second and third order change. Hence, both camps' positions are in need of qualifying. For the most part, what has been described as paradigmatic change is in contradiction with the empirical reality that these changes have not undermined the hierarchy of goals that Euro Area policies are geared to. And advocates of a *lock-in* are well-advised to enlarge their focus so as to account for strategic policy instruments that transcend the sphere of routinized policy-making, most of which we have witnessed at the European Central Bank. Importantly, however, the ECB was com-pelled to perform these first and second order changes precisely because of the limited change in terms of fiscal policy: the mere reinforcement of fiscal rules, instead of larger-scale coordination to restore financial stabil-ity, is a major reason why monetary policy had to become 'unconven-tional' (Schelkle 2014). In this vein, future research should start from a more thorough assessment of the linkages between supposedly strictly separated policy fields and the different orders of policy change, espe-cially in how far first and second order change may ultimately induce third order shifts (and whether this process itself might sensibly be subdi-vided in different logical steps; cf. Oliver and Pemberton 2004).

While I consider this a robust result, a number of limitations should also be discussed. Several critiques are in order, of which the follow-ing two caveats are particularly relevant. Firstly, Hall's (1993) origi-nal account of policy paradigms is, first and foremost, concerned with the impact of these notions on actions of 'the state' (here the United Kingdom), thus contributing to influential state-centrist theories of the time (cf. Krasner 1984; Evans, Rueschmeyer and Skocpol 1985). This raises the question in how far, and whether at all, theoretical concepts that originally examined the properties and behaviour of 'states' can actually be transferred to the study of a supranational union that does not fit narrow statist definitions. However, there shall be no confusion about the meaning and content of 'state' as evoked by said scholars: what is referred to in this literature is the structure that we may also call 'public administration' or 'the public sector', i.e. the actors respon-sible for devising and implementing public policy in a given polity. The existence of such structures is by no means limited to rigidly defined *nation*-states, but can evidently also be attested to the European Union and its institutions. Crucially, not only individual member states but also the union as a whole provides public goods for European citizens, as shown by the different contributions to this book. Lastly, what justified Hall's case selection of macroeconomic policy in the UK was the 'closed bureaucracy' of the British public sector as well as the technical, knowledge-intensive character of the chosen public policy field of economic policy (1993: 277). There is no particular reason to assume that these properties are not fulfilled by EMU macroeconomic policy-making, performed by the administrations of the ECB, the European Commission and the Council.

Secondly, with regard to the case selection, one can always stress the difficulty of making inferences from just a single or two cases. This calls for additional justification of why precisely my two cases have been chosen as representative for Euro Area crisis responses more generally. While I am aware of other policy responses that could have made for interesting examinations (e.g., the European Stability Mechanism[34] or the still incomplete banking union) I feel it is not too far-fetched to consider the ECB's OMT programme as one of the most profound policy changes thus far, if not the single most profound. The remarkable success that its mere announcement has produced (cf. Altavilla et al. 2014), as well as the overt controversy that it has provoked, testifies to this quite convincingly. On the other hand, the intergovernmental Fiscal Compact (TSCG) can also be seen as exemplary for the 'disciplinarian approach' in response to the crisis of monetary union (Schelkle 2013): national governments are preoccupied with preventing one another from exceeding debt and deficit limits in a unitary, sometimes unreflecting fashion, without sufficient will to pursue truly concerted policies through supranational institutions. This collective action problem ultimately results in the underprovision of the public good of financial and monetary stability in the Euro Area.

With these caveats in mind, new questions arise in the search for alternative paradigms in the Euro Area. An issue that merits particular scrutiny is the interaction between monetary and

---

[34]See Spörer in this volume for a discussion of the ESM.

fiscal policy-making in EMU, which arises not least from the euro's nature as the Euro Area's hard budget constraint. If we think of the ECB's supply of euros as the common resource good that constitutes the budget constraint for firms, households and governments, this raises important implications for the governance of the Euro Area. While firms and households can theoretically arrive at efficient solutions via markets, the same logic is not applicable to governments that narrowly pursue the 'national' interests of their constituencies. The reason is that, in theory, market participants act according to a logic of allocating private goods without externalities, whereas the collective efforts of governments are concerned with public goods that do entail externalities (Collignon 2003: 49). The tension that arises from this is that the euro has, through its nature as a hard budget constraint, effectively established a euro-wide economy by way of completing the single market. Yet, this development has not been accompanied by the concomitant creation of a euro-wide governance structure that could alleviate the problems of collective action among governments (ibid.). This situation is bound to produce enduring inefficiencies and lead to preference frustration among European societies, since the problem of externalities remains unresolved. If such deficiencies persist, it can hardly be surprising that countries contemplate an exit from either the monetary union (as in the case of Greece) or the EU project altogether (as for the UK).[35]

In conclusion, the persistence of the Euro Area's stable-money-sound-finances paradigm raises questions for the monetary union's adaptability in the face of mounting challenges. Much of the union's belated crisis responses may be associated with decision-makers' shared beliefs about the virtues of policies that do little to stabilize an ailing EMU. In this vein, the chapters of this book can very much be seen as advancing alternative analyses of EMU's ailments and generating new perspectives on how to resolve them. By invoking a republican paradigm and different views on the management of European public goods—beyond a narrow focus on

---

[35]Note, however, that the crucial difference between a theoretical 'Grexit' and the actual 'Brexit' is that the former is squarely about removing the monetary hard budget constraint, while the latter implies extricating oneself from all aspects of the union's governance structure.

the goods of mere price stability and fiscal 'asceticism'[36] which remain at the core of EMU's prevailing paradigm—we hope to do our bit to contribute to the academic and political debate about how to fix the E(M)U.

References

Altavilla, C., Giannone, D., & Lenza, M. (2014). The financial and macroeconomic effects of OMT announcements, ECB (Working Paper Series 1707). Frankfurt: European Central Bank.

Anderson, C. (1978). The logic of public problems: Evaluation in comparative policy research. In D. Ashford (Ed.), *Comparing public policies* (pp. 19–41). Beverly Hills: Sage.

Armingeon, K., & Baccaro, L. (2012). The sorrows of young Euro: The sovereign debt crises of Ireland and Southern Europe, In N. Bermeo & J. Pontusson (Eds.), *Coping with crisis: Government reactions to the great recession* (pp. 162–197). New York: Russel Sage.

Barnes, L., & Wren, A. (2012). The liberal model in (the) crisis: Continuity and change in great Britain and Ireland. In N. Bermeo & J. Pontusson (Eds.), *Coping with crisis: Government reactions to the great recession* (pp. 287–324). New York: Russel Sage.

Barro, R. J., & Gordon, D. B. (1983). A positive theory of monetary policy in a natural-rate model. *Journal of Political Economy, 91*(4), 589–610.

Béland, D., & Cox, R. H. (2011). Introduction: Ideas and politics. In D. Béland & R. H. Cox (Eds.), *Ideas and politics in social science research* (pp. 3–20). New York and Oxford: Oxford University Press.

Béland, D., & Cox, R. H. (2013). Introduction to special issue: The politics of policy paradigms. *Governance, 26*(2), pp. 193–195.

Berman, S. (2013). Ideational theorizing in the social sciences since "Policy paradigms, social learning, and the state". *Governance, 26*(2), 217–237.

Bermeo, N., & Pontusson, J. (Eds.). (2012). *Coping with crisis: Government reactions to the great recession*. New York: Russel Sage.

Blyth, M. (2013). Paradigms and paradox: The politics of economic ideas in two moments of crisis. *Governance, 26*(2), 197–215.

---

[36]See Dyson (2014: 275–276).

Boyer, R. (2013). The Euro crisis: Undetected by conventional economics, favoured by nationally focused polity. *Cambridge Journal of Economics, 37*(3), 533–569.

Buti, M., Röger, W., & Turrini, A. (2009). Is Lisbon far from Maastricht? Trade-offs and complementarities between fiscal discipline and structural reforms. *CESifo Economic Studies, 55*(1), 165–196.

Cameron, D. R. (2012). European fiscal responses to the great recession. In N. Bermeo & J. Pontusson (Eds.), *Coping with crisis: Government reactions to the great recession* (pp. 91–129). New York: Russel Sage.

Chang, M. (2006). Reforming the stability and growth pact: Size and influence in EMU policymaking. *Journal of European Integration, 28*(1), 107–120.

Claeys, G. (2014). The (not so) Unconventional monetary policy of the European central bank since 2008, European parliament economic and monetary affairs committee homepage, accessible online at (Last Access September 20, 2017): http://www.europarl.europa.eu/RegData/etudes/IDAN/2014/518781/IPOL_IDA(2014)518781_EN.pdf.

Clift, B. (2012). French responses to the global economic crisis: The political economy of "Post-Dirigisme" and new state activism. In W. Grant & G. K.Wilson (Eds.), *The consequences of the global financial crisis: The rhetoric of reform and regulation* (pp. 206–225) New York and Oxford: Oxford University Press.

Collignon, S., & Schwarzer, D. (2003). *Private sector involvement in the Euro: The power of ideas.* London: Routledge.

Cooper, R., & John, A. (1988). Coordinating coordination failures in a keynesian model. *The Quarterly Journal of Economics, 103*(3), 441–463.

Darvas, Z. (2010). The impact of the crisis on budget policy in central and Eastern Europe. *OECD Journal on Budgeting, 10*(1), 1–42.

Darvas, Z., & Merler, S. (2013). The European Central bank in the age of banking union. *Bruegel Policy Contribution, 2013*(13), 1–18.

De Grauwe, P. (2006). What have we learnt about monetary integration since the Maastricht treaty? *Journal of Common Market Studies, 44* (4), 711–730.

De Grauwe, P. (2012). *Economics of monetary union* (9th ed.). Oxford: Oxford University Press.

De Grauwe, P. (2013). The political economy of the Euro. *Annual Review of Political Science, 16*, pp. 153–170.

De Grauwe, P. & Ji, Y. (2013). Fiscal implications of the ECB's bond buying program. *Open Economies Review, 24* (5), pp. 843–852.

Dullien, S., & Guérot, U. (2012). The long shadow of ordoliberalism: Germany's approach to the Euro crisis. *European Council on Foreign Relations Policy Brief, 49*, 1–15.

Dyson, K. (2014). *States, debt, and power: 'Saints' and 'Sinners' in European history and integration*. Oxford: Oxford University Press.

Dyson, K., & Featherstone, K. (1999). *The road to Maastricht: Negotiating economic and monetary union*. New York and Oxford: Oxford University Press.

Eckstein, H. (1975). Case studies and theory in political science. In F. I. Greenstein & N. W. Polsby (Eds.), *Handbook of political science 7. Political science: Scope and theory* (pp. 94–137). Reading, MA: Addison-Wesley.

Eichengreen, B., & Frieden, J. (Eds.). (1998). *Forging an Integrated Europe*. Ann Arbor, MI: University of Michigan Press.

European Central Bank. (2011a). ECB announces measures to support bank lending and money market activity, Press Release 8 December, Frankfurt: European Central Bank, Directorate Communications.

European Central Bank. (2011b). *Hearing before the plenary of the European Parliament on the occasion of the adoption of the resolution on the ECB's 2010 annual report*. Frankfurt: European Central Bank, Directorate Communications.

European Central Bank. (2012a). *Technical features of outright monetary transactions*, Press Release 6 September, Frankfurt: European Central Bank, Directorate Communications.

European Central Bank. (2012b). *Verbatim of the remarks made by Mario Draghi at the global investment conference in London, 26 July 2012*, Frankfurt: European Central Bank, Directorate Communications.

European Commission. (2017). *Timeline: The EU economic governance*, Directorate general for economic and financial affairs homepage, accessible online at (Last Access September 20, 2017): https://ec.europa.eu/info/business-economy-euro/economic-and-fiscalpolicy-coordination/eu-economic-governance-monitoring-prevention-correction/timeline-evolution-eu-economic-governance_en.

Eurostat. (2013). Macroeconomic Imbalances Procedure Scoreboard: Eurostat Publishes Latest Indicators for Early Detection of Macroeconomic Imbalances, Press Release STAT/13/166, Brussels: Eurostat Press Office.

Evans, P. B., Rueschmeyer, D., & Skocpol, T. (Eds.). (1985). *Bringing the State Back In*. Cambridge: Cambridge University Press.

Featherstone, Kevin. (2012). *Le choc de la nouvelle? Maastricht, déjà vu and EMU reform, LSE 'Europe in Question'* (Discussion Paper 52). London: London School of Economics.

Fitoussi, J.-P., & Saraceno, F. (2004). *The Brussels-Frankfurt-Washington consensus: Old; new tradeoffs in economics.* Paris: Observatoire Français des Conjunctures Economiques, OFCE Working Document.

Fitoussi, J.-P., & Saraceno, F. (2013). European economic governance: The Berlin-Washington consensus. *Cambridge Journal of Economics, 37*(3), 479–496.

Garrett, G., & Weingast, Barry. (1993). Ideas, interests, and institutions: Constructing the European community's internal market. In J. Goldstein & R. O. Keohane (Eds.), *Ideas and foreign policy* (pp. 173–206). Ithaca: Cornell University Press.

Gerring, J. (2007). Is there a (Viable) crucial-case method? *Comparative Political Studies, 40*(3), 231–253.

Giavazzi, F., & Pagano, M. (1988). The advantage of tying one's hands: EMS discipline and central bank credibility. *European Economic Review, 32*(5), 1055–1082.

Goodhart, C. (1998). The two concepts of money: Implications for the analysis of optimal currency areas. *European Journal of Political Economy, 14*(3), 407–432.

Gourevitch, P. (1986). *Politics in hard times.* Ithaca, NY: Cornell University Press.

Grant, W., Wilson, G. K. (Eds.). (2012). *The consequences of the global financial crisis: The rhetoric of reform and regulation.* New York and Oxford: Oxford University Press.

Hall, P. A. (Ed.). (1989). *The political power of economic ideas: Keynesianism across nations.* Princeton, NJ: Princeton University Press.

Hall, P. A. (1993). Policy paradigms, social learning, and the state: The case of economic policymaking in Britain. *Comparative Politics, 25*(3), 275–296.

Hall, P. A. (2013a). The political origins of our economic discontents: Contemporary adjustment problems in historical perspective. In M. L. Kahler & D. A. Lake (Eds.), *Politics in the new hard times: The great recession in comparative perspective* (pp. 129–149). Ithaca, NY: Cornell University Press.

Hall, P. A. (2013b). Commentary: Brother, can you paradigm? *Governance, 26*(2), 189–192.

Hall, P. A., & Taylor, R. (1996). Political science and the three new institutionalisms. *Political Studies, 44*(5), 936–957.

Hay, C. (2011) Ideas and the construction of interests. In D. Béland & R. H. Cox (Eds.), *Ideas and politics in social science research* (pp. 65–82). New York and Oxford: Oxford University Press.

Heclo, H. (1975). *Modern social politics in Britain and Sweden: From relief to income maintenance.* New Haven: Yale University Press.

Hodson, D., & Mabbett, D. (2009). UK economic policy and the global financial crisis: Paradigm lost? *Journal of Common Market Studies, 47*(5), 1041–1061.

Howarth, D. (2012). Defending the Euro: Unity and disunity among Europe's central bankers'. In J. Hayward & R. Wurzel (Eds.), *European disunion—Between sovereignty and solidarity* (pp. 131–145). Houndmills: Palgrave.

Issing, O. (2006). The ECB's monetary policy strategy: Why did we choose a two pillar approach? Contribution to 4th ECB central banking conference: The role of money: Money and monetary policy in the twenty-first century, November 10, Frankfurt: ECB.

Jabko, N. (2010). The hidden face of the Euro. *Journal of European Public Policy, 17*(3), 318–334.

Jones, E. (2013). The collapse of the Brussels-Frankfurt consensus and the future of the Euro. In V. A. Schmidt & M. Thatcher (Eds.), *Resilient liberalism in Europe's political economy* (pp. 145–170) New York and Cambridge: Cambridge University Press.

Kahler, M. L., & Lake, D. A. (Eds.). (2013). *Politics in the New Hard Times: The great recession in comparative perspective.* Ithaca, NY: Cornell University Press.

Katzenstein, P. (Ed.). (1997). *Tamed power: Germany in Europe.* Ithaca, NY: Cornell University Press.

Kornai, J. (1980). *Economics of shortage.* Amsterdam: North-Holland.

Krasner, S. (1984). Approaches to the state: Alternative conceptions and historical dynamics. *Comparative Politics, 16*(2), 223–246.

Kuhn, T. (2012[1962]). *The structure of scientific revolution* (50th anniversary ed.). Chicago and London: University of Chicago Press.

Kydland, F. E., & Prescott, E. C. (1977). Rules rather than discretion: The inconsistency of optimal plans. *Journal of Political Economy, 85*(3), 473–491.

Levy, J. S. (2008). Case studies: Types, designs, and logics of inference. *Conflict Management and Peace Science, 25*(1), 1–18.

Lindblom, C. E. (1968). *The policy-making process*. Englewood Cliffs, NJ: Prentice Hall.

Lindvall, J. (2012). Politics and policies in two economic crises: The nordic countries. In N. Bermeo & J. Pontusson (Eds.), *Coping with crisis: Government reactions to the great recession* (pp. 233–261). New York: Russel Sage.

Lombardi, D., & Moschella, M. (2015) The government bond buying programmes of the European central bank: An analysis of their policy settings. *Journal of European Public Policy* (early view, article first published online 14 August 2015).

Ludlow, P. (1982). *The making of the European monetary system: A case study of the politics of the European community*. London: Butterworths.

Mabbett, D., & Schelkle, W. (2007). Bringing macroeconomics back in to the political economy of reform: The Lisbon Agenda and the 'fiscal philosophy' of EMU. *Journal of Common Market Studies, 45*(1), 81–103.

Mabbett, D., & Schelkle, W. (2014). *Searching under the lamp-post: The evolution of fiscal surveillance, LSE 'Europe in Question'* (Discussion Paper 75). London: London School of Economics.

Marcussen, M. (1999). The dynamics of EMU ideas. *Cooperation and Conflict, 34*(4), 383–411.

Martin, C. J., (2012). Social Solidarity in Scandinavia after the Fall of Finance Capitalism. In W. Grant & G. K.Wilson (Eds.), *The consequences of the global financial crisis: The rhetoric of reform and regulation* (pp. 187–205). New York and Oxford: Oxford University Press.

Maskin, E. S. (1999). Recent theoretical work on the soft budget constraint. *American Economic Review, 89*(2), 421–425.

McKeown, T. J. (1999). Case studies and the statistical worldview: Review of king, Keohane, and Verba's designing social inquiry: Scientific inference in qualitative research. *International Organization, 53*(1), 161–190.

McNamara, K. R. (1998). *The currency of Ideas: Monetary politics in the European union*. Ithaca, NY: Cornell University Press.

McNamara, K. R. (1999). Consensus and constraint: Ideas and capital mobility in European monetary integration. *Journal of Common Market Studies, 37*(3), 455–476.

McNamara, K. R. (2006). Economic governance, ideas and EMU: What currency does policy consensus have today? *Journal of Common Market Studies, 44*(4), 803–821.

Moravcsik, A. (1998). *The choice for Europe: Social purpose and state power from Messina to Maastricht*. Ithaca, NY: Cornell University Press.

Moss, B. H. (Ed.). (2004). *Monetary union in crisis: The European union as a Neo-liberal construction*. Basingstoke: Palgrave Macmillan.

Oliver, M. J., & Pemberton, H. (2004). Learning and change in 20th-century British economic policy. *Governance, 17*(3), 415–441.

Padoa-Schioppa, T., King, M., Paelinck, Jean-H. P., Papademos, L. D., Pastor, A., & Scharpf, F. W. (1987). *Efficiency, stability and equity: A strategy for the evolution of the economic system of the European community*. Brussels: European Commission.

Puetter, U. (2012). Europe's deliberative intergovernmentalism: The role of the council and European Council in EU economic governance. *Journal of European Public Policy, 19*(2), 161–178.

Puntscher Riekmann, S., & Wydra, D. (2013). Representation in the European state of emergency: Parliaments against governments? *Journal of European Integration, 35*(5), 565–582.

Quiggin, J. (2012). *Zombie economics: How dead ideas still walk among Us* (2nd ed.). Princeton, NJ: Princeton University Press.

Regulation (EU) No. 1174/2011: Regulation of the European Parliament and of the Council of 16 November 2011 on enforcement measures to correct excessive macroeconomic imbalances in the euro area. Official Journal of the European Union L 306/8, 23.11.2011, Brussels.

Regulation (EU) No. 1176/2011: Regulation of the European Parliament and of the Council of 16 November 2011 on the prevention and correction of macroeconomic imbalances. Official Journal of the European Union L 306/25, 23.11.2011, Brussels.

Rohlfing, I. (2012). *Case studies and causal inference: An integrative framework*. Basingstoke: Palgrave Macmillan.

Sandholtz, W. (1993). Choosing union: Monetary politics and Maastricht. *International Organization, 47*(1), 1–39.

Sapir, A., Aghion, P., Bertola, G., Hellwig, M., Pisani-Ferry, J., & Rosati, D. et al. (2004). *An Agenda for a growing Europe: The sapir report*. Oxford: Oxford University Press.

Schäfer, D. (2016). A banking union of ideas? The impact of ordoliberalism and the vicious circle on the EU banking union. *Journal of Common Market Studies, 54*(4), 961–980.

Schelkle, W. (2011). A Tale of two crises: The Euro area in 2008/09 and in 2010. *European Political Science, 10*(3), 375–383.

Schelkle, W. (2012a). European fiscal union: From monetary back door to parliamentary main entrance. *CESifo Forum, 1*/2012, 28–34.

Schelkle, W. (2012b). Policymaking in hard times: French and German responses to the Eurozone crisis. In N. Bermeo & J. Pontusson (Eds.), *Coping with crisis: Government reactions to the great recession* (pp. 130–161). New York: Russell Sage.

Schelkle, W. (2013). Monetary integration in crisis: How well do existing theories explain the predicament of EMU? *Transfer, 19*(1), 37–48.

Schelkle, W. (2014). Fiscal Integration by Default, In P. Genschel & M. Jachtenfuchs (Eds.), *Beyond the regulatory polity? The European integration of core state powers* (pp. 105–123). New York and Oxford: Oxford University Press.

Schelkle, W., & Hassel, A. (2012). The policy consensus ruling European political economy: The political attractions of discredited economics. *Global Policy, 3*(1), 16–27.

Schmidt, V. A. (2010). Taking ideas and discourse seriously: Explaining change through discursive institutionalism as the fourth 'New Institutionalism'. *European Political Science Review, 2*(1), 1–25.

Schmidt, V. A. (2011). Reconciling ideas and institutions through discursive institutionalism. In D. Béland & R. H Cox (Eds.), *Ideas and politics in social science research* (pp. 47–64). New York and Oxford: Oxford University Press.

Schmidt, V. A. (2012). What happened to the State-Influenced Market Economies (SMEs)? France, Italy, and Spain confront the crisis as the good, the bad, and the ugly. In W. Grant & J. White (Eds.). (2014), *Politicizing Europe: The challenge of executive discretion, LSE 'Europe in Question'* (Discussion Paper 72). London: London School of Economics.

Schmidt, V. A. (2014). Speaking to the markets or to the people? A discursive institutionalist analysis of the EU's sovereign debt crisis. *British Journal of Politics and International Relations, 16*(1), 188–209.

Schmidt, V. A. & Thatcher, M. (2013). Theorizing ideational continuity: The resilience of Neo-liberal ideas in Europe. In V. A. Schmidt & M. Thatcher (Eds.), *Resilient Liberalism in Europe's political economy* (pp. 1–50). New York and Cambridge: Cambridge University Press.

Siems, M., & Schnyder, G. (2014). Ordoliberal lessons for economic stability: Different kinds of regulation not more regulation. *Governance, 27*(3), 377–396.

Sinn, H.-W. (2014). *The Euro trap: On bursting bubbles, budgets, and beliefs.* Oxford: Oxford University Press.

Stark, J. (2013). Lessons from the European crisis. *Cato Journal, 33*(3), 541–562.

Torres, F. (2008). The long road to EMU: The economic and political reasoning behind Maastricht. In S. Baroncelli, C. Spagnolo, & L. S. Talani (Eds.), *Back to Maastricht: Obstacles to constitutional reform within the EU treaty (1991–2007)* (pp. 196–220). Newcastle: Cambridge Scholars Publishers.

Vail, M. I. (2014). Varieties of Liberalism: Keynesian responses to the great recession in France and Germany. *Governance, 27*(1), 63–85.

Van Evera, S. (1996). *Guide to methodology for students of political science.* Cambridge, MA: MIT Press.

Verdun, A. (1999). The role of the Delors Committee in the creation of EMU: An epistemic community? *Journal of European Public Policy, 6*(2), 308–328.

Wolff, G. B. (2013). The ECB's OMT programme and German constitutional concerns. In Brookings Institution (Ed.), *Think tank 20: The G-20 and central banks in the new world of unconventional monetary Policy* (pp. 26–31). Washington, DC: Brookings Institution.

Woodford, M. (2009). Convergence in macroeconomics: Elements of the new synthesis. *American Economic Journal: Macroeconomics, 1*(1), 267–279.

White, J. (2014*). Politicizing Europe: The challenge of executive discretion, LSE 'Europe in Question'* (Discussion Paper 72). London: London School of Economics.

Woodruff, D. M. (2014). *Governing by Panic: The politics of the Eurozone Crisis, LSE 'Europe in Question'* (Discussion Paper 52). London: London School of Economics.

Young, B. (2014). The Power of Ordoliberalism in the Eurozone crisis management. In D. Daianu, C. D'Adda, G. Basevi, & R. Kumar (Eds.), *The Eurozone crisis and the future of Europe: The political economy of further integration and governance* (pp. 126–137). Basingstoke: Palgrave Macmillan.

5

Principals and Agents in European Democracy

Benjamin Spörer

European integration has progressed significantly both economically and politically since the 1980s. Economically, the most substantial steps have been the creation of the European internal market, the creation of the Economic and Monetary Union and the introduction of the Euro as a single currency. Politically, the structure of the EU has also changed to become more democratic, as seen by the introduction of qualified majority voting and the strengthening of the European Parliament. However, many analysts have commented that despite the expansion of EU competences, the democratization of the EU system has lagged behind. The outbreak of the Euro crisis raised the issue of the EU's democratic legitimation and political mistrust surged all around Europe (Eurobarometer 2011, 2014).

B. Spörer(✉)
University of Hamburg, Hamburg, Germany
e-mail: benjamin.spoerer@gmail.com

© The Author(s) 2017
S. Collignon, *The Governance of European Public Goods*,
DOI 10.1007/978-3-319-64012-9_5

The debate on the European Union's democratic deficit can be summarized through three major voices—Andrew Moravcsik, Giandomenico Majone and Simon Hix.[1] Both Moravcsik (2002, 2004) and Majone (1998) deny the existence of a democratic deficit, while Hix adopts a more critical view, arguing that political contestation, a central characteristic of all democracies, is underdeveloped and lacking in the EU.

This chapter aims to examine the deadlock between the dominating views by applying the Principal Agent theory developed by Mark A. Pollack. Approaching the question of the efficient provision of public goods and their democratic governance, I will show that the principal-agent theory reveals weaknesses inherent in the different arguments of the debate on the democratic deficit. It becomes clear that certain assumptions lead to mutual incomprehension. We therefore need an honest reassessment of the meaning of the democratic deficit.

My argument is divided into three parts. Part one starts by giving a broad overview of the 'pre-crisis' discussion of the democratic deficit of the EU. It outlines and contrasts the contributions of the three authors mentioned above and highlights the differences in their arguments and underlying assumptions. It also examines how principal-agent theory provides some valid contribution to the discussion.

Part two focuses on the principal-agent theory and examines how it is applied to the political system of the EU. I first apply it to the EU by accepting member states as ultimate principals, and I then move forward by focusing on citizens as ultimate principals.

The last part analyses the democratic deficit in the context of the Euro crisis. It is frequently stated that the Euro crisis led the governments of member states to adopt certain reforms, which dangerously overstretched the democratic deficit (Habermas 2014; Offe 2013). I conclude that the Euro crisis is a useful test ground for principal-agent theory. Examining the Euro crisis from the principal-agent perspective, and contrasting the results with the argumentations of Moravcsik, Majone, and Hix, including post-crisis comments of these scholars, reveals deeper causes behind the deadlock in present policy discussions.

---

[1]Although recent, their contributions to the debate notably predate the financial crisis and must therefore be understood in this context.

The Pre-crisis Discussion About the Democratic Deficit of the European Union

Within the debate, the term 'democratic deficit' has taken on different connotations and meanings (Milev 2004). This section will first explain the standard version of the democratic deficit, then moves on to explain the main arguments by Moravcsik (2002, 2004, 2008), Majone (1998), Hix (2008), and Follesdal and Hix (2006).

Discussing Europe—The Standard Version of the Democratic Deficit

The basic problem behind most of the criticisms concerning the democratic credentials of the EU is the lack of responsiveness and the insufficient possibility for European citizens to influence European policy outcomes (Sonnicksen 2014).

Throughout the process of European integration, the executive powers of EU institutions have strengthened at the expense of the powers of national parliaments. Policy-making in the EU is now dominated by national ministers in the Council and by government appointees in the European Commission. The degree of control by national parliaments is limited, which goes against a fundamental principle in democracies— the direct accountability of decision-makers to electoral constituencies (Auel and Benz 2007; Baker et al. 2002; Andersen and Burns 1996; Raunio 1999).

Although this loss of influence has been compensated by strengthening the European Parliament in some domains, the power of the European Parliament is still weak when compared to the Council or the Commission, because it lacks substantial competences in key policy areas. Although the appointment of the Commission as a whole requires the approval of the European Parliament (article 17 (7) TEU-Lisbon), each Commissioner is still nominated by national governments. Hence, the Commission does not qualify as a directly or indirectly elected executive government by national standards (Mair and Thomassen 2010; Magnette 2001; Wallace and Smith 1995).

European Parliament elections are thus usually considered as 'mid-term' or 'second-order' elections, with parties competing mainly on national, instead of European, issues.

Another explanation for the EU's democratic deficit is the institutional, geographical and psychological distance between the EU and its citizens. The EU's complex structure and it's obscure legislation process make it difficult for citizens to understand the system and participate accordingly. EU citizens' lack of understanding is aggravated by two perceptions. First, EU citizens believe that national governments use the EU as a backdoor to implement policies they cannot achieve or legitimate at national level. Secondly, they also believe that policymakers at the EU-level often neglect the social concerns of EU citizens. Indeed, various scholars have found that policy outcomes in the EU usually favour well-organized interest groups rather than citizens' preferences (Follesdal and Hix 2006; Scharpf 1997, 1999; Streeck and Schmitter 1991).

Examining the Deadlock Between Majone, Moravcsik and Hix

I shall now examine the deadlock between Majone, Moravcsik and Hix by analysing the key points of their arguments.

Policymaking in the EU—Regulatory or Redistributive?

One topic of disagreement between Majone and Hix is the nature of EU competences. On the one hand, Giandomenico Majone believes that the EU plays the role of a "regulatory agency", whose competences are limited to the regulation of economic policy and market related policy fields with the aim of achieving Pareto-efficiency. In this sense, the EU is no different from domestic regulatory agencies such as competition or telecommunication agencies, which are also isolated from the political process. He warns that if such institutions were directly elected, regulatory policy-making would be politicized and result in Pareto-inefficient policy outcomes, which will in turn undermine the legitimacy of the EU (Majone 2002).

Hix, however, argues that even though institutions isolated from the majoritarian democratic process may best provide purely Pareto-improving policies, European economic and social policies also have significant redistributive consequences.[2] EU policies are neither purely Pareto-improving, nor are they a priori unimportant to voters. For example, EU expenditure policies have huge redistributive effects where net-contributors and net-beneficiaries from the EU budget can clearly be identified. Another example would be trade liberalization policies, where private producers for domestic markets stand to 'lose' from the process. Thus, democratic contestation and participation cannot be judged only by the formal list of competences assigned to the EU, but rather we must take into account the effects that these policies have on the lives of EU citizens and how they perceive this impact (Hix 2008).

Policy Outcomes or Process?

One of the central arguments by Andrew Moravcsik denying the existence of a democratic deficit in the EU is that policies are pursued by democratically legitimated governments and there are sufficient institutional checks and balances that are embedded in the European governance structure due to the horizontal and vertical divisions of power. As such, the EU institutions are tightly constrained by a "set of substantive, fiscal, administrative, legal and procedural constraints" (Moravcsik 2008: 334). This ensures that policy decisions are only taken when there is a 'supermarjority' of not only national representatives, but also technocrats, judges and parliamentarians. The result of having a 'supermajority' is that EU policy outcomes tend to be rather centrist in nature.

Hix disagrees with Moravcsik's assumption that a majority of citizens would support such centrist policy outcomes. He stresses two specific

---

[2]Also Majone points out that efficiency-enhancing policies are indeed very likely to have some redistributive impacts, but that this is not a serious problem as long as efficiency gains are large enough to compensate the losers (Majone 1998).

problems in this regard. First, he points out that voters' preferences are neither fixed nor exogenously determined; instead they are continuously shaped through the process of deliberation and party contestation, which are essential elements of all democracies. However, EU policy outcomes "may not be those policies that would be preferred by a political majority after a debate" (Follesdal and Hix 2006: 545). This leads to his second point: the legitimacy of an institution is not only based on final outcomes, but rather on mechanisms that can reliably ensure that future outcomes are acceptable, even when voters' preferences change. This is exactly what the EU lacks—sufficient democratic contestation that allows the formation of voters' preferences.

Electoral Salience

Moravcsik also raised the point that EU competences are mostly regulatory in nature and focus mainly on the "regulation of policy externalities resulting from cross border economic activity" (Moravcsik 2002: 607). Although this is similar to Majone's point about EU competences being more of a technical matter, Moravcsik goes one step further by concluding that such competences are "relatively unimportant to voters" (Moravcsik 2008: 333) and are thus of low electoral salience.[3] This explains why European elections are usually considered as second-order elections and electoral turnout is so low. Furthermore, he asserts that all salient policy issues remain fully in the hands of member states' governments and he believes it is unlikely that EU policies would be opposed to any important national interest because national governments have veto power. He claims that "any effort to expand participation is unlikely to overcome apathy" (Moravcsik 2002: 615).

By contrast, Hix points out that the salience of policies is endogenous to the political process. In other words, salience of an issue is dependent on the political process and the articulation of different and opposing

---

[3]Moravcsik stresses that the EU treaties explicitly exclude the most salient policy issues like health care provision, taxation, law and order, education policy and social security policy from the EU's competences (Moravcsik 2002).

positions through a debate. Thus, when voters are deprived of a broad debate and different views are not articulated, the issue would inevitably lack voter salience.

Another problem with the lack of democratic debates is that voters believe that there is no visible opposition to EU policies at the EU-level. Due to the dearth of preference revelation and dissatisfaction at the EU-level, citizens have difficulty in distinguishing between parties opposing certain EU policies and parties opposing the EU system as a whole. This explains increasing Euro scepticism and the rise of anti-EU parties all over Europe. National political parties exploit the lack of opportunities for voters to choose between rival policy agendas at the EU-level and mobilize voters by presenting themselves as opposition to the entire EU establishment.

Hix believes that political contestation and the possibility of choice would lead to a broader debate, which will increase the salience of the respective issues and shape voters' preferences, which in turn would increase electoral turnout and finally ensure that policy outcomes are more strongly supported by a majority of citizens. Hence, contested politics would increase the democratic legitimacy of the EU (Hix 2008).

Discussion of the Deadlock

It is clear that the common theme of these three scholars is the logic of delegation and the costs, risks and benefits of delegation. In the views of Majone and Moravcsik, delegation of regulatory competences to the EU is justified—it significantly reduces transaction costs of decision-making, increases efficiency and ensures credible commitments from member states by monitoring compliance (Moravcsik 2004; Majone 1998). Since the competences delegated to the EU are limited to those that are regulatory in nature and tightly constrained by sufficient checks and balances, the EU's democratic deficit is nothing but a myth.

Hix on the other hand, advocates the examination of the EU from a more functional perspective and advocates judging the EU system with the main criteria of democracy. The fundamental factor, he argues, is the role of citizens in the overall chain of delegation, which Majone and Moravcsik have failed to take into account sufficiently.

I shall now explain how principal-agent theory, developed by Mark A. Pollack as the 'Theory of Delegation, Agency and Agenda Setting', may contribute to overcoming the deadlock. This theory allows us to examine the logic of delegation within the EU system and provides further insights and contributions to the examination of the EU's democratic deficit.

Applying the Principal-Agent Model to the Debate on Democratic Deficit

Explaining the Principle-Agent Model

The Principle-Agent Model derived from Rational Choice Institutionalism (RCI), one of the more recent approaches to the study of European integration. RCI adopts a functionalist approach whereby the type of institutions that member states choose is determined in terms of the supposed functions of an institution and their expected effects on policy outcomes (Pollack 1997).

The Principal-Agent Model, developed within the domain of microeconomics, models the contractual relationship and the strategic interaction between two actors: the principal, who delegates powers to the agent, and the agent, who acts on behalf of the principal (Dür and Elsig 2011; Hawkins et al. 2006; Pollack 2003; Pratt and Zeckhauser 1991).

The main principals of Pollack's model are member states. He asserts that member states lead the process of European integration by concluding the various founding treaties and play a central role in delegating to supranational agents in both the European Council and the Council of the European Union (Council) (Pollack 2003). The principal-agent model provides certain reasons as to why member states, as principals, delegate certain powers to supranational agents.

Benefits and Costs Associated with Member States Delegation to Supranational Agents

To explain the reasons for delegation, the principal-agent model assumes that principals are rational actors and thus base their decision on a cost-benefit analysis (Pollack 1997; Pratt and Zeckhauser 1991).

The main purpose of delegation is to overcome collective action problems, reduce uncertainty, enhance the principal's own credibility, and increase efficiency of policy-making. By delegating monitoring and enforcement responsibilities to a supranational agent, transaction costs are reduced for member states and non-compliance is penalized, thereby ensuring that mutually advantageous agreements can be reached (Pollack 2003). Member states are likely to delegate four specific key functions: monitoring compliance, solving the problem of incomplete contracting, regulation, and agenda setting.

However, while delegation helps to reduce transaction costs and increase efficiency, there are also costs associated with the act of delegation. The principal might incur losses if there is what Pollack calls 'agency slack'.[4] This occurs when the agent pursues an outcome that is divergent from or non-compliant with the principal's preferences. To avoid agency slack, the principal needs to put control mechanisms in place; one of them is oversight procedures, although they will generate additional costs associated with the act of delegation and asymmetric information.

---

[4]Agency slack as an independent action by the agent that is undesired by the principal occurs mainly in two forms: shirking and slippage. Shirking refers to a situation in which the agent minimizes the effort it expends on the principal's behalf and instead behaves opportunistically, pursuing its own interests (Hawkins et al. 2006; Pollack 1997). According to Pollack, shirking emerges as the primary source of agency losses (Pollack 1997). Slippage, on the other hand, refers to a situation in which the structure of delegation and the contractual conditions actually provide distorted incentives for the agent to shift policies away from its principal's preferred outcome and towards its own preferences (Hawkins et al. 2006; Pollack 1997).

What Does Principal-Agent Theory Tell Us About the EU's Democratic Deficit?

If we apply the principal-agent theory to Majone and Moravcsik arguments, we can see that both authors share a similar view with Pollack in that they see the relationship between member states and EU institutions through the logic of delegation. Member states are the main principals in the EU system, whereas supranational institutions are considered unitary and competence-maximizing agents—an assumption that is widely accepted because all supranational institutions have pursued a broadly integrationist agenda.

Various tasks or competences are assigned to these agents through the unanimous conclusion of EU treaties by member states and in the form of legislative acts decided by the Council. Given that they are treated as principals, member states assign tasks to agents to reap the benefits of more efficient decision-making.

However, with every act of delegation, member states also establish various control mechanisms to reduce the risk of agency slack and to ensure favourable policy outcomes. Both Majone and Moravcsik believe that within the EU, such control mechanisms are sufficient in ensuring the agent's responsiveness and accountability to the member states. Majone and Moravcsik emphasize that delegation in the EU is consistent with today's practice of most modern democracies (Moravcsik 2002). Majone goes even further by concluding that in terms of transparency and accountability, delegation in the EU is even more advanced than within the member states (Majone 1998).

With principal-agent theory however, Pollack is able to examine the EU by going beyond the arguments of Majone and Moravcsik. He sees the act of delegation as far more complex and associated with its own problems. In his model, the question of democratic legitimacy deals with how delegation is structured, rather than with the question of delegation itself.

One defining feature of Pollack's theory is that he highlights the role of the agent's preferences in the act of delegation. He warns that the preferences of the agent can diverge from the principal's, which results in a certain degree of mistrust between both parties. The principal thus tries to overcome this by putting in place certain control mechanisms and safeguards.[5] But how much control such control mechanisms have is very much dependent on a number of factors, such as the amount of information that the principals have at the time and the political costs that is associated with sanctioning the agent.

Pollack concludes that the act of delegation is not as straightforward as Majone and Moravcsik believe it to be. Instead, member states have to take into account many factors when calculating the trade-off between control, on the one hand, and speed and efficiency of decision making, on the other. In doing so, control mechanisms are constantly recalibrated to achieve the best policy outcome.

This was exactly what Pollack found when examining the period where the old comitology system was in place. He saw that member states had far-reaching and direct control over the Commission due to the various control mechanisms that they have put in place. These were in the form of committee procedures, with each procedure having a different degree of control.

However, member states constantly adjusted such control mechanisms. For example, they "sometimes 'tightened' committee procedures in response to Commission shirking" (Pollack 1997: 115). Member states also regularly adjusted the Commission's mandate, by reinforcing safeguards and by putting procedures that are more restrictive into place, and even assuming some of the Commission's executive powers. Pollack concludes that within the comitology system, member states "tailor their comitology preferences according to the specific issue area or even the specific piece of legislation at hand as a function of their substantive interests in a given issue area and their estimation of the Commission likely behavior in that area" (Pollack 2003: 139).

Therefore, by highlighting the role of the agent's preferences in the whole act of delegation, Pollack highlights the fundamental weakness of the functional approach, which is the "assumption that the institutions adopted are those that most efficiently perform the tasks set out for them by their creators and are chosen for that reason" (Pollack 1997: 107).

---

[5]Popular control mechanisms to constrain the agent's behaviour, thus reducing the risk of agency losses, are screening, monitoring, and sanctioning mechanisms.

Pollack's principal-agent theory reveals certain weakness in Moravcsik's and Majone's arguments. Majone claims that EU institutions should be shielded from the political process and should not rely on majority rule because EU institutions are only assigned competences that are "regulatory in nature" (Majone 1998). Instead, Pollack has shown that the principal's control over the agent is not always perfect and anticipated policy outcomes are not always reached.[6] Thus, a more flexible system which allows principals to constantly recalibrate their control over the agent is needed.

Moravcsik, on the other hand, assumes that because policy outcomes in the EU are usually centrist in nature and therefore supported by a majority, there must be adequate control and oversight mechanisms put in place by member states. However, Moravcsik neglects the fact that the types of control mechanism and their associated degrees of control are also the result of an intergovernmental bargaining process that is far from perfect. Each member state has different preferences concerning the various control and oversight mechanisms and Majone finds that intergovernmental bargaining usually favours the states with stronger negotiating positions.

Moreover, there are some decisions by which member states create lock-in effects, constrain future actions, and prevent any improvement of either delegation itself or of the respective control mechanisms. Such lock-in effects constrain future governments more thoroughly than national constitutions. This is especially so in the case of EU treaties, where any revision requires unanimity among all member states. According to Hix, the process of making decisions regarding the necessity of reforms has often resulted in policy gridlock until the Lisbon Treaty came into force (Hix 2008), although it is not clear that the situation has improved since then. Clearly, member states do not intend to create gridlock effects; these effects are the unintended consequences resulting from member states' focus on control mechanisms, such as veto rights and the costs of sanctions and the need for finding compromises.

---

[6]"[T]his is [also] why member states and the Commission often disagree on the choice of procedures, and it is why member states sometimes 'tighten' committee procedures in response to Commission shirking" (Pollack 1997: 115).

Reforms in the Lisbon Treaty

Since Majone and Moravcsik formulated their theories, important changes in the EU governance have occurred in the form of the Lisbon Treaty. This treaty significantly altered the EU's decision-making process and the influence that member states have over policy outcomes. This section will examine the various reforms that have taken place.

First, the Lisbon Treaty extended the ordinary legislative procedure to new areas. Qualified majority voting in the Council was significantly extended. Second, the ordinary legislative procedure gives the European Parliament the role of co-decider, thus affording it with a more balanced position with the Council (article 291 TFEU-Lisbon). The legislative powers of the European Parliament have increased and were even extended to areas like the EU budget, common agricultural policy, as well as justice and home affairs (Horeth 2010).[7] Third, the Lisbon Treaty has also removed the old comitology system. The Council and the European Parliament are now treated as equal in their control of delegated acts (Article 290 TFEU-Lisbon). Both now enjoy the right to veto and to revoke the delegation to the Commission. The policy analysts Corina Stratulat and Elisa Molino assess "[t]he need to agree on the terms of delegation, as well as the right to object to any delegated act on whatever grounds, boosts the legislators' power of scrutiny and increases democratic deliberation in the co-decision phase of the EU policy cycle" (Stratulat and Molino 2011: 3). Undoubtedly, this has made the EU more majoritarian, which Majone and Moravcsik view as negative.

---

[7]Actually, most European policies are affected by the extension of qualified majority voting. The Lisbon Treaty extends the ordinary legislative procedure also to areas such as freedom, security, and justice (articles 77-88 TFEU-Lisbon)—areas where the Council traditionally adopted measures unanimously—which, according to Moravcsik, are rather salient policy fields (Moravcsik 2004).

What Does Pollack Say About the European Parliament?

Pollack argues that although the member states have created the European Parliament and assigned various legislative and budgetary powers to this body, it cannot be considered as an agent of the member states. Individual members of the European Parliament (MEPs) are not appointed by the member states' governments but are instead elected (since 1979) by the EU citizens. As such, the European Parliament is an agent of its electorates.

Moreover, the member states have not established any oversight mechanisms and the only way to sanction the European Parliament is through the relatively difficult means of treaty amendments, which require unanimity and ratification by national parliaments and electorates. The question then arises as to why would member states create such a relatively powerful body that is largely independent? Pollack (2003) explains that this is due to member states' ideological concerns about the democratic character of EU decision-making rather than for pure functionalist motivations. This shows that a pure rational choice approach to delegation is too simplistic; it must be seen in the context of the current sociopolitical values.

Therefore, the principal-agent theory is rather weak in explaining the reforms of the Lisbon Treaty. If one takes ideology into account and consider the traditions of Western democracies and European values, the citizens are often referred to as the ultimate principals (Scharpf 2009, 2012; Collignon 2013a). Assuming a two-step, sequential model of preference formation (first Appendix, Fig. A.1 and then Appendix, Fig. A.2), even Pollack as well as Moravcsik implicitly acknowledge this fact as citizens determine national governments, which they view as the ultimate principals in their theories (Pollack 2001; Moravcsik 1993).

Let us now examine if principal-agent theory can provide any further insights if we consider citizens as the ultimate principals instead of member states.

Citizens as Ultimate Principals

Since the Maastricht Treaty, opinion polls reveal that the public perception of the democratic credentials of the EU has continuously deteriorated (Hix 2008). This indicates the inaccuracy of Moracvsik's view that the competences assigned to the EU are not salient to citizens. It also debunks Majone's claim that EU policies are Pareto-efficient. We need to understand why EU citizens are increasingly viewing the EU as undemocratic. In other words, what are the criteria against which we can judge democratic credentials? Here, we can bring in another theory, namely the functional logic of the provision of public goods.

Citizens as Owners of Public Goods

The theory of public goods says that the ultimate function of a state is the provision of public goods. Within a democratic system, the citizens are the common owners of national public goods and they determine the administration of such goods through the democratic process. In other words, according to principal-agent theory, citizens are the ultimate principals who aim to reduce transaction costs by delegating the task of supplying public goods to agents through the electoral process. This process is illustrated in Fig. 5.1.

In the context of European integration, member states have transferred the responsibility for the provision of certain goods to the European level and delegate European institutions as their agents in order to reduce transaction costs. In this scenario, member states are the ultimate principals, as member states alone can authorize the delegation of power and determine the administration. The chain of delegation at EU level, as illustrated in Fig. 5.2, corresponds to Pollack's vision.

Clearly, there is a significant change of ownership of public goods when the administration of such goods moves from the national level to the European level. Because of the predominance of the member states within the political system of the EU, member states, not citizens, are now the owners of European public goods (Collignon 2013a).

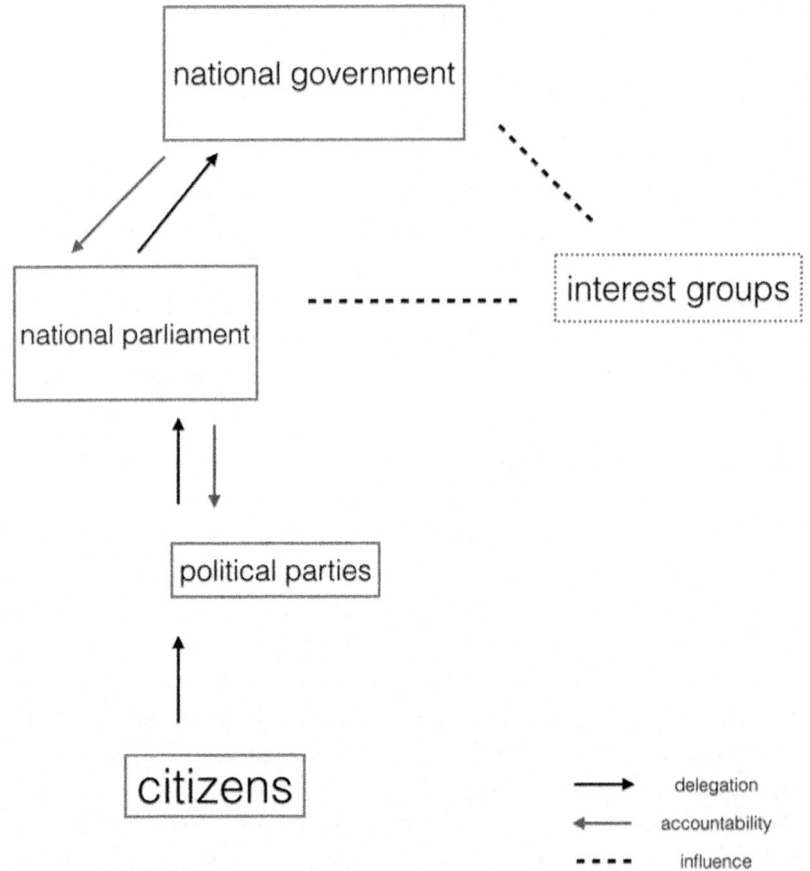

Fig. 5.1 Chain of delegation within nation states

However, if citizens are the ultimate principals, it becomes clear that Pollack's model is oversimplified due to one problematic assumption—that member states' governments always fully represent the preferences of their constituencies. This assumption is not a given as national political systems are also based on chains of delegation which are susceptible to agency slack. The risk of agency slack depends on the degree of control, which in turn also depends on the amount of principals'

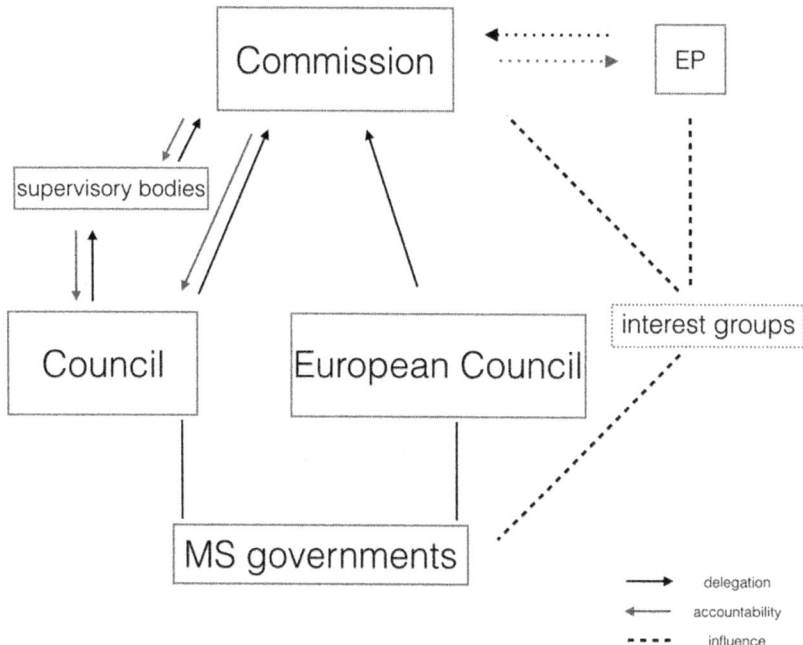

Fig. 5.2 Chain of delegation at European level as envisioned by Pollack

information (Pollack 1997). In other words, because each agent has its own preferences that may be divergent from its principal's, there is a risk of imperfect policy outcomes at each act of delegation. This risk is multiplied when several chains are built upon one another (Vaubel 2006).

The various chains of delegation are illustrated in Fig. 5.3.

In reference to Fig. 5.1, citizens face only two channels of delegation—one through national parties, which in turn delegate to the national parliament. In Fig. 5.3, however, citizens face two different channels of delegation: one through the European Parliament and one through national parliaments. Moreover, each act of delegation differs substantially in terms of the strength of control and sanction mechanisms. Yet, citizens' risk of agency slack is significant, as first of all, controls and sanctions concerning the Commission remain in the hands of member states' governments and, second, European citizens are not fully equipped to control their governments within

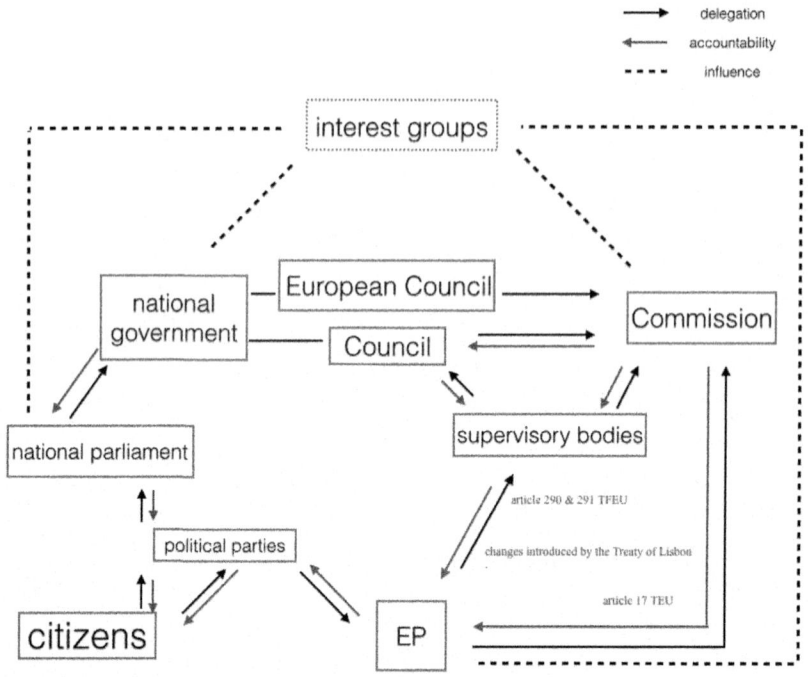

Fig. 5.3 Chain of delegation within the political system of the EU and its member states

the intergovernmental setting. Principal-agent theory tells us that the two factors affecting the probability of agency slack are the amount of principals' information and their perception of costs and benefits (Pollack 1997). This has huge implications for the legitimacy of any democracy—whether national or European.

Delegation and Legitimacy—The Principals' Perception and the Centrality of the Public Discourse

Three variables determine democratic legitimacy: input-legitimacy, output-legitimacy, and throughput-legitimacy. Input legitimacy is the degree of institutional responsiveness to citizen's concerns resulting from people's democratic involvement. Scharpf (1988) found that there is a trade-off between the efficiency of the system and citizen participation in deliberation. Output legitimacy focuses on how policy outcomes meet peoples' preferences. Throughput-legitimacy refers to the policy process between input and output, and whether the process enables the fair and appropriate inclusion of preferences (Schmidt 2010; Wimmel 2009; Jones 2009). Obviously, agency slack will reduce both output-legitimacy and throughput legitimacy, but some scholars have concluded that this could be compensated by greater input legitimacy. The reason is that because as a means of democratic contestation public discourses can shape the perceptions of citizens, both *ex ante* and *ex post*, and therefore may be seen as the crucial element for each single category of legitimacy (Scharpf 2004, 2009, 2012; Schmidt 2010; Hix 2008).

Within a democratic state, parliamentary opposition and the media act as the most important control agents for forcing the government to explain itself and to justify certain policies. This sparks public discourses between opposing forces and in turn shapes the perceptions of citizens (Schmidt 2010; Collignon 2003). It is only through this process of debating policy pros and cons that citizens can assess whether their government is acting in their interest.

This sort of public deliberation does not exist in the EU and this explains why people perceive a democratic deficit. Member states' governments are more successful in shaping their democratic legitimacy through public discourses than European institutions. The next section would investigate why the EU is not able to generate the same type of public discourse that member states have.

Institutional Discourses in the European Union

It is necessary to distinguish two different types of political discourses. In a 'coordinative discourse', various actors focus on achieving an agreement among themselves and on convincing key constituencies of necessity and appropriateness of the issue at stake (Schmidt and Radaelli 2004). By contrast, in a 'communicative discourse' an actor focuses on convincing the entire public of the necessity and appropriateness of certain policies. Schmidt (2010) found that within the EU system, the coordinative discourse tends to be more common, especially within the Council, but also between the Commission, the Council and the European Parliament. A more communicative discourse is mostly left to national politicians, but would be needed for greater policy acceptance.

The Council is unlikely to provide a communicative discourse as the intergovernmental negotiation and bargaining that occurs is not transparent and unknown to the public (Pollack 2003). Therefore, member states' governments have extensive discretion within the Council, making it almost impossible for national parliaments or for citizens to hold their governments accountable for their work at the EU level. Qualified majority voting was supposed to make it easier to avoid veto playing by national interests, but this highlights the dilemma of the European governance: national governments alone cannot set policies, but the overlapping consensus for all, or most, is minimal. The opaqueness of the Council's negotiation process means that even when governments report to their respective parliaments, they frame these reports to highlight their own role in finding successful outcomes, or to blame EU institutions in failures (Hobolt and Tilley 2014; Down and Wilson 2008). As such, the policy discourses are based on a narrow and biased lens of the Council's decision-making process and shape EU citizens' perceptions of the EU and its institutions negatively.

Instead, the Commission has sought to increase its legitimacy by reinforcing its communicative component through clarifying discourses on EU policies, largely by producing a pile of technical papers for and about the intergovernmental coordination and by inviting NGOs and civil society to comment on these initiatives. However, Schmidt and Radaelli concluded in their 2004 study that this approach has not been successful as the Commission faces difficulties in challenging national discourses. Instead, the primary focus of the Commission's policy discourse remains in the coordinative realm, mainly within governmental and non-governmental networks.

The European Parliament is the institution with the greatest potential to move to the much-needed communicative discourse in the EU. It is an institution where open debates on EU issues occur and these debates can shape citizens' perceptions of the policy process as well as the content of respective policies. These public discourses can also force the executive agents of the EU—the Commission and member states' governments—to publicly justify and explain themselves. In reality, however, a communicative discourse has not occurred within the European Parliament. According to Hix (2008), this is due to the lack of political contestation in the EU.

The Discussion About the Democratic Deficit After the Lisbon Treaty

The Lisbon Treaty has improved the politicization of European discourses regarding the governance of European goods. The previous Treaty of Nice had stated under articles 201 and 214 (2) TEC that the designation of the European Commission was decided by national governments and required the approval by a majority of the European Parliament. The European Parliament also had the power to withdraw its confidence from the Commission as a whole. At first glance, it seems that the Commission became dependent on the European Parliament, but because the principal is still the European Council, this was not an act of delegation in accordance with principal-agent theory. For this reason, no communicative discourse emerged from the European Parliament—in contrast to national parliaments. Although in principle the European Parliament could have had the potential to launch communicative discourses, the weak power of delegation between the European Parliament and the Commission prevent this. The Commission did not depend on the support of the European Parliament and the European Parliament had no means of controlling its agent, the Commission, in accordance with the preferences of their respective constituencies. Thus, due to the lack of competences, the European Parliament could not fulfil functions similar to national parliaments (Sonnicksen 2010, 2014; Mair and Thomassen 2010).

Moreover, the Treaty of Nice also placed member states' governments in the most dominant role because of the central position assigned to the Council between the Commission and the European Parliament. These two factors—the weak delegation link between the European

Parliament and the Commission, and the central position of the Council—all changed with the Lisbon Treaty.

The Lisbon Treaty significantly weakened the role of the Council and strengthened the role of the European Parliament. The Parliament now acts as a counterweight to the Council as the ordinary legislative procedure was extended and the changes in the comitology system place the Parliament on equal footing as a co-decider with the Council. Furthermore, the Lisbon Treaty has increased the European Parliament`s capacity to control and influence the Commission.

Moreover, the Lisbon Treaty has also made the Council's work more transparent. Article 16(8) TEU-Lisbon states that "the Council shall meet in public when it deliberates and votes on a draft legislative act". Instead of relying on the reports of officials acting in the Council, national parliaments and EU citizens can now hold their government accountable based on their own judgment. This increases the accountability of member states' governments and reduces the risk of agency slack.

However, of all the reforms introduced by the Lisbon Treaty, the most important consequence is the emergence of a new chain of delegation between the European Parliament and the Commission.

First, Article 17(7) TEU-Lisbon states the following:

1. The President of the Commission's is nominated by a qualified majority of the member states' governments in the European Council.
2. Before the nomination, the member states' governments in the European Council must take into account the election results of the European Parliament and hold appropriate consultations before the European Council proposes to the European Parliament a candidate.
3. A majority of the members of the European Parliament must then agree on the candidate.

Second, Article 17(8) TEU-Lisbon states that the Commission shall be responsible to the European Parliament.

Hence, for the very first time, the Lisbon Treaty gives European citizens the ability to influence the formation of the main executive agent and gain full-ownership of European public goods in the policy areas. The Commission now must be more responsive to the expressed preferences of the citizen principals and must adopt a "communicative discourse" with the citizen principals by explaining and justifying certain actions and policy choices. However, the European Parliament still lacks competences for important policies such as budget and fiscal policy, immigration and external security. Unfortunately, these are precisely the areas where policy issues are most salient.

Hix had warned in 2008 that procedural changes do not directly entail substantive increases in political contestation within the EU. Instead, a commitment from the political elites must open the door for more politicization, for example, via a battle for the position of the Commission's presidency with governments, national and European parties supporting different candidates (Follesdal and Hix 2006). In fact, during the first European Parliament elections held in May 2014, after the Lisbon Treaty came into force, European political parties put forward their top candidates (*Spitzenkandidaten*) for the position of the President of the Commission. This was unprecedented. However, soon a spell of disillusionment followed the initial enthusiasm when some member states' governments seemed unwilling to nominate the winning party's candidate, Jean Claude Juncker, and started coming up with different proposals. However, citizens were now empowered and engaged in the election process and pressured the governments,[8] which eventually accepted Juncker, who was the elected by a majority of the European Parliament based on a great coalition between EPP and S&D. Although achieving the level of political contestation claimed by Hix is still work in progress, the Lisbon Treaty is a major step forward.

---

[8]See The Guardian, Friday 6 June 2014 (http://www.stefancollignon.de/PDF/The-guardian_letter-juncker-6-June-2014.pdf).

'The Euro Crisis' or 'How Member States Took the Power Away from the People'

According to one interpretation, the Euro crisis was a sovereign debt crisis that emerged from the global financial crisis, starting with the bankruptcy of Lehman Brothers in 2008. However, after his election as the new Greek Prime Minister in 2009, George Papandreou revealed that his predecessor government had run budget deficits up to 12% of GDP. Consequently, the credibility of the European budget rules and governance were seriously discredited. Greece fell into a debt crisis in 2010, which triggered further uncertainty in the financial market. This entailed certain domino effects on other Euro Area members, which also had to face solvency problems. In the further course, the crisis transformed into a massive economic crisis in several EMU member states (Offe 2013).[9] This has shown that economic stability and the stability of the Euro are European public goods, where the uncoordinated actions of single member states generate significant negative externalities (Collignon 2013a).

The next section will mention some explanatory aspects concerning the Euro crisis, but I shall not aim at providing an in-depth explanation of the crisis. The crisis' complexity caused a broad discussion among academics concerning causes and effects. While two main explanatory branches with different theoretical foundations can be identified, namely a monetarist and a 'fundamentalist' explanation (Collignon 2012b, 2013b), other scholars have highlighted the various misunderstandings, which are continuously occurring within the academic and public debates (Collignon 2012a, b, 2013b). Therefore, the interpretation of the crisis as a sovereign debt crisis is rightly criticized as being too narrow and excluding major aspects. Nevertheless, in 2012 member state governments set up an additional Treaty on Stability, Coordination and Governance in the Economic and Monetary Union, which introduced as a new stricter version of the Stability and Growth Pact. This was a major

---

[9]Particularly in Greece, Ireland, Italy, Portugal and Spain (GIIPS countries).

step away from public politicized debates on fiscal policy; instead, fiscal policy, the heart of democracy, was treated like a regulatory arrangement in the sense of Majone.

One major aspect, which has been ignored previously, was the existence of significant macroeconomic imbalances within the Euro Area. However, it became quickly apparent that the debt problems in Greece and Portugal were of a different nature from those in Ireland and Spain. In the first case, budget deficits had been too high, in the second private borrowing during the property boom was excessive. For this reason, the macroeconomic imbalance procedure (MIP), aimed at identifying, preventing and addressing the emergence of potentially harmful macroeconomic imbalances that could adversely affect economic stability in the Euro Area, was introduced in 2011. It is possible that acknowledging macroeconomic imbalances earlier could have led to a different policy response, especially by targeting both deficit and surplus countries (Schwarzer 2013; Collignon 2012a, 2013b). However, this new procedure re-enforces the intergovernmental governance of the Euro Area, despite the fact that the Commission leads the process, because it only monitors national government policies but does not give discretionary executive functions to a European agent.

An important aspect of the controversial discussions among Europe's elites about the causes of the crisis is the increased uncertainty it provokes. Recent studies suggest that this uncertainty originates not only from the real economic development and the indecisive behaviour of politicians (Collignon et al. 2013), but also from the dissent among academics and stakeholders about the causes and the most appropriate policy responses (Collignon 2013b; Scharpf 2011; Jones 2009). Keeping in mind the crucial role of the principals' (i.e. citizens') perception and taking into account that the crisis has dominated public attention for a long time—with many European citizens being affected in an existential way—it does not come as a surprise that the increased public uncertainty correlates with declining trust in European political institutions (Jones 2009).

Before turning to the Euro crisis and the political response by member states, the next section gives a broad overview about the development of the citizens' perception in the face of the progressing European integration.

The European Union and the Erosion of the Permissive Consensus

From the beginning, the project of European integration was based on the idea that it was a "process of creating an ever closer union among the peoples of Europe" (paragraph 14, Preamble TEU Lisbon) that would not only create peace, but also greater prosperity. The creation of the internal market, for example, was seen as a positive sum game that would foster economic growth and prosperity in all member states. In the early days, the severe lack of democratic structures seemed tolerable because integration was supported by the so-called permissive consensus and output legitimacy.

However, as the European integration proceeded, the picture has changed radically. Questions changed from the pros and cons of an internal market to whether the internal market should be regulated or deregulated, resulting in an increasingly politicized atmosphere (Craig 2010; Hix 2008). This politicization has become more intense due to the "increasing tendency for EU policy decisions to impinge on the life of individuals, and, the tendency of governments to scapegoat the EU for unpopular policy decisions" (Down and Wilson 2008: 30). This radical shift became most evident with the negative outcome of the referendum on the European Constitutional Treaty in 2005. Hix (2008) has pointed out that more conflict is inevitable as the EU shifts from Pareto-efficient to redistributive polies. The impact of monetary union on the European economy has been broadly positive, as it helped foster monetary stability, create new jobs, and increase general welfare. Yet, unfortunately, due to its incomplete governance structure, the management of the crisis has turned monetary union into a negative sum game, and risks eliminating the benefits that integration has achieved thus far (Collignon 2013b; Hix 2008).

On the one hand, the constraints imposed on member states frequently conflict with policies that represent national constituencies, because they prohibit actions and force governments (agents) to adopt policies that they, nor their voters, would have freely chosen (Mair 2009; Strom 2003). On the other hand, European policies, practically for the first time in European history, have a direct and massive impact on the lives of European citizens, while the main authors of these European policy-decisions are perfectly visible but non-revocable (Scharpf 2012). Consequently, the deficient crisis management has not only decreased citizens' confidence in the capability of the EU institutions and member states to solve the crisis and to incorporate the citizens' preferences and concerns, but also the mutual trust between the member states in terms of solidarity has suffered (Habermas 2014).

While the earlier permissive consensus reflected output legitimacy where all member states were benefitting from European integration, the Euro crisis appears as a peak of constraining dissent (Hooghe and Marks 2009). Citizens in the Southern crisis countries find themselves in disastrous situations[10] and often believe that they would have managed the crisis better without the Euro (Jones 2009). Nevertheless, national governments remain responsible for protecting the public goods on behalf of their citizens. Because they have lost their capacity of action in the national domain, and therefore delegate to supranational and intergovernmental institutions, they should be able to provide good output-oriented arguments and to justify these policy decisions (Scharpf 2012; Schmidt 2010; Jones 2009).

However, during the Euro crisis, national governments did the opposite. Taking the intergovernmental pathway to deal with the crisis, they have not only shown that they are incapable of administering European public goods efficiently, but also that they have widened the democratic deficit. This is leading to the emergence of a second deficit: social justice. Both deficits undermine the acceptability and the efficiency of the EU (Collignon 2013a).

Europe and Its Political Response to the Euro Crisis

Before the Euro crisis, the EU mostly limited itself to influencing national developments through soft forms of governance, meaning promoting best practice and giving non-binding recommendations on national wage and labour market policies (Busch et al. 2013). This picture changed radically in the course of the crisis.

---

[10]Disastrous situation refers to double-digit and rising rates of unemployment, massive real-wage cuts, rising social inequality, enormous cuts in public pensions, and growing poverty in Southern Europe which surely does not generate outcome satisfaction (Busch et al. 2013; Neal and Concepción 2013; Schwarzer and Wolff 2013; Scharpf 2011).

Given the non-bail-out clause (article 125 TFEU), whereby every member state is responsible for its own debt, Greece was threatened with bankruptcy when financial markets reacted to Greece's sovereign debt problems. The EU was facing an unexpected situation for which it had neither the instruments nor competences. A federal government that could have mitigated the effects did not exist. Therefore, the problem was passed on to the member states' governments, which were hesitant to acknowledge Greece's problem as a European problem. Only when it became clear that Greek's bankruptcy might have a fatal impact on the solvency of the creditor banks and might trigger domino effects in other member states, the surplus countries finally acknowledged the Greek sovereign-debt crisis as a threat to the Euro[11] and to European integration itself. In subsequent European Council summits, all Eurozone governments agreed to ignore various contractual constraints such as the no-bail-out clause, and went beyond a regulatory structure of EMU (Scharpf 2012; Klump 2011).[12] Thus, the EU treaties were not sufficient to solve the crisis.

What happened next was a major step in European economic integration. However, instead of transferring more sovereignty to the EU level in terms of a deeper economic integration of the Eurozone, as recommended by the Commission (Barroso 2011; Rehn 2011), member states opted for a combination of European rules and

---

[11]The Commission, the European Central Bank (ECB) as well as the governments of the surplus countries assessed the exit of Greece or any other deficit country from the Monetary Union as not being an option for various reasons. They were not only concerned that an exit of any state would be perceived as major setback for European integration, but that it would also encourage speculative attacks on other member states and therefore threaten all EMU states. Furthermore, the bankruptcy of any deficit state would also tie in heavy losses for the ECB as well as banks in surplus countries, and finally might provoke currency fluctuations that would hurt export industries in surplus countries that profit from an undervalued real exchange rate (Scharpf 2011).

[12]It should be noted that the ECB, conducting Europe's monetary policy, has played an important role in dealing with the crisis (see Diessner in this volume). As part of the Troika, together with the Commission and the IMF, the ECB played a crucial role in monitoring the sovereign bailout programs to the GIIPS countries. Although the role of the politically independent ECB—as it is based on a onetime target-oriented delegation act providing the ECB a maximum of discretion—as well as its policies have frequently been subject to critical questions concerning their legitimacy, the ECB is largely excluded from this examination of the Euro crisis due to the limited scope of this chapter.

intergovernmental agreements complemented by domestic constitutional changes (Schwarzern 2013; Schwarzer and Wolff 2013).

Concerning the intergovernmental negotiations and the following policy-decisions, it is important to consider two aspects. Firstly, the Greek case seemed to confirm the political diagnosis of the Euro crisis, namely that the sovereign debt crisis was the result of irresponsible national budgetary policies. Although this explanation is only partly true for Greece and almost entirely wrong for the other GIIPS countries such as Spain and Ireland, it kept dominating the debate (Schwarzer 2003; Scharpf 2011, 2012). Secondly, since the surplus countries were required to provide expensive guarantees and credits to the struggling deficit countries to prevent their bankruptcy and to protect the Euro, the previous balance of power within the European Council was disrupted as the "bailing-out" countries were in a stronger negotiating position (Scharpf 2011; Hassel and Lütz 2010).[13] Consequently, the rescue operations, largely driven by the surplus countries' analysis of the crisis, have been targeting almost exclusively the sovereign debt crisis rather than the crisis of real economies (Schwarzer 2013; Scharpf 2012). Thus, the summit resolutions and Council agreements had the character of take-it-or-leave-it offers that no struggling member state could afford to reject (Scharpf 2012; Silva 2011); economic adjustment was left to the deficit countries (Schwarzer and Wolff 2013).

The Crisis Management—What Has Been Done Exactly?

Other than various market regulations and oversight mechanisms offering macro prudential oversight of the financial market,[14] the most remarkable changes since 2008 are the following on:

---

[13]Especially the German government has been widely considered to be the dominant player as every EU-wide approach to resolve the crisis required the approval of the government of Europe's strongest economy (Collignon et al., forthcoming; Habermas 2014; Schwarzer and Wolff 2013; Scharpf 2011, 2012).

[14]The most important steps in this regard were the establishment of the European Systemic Risk Board, the establishment of three European supervisory authorities—the European Banking Authority, the European Insurance and Occupational Pensions Authority, and th1)e European Securities and Markets Authority, and finally the creation of the Banking Union (Schwarzer 2013). However, since this chapter focuses on agency slack within the political chain of delegation, these market-regulating innovations are of lesser interest.

First, member states had to find ways for preventing successfully the bankruptcy of any EMU member state by quickly establishing stabilization mechanisms by setting up the EFSM and the EFSF.[15] Both stability funds became a permanent rescue mechanism for emergencies, the European Stability Mechanism (ESM). Member states were only entitled to rescue funds under strict conditions defined at EU level. These conditions were specified in a number of "Memorandums of Understanding on Specific Economic Policy Conditionality". By analysing the financial and economic situation, by defining necessary policy decisions, and by monitoring the adaption progress, the Commission exercises control concerning the compliance with the conditions (article 5 (6g), and 13 ESM Treaty). Although the Commission is supposed to do all this in close consultation with the respective member state, the bargaining power of the member state in the case of disagreement is minimal (Scharpf 2011). The voting procedures of the Board of Governors, the highest organ of the ESM and consisting of the finance ministers of the member states, also reflect this unequal bargaining power. Although the ministers are normally taking decisions unanimously, article 4 ESM Treaty states that decisions may also be taken with qualified majority when the Commission or the ECB assesses them as a matter of urgency. The "the voting rights of each ESM Member [...] shall be equal to the number of shares allocated to it in the authorized capital stock of the ESM" (article 4 (7) ESM Treaty). Thus, a qualified majority does not require a majority of member states, since an alliance of the biggest shareholders shall be sufficient.

Second, to prevent future occurrences of solvency problems, governments decided to enhance budgetary and economic policy surveillance. On the one hand, they set up the "European Semester", which is basically a revised policy coordination timetable that allows an earlier analysis of the member states' economic and fiscal policies as well as financial developments and, therefore, enhances the means to timely influence policy choices (Schwarzer 2013; Collignon 2012a). On the other hand, as mentioned above, member states (in part together with the European

---

[15]The European Financial Stabilization Mechanism and the European Financial Stability Facility.

Parliament) adopted a number of legislative packages known as the "Six Pack" and "Two Pack" as well as the Macroeconomic Imbalance Procedure (MIP), and further drew up the intergovernmental Fiscal Compact.[16]

What Are the Implications?—A Discussion

It becomes clear that the overwhelming majority of the crisis measures focused on the need to control national policies and expenses. The central mechanisms are, on the one hand, the reinforcement of budgetary discipline by determining that sanctions will be imposed earlier and in a more consistent manner, and on the other hand, the prevention and correction of economic imbalances through the detection of unsustainable national policies and their ensured correction (Schwarzer 2013).

In view of the underlying diagnosis (esp. in the case of Greece), the member states' political response may seem appropriate as all measures together aim to streamline national policies and to limit the scope of national discretion. In this way, member states protect themselves against externalities. They minimize the risk that any form of irresponsible behavior by any individual member state may negatively affect important European public goods such as economic stability or the stability of the single currency (Collignon 2013a; Schwarzer 2013). In contrast, many scholars see the emergence of macroeconomic imbalances as one of the crucial causes of the crisis and stress the corresponding lack of proper EU-wide economic governance as one of the central weaknesses of the EMU system.[17] Nevertheless, especially the Six-Pack regulations with which member states attempt to solve this problem have

---

[16]See Diessner in this volume for an in-depth discussion of these measures, which are broadly in line with the eurozone's established policy paradigm.

[17]The bottom line of most of the criticisms is that the one-size-fits-all approach of the ECB in conducting monetary policy is very likely to lead to macroeconomic imbalances as the Eurozone is not an optimal currency area and economic policies remain in the hands of the member states (Majone 2012; Moravcsik 2012; Saito 2013; Scharpf 2011, 2012, 2013). For a contrary view see Collignon (2013a, b).

been subject to extensive critique. Concerning the MIP, Fritz Scharpf stresses that various indicators and balances listed in the Commission's scoreboard are practically not under direct control of the EMU member states' governments. He points out that before entering the EMU, member states used to influence, for example, the rise of house prices or of private sector debt indirectly through the monetary, fiscal and exchange-rate instruments available to them for macroeconomic management. Since these instruments are no longer available to EMU member states as they have been transferred to the ECB, he raises the question of what governments should have done to prevent imbalances in the past (Scharpf 2012). Furthermore, the Commission's scoreboard evaluating member states' current account balances does not assess deficits and surpluses equally as imbalances. With a threshold of +6% of GDP and −4% of GDP, deficits seem to be more problematic than surpluses, which partly reflects the stronger negotiation position of the surplus countries. However, Collignon argues that the focus on current account balances is a mistake because it confusingly treats financial flows within the Euro Area as if they were international flows, thereby ignoring the basic functioning of a monetary union.

Various scholars have also criticized these reforms as being contrary to the democratic traditions of EU member states as they largely lack any form of democratic legitimacy (Habermas 2014; Collignon 2013a, b; Scharpf 2011, 2012; Busch et al. 2013; Schwarzer 2013; Schwarzer and Wolff 2013; Offe 2013; Mair and Thomassen 2010; Mair 2009). A central criticism is the democratic dilemma to which these reforms are likely to lead. This is because in reacting to the crisis, reforms that not only aim to constrain national governments, but that also empower the Commission to intervene and enforce certain domestic policy decisions, whereas the European Parliament has little to say. The problem here is that member states have limited their own control and power by granting extensive discretion to the Commission through the "reverse qualified majority" voting, while on the other hand the Commission is not (yet) fully democratically accountable to the Parliament and has no incentive to be politically responsive to the affected citizens. In other words, member states' governments may find themselves in a dilemma as they face opposed preferences and political demands with the Commission on the one side and their constituents on the other (Scharpf 2011). Scharpf highlights the legitimacy problem as follows:

> [M]acroeconomic management creates the possibility for a democratic dilemma: By attempting to maintain output legitimacy through functionally effective policy choices, governments may undermine their input legitimacy and vice versa. In actual practice, however, the intensity of the dilemma depends not only on the type of economic challenges but also on the choice between the Keynesian or monetarist models or paradigms of macroeconomic management. (Scharpf 2011: 4)

Scharpf is referring to the way by which the Commission comes to its recommendations regarding national policy decisions. He highlights that under criteria of republican as well as liberal constitutionalism discretionary authority either must be subject to democratic accountability or narrowly defined. However, the Commission is neither constrained by any predefined rule nor bound to a commonly shared economic paradigm. In fact, the Commission can give any recommendation it considers economically useful. Furthermore, the Commission's decision-making process does not provide any public communicative discourse, but rather leaves the task of explaining and defending the reforms to the respective member states' governments (Scharpf 2012). Given that the policy outcomes have mainly consisted of radical supply-side reforms— with the effect that GIIPS economies are still in recession after 7 years of crisis and still face unemployment rates up to 25%[18]– regardless of their functional necessity, it is not surprising that the governments lose the support of their voters (Scharpf 2009, 2011, 2012). Stressing the importance of proper communication concerning the question of legitimacy, Scharpf (2011: 31) points out that *"the program [adopted by* member states' *governments] amounts to a greatly radicalized version of the supply-side reforms adopted in Germany during its (much milder) recession before 2005 [...]. But whereas [the German government] had the chance of*

---

[18](Statista 2015: Unemployment rate in member states of the EU in November 2014) In 2011, Spain's unemployment rate for workers under the age of 25, according to Eurostat, was around 46.2%, by far the highest in Europe (Neal and Concepción 2013).

developing and defending self-chosen reforms, the governments of [...] [the GIIPS countries] must implement policies likely to be seen as dictates from Commission bureaucrats and self interested foreign governments trying to protect their own banks, investors and export industries."

The lack of a communicative discourse is particularly important as the various intergovernmental meetings were the focus of public attention. Furthermore, according to Germany's dominant economic position, the government of Angela Merkel has been publicly acknowledged as being the dominant player in the negotiation process. Once it became clear that Germany had little choice but to provide financial assistance in order to protect the Euro, the Merkel government publicly took over the leading role in the negotiation process and started propagating the necessity of a European stability culture. For the German government the significant construction error of the EMU was the lack of sanction mechanisms to ensure compliance with the SGP. Thus, the German insistence on the enforcement of such a stability culture—through conditionality and sanctions—was the compromise the Merkel government was willing to offer (Howarth and Rommerskirchen 2013).[19] Therefore, from the perspective of the citizens in the GIIPS countries, suffering under the imposition of harsh austerity policies regardless of the national party in power, the authors of these dictates have the faces of Angela Merkel, Wolfgang Schäuble and Jose Manuel Barroso, none of whom can be sanctioned by the voters in the countries concerned (Scharpf 2012).

---

[19]Highlighting the importance of propagating such a stability culture as part of the German political culture, the scholars David Howarth and Charlotte Rommerskirchen (2013) point out how the German government made sure that such a culture would be systemically integrated in the reforms. For example, "[a]ddressing the newly created rescue fund, Finance Minister Wolfgang Schäuble (2010) argued that the unanimity principle under which the facility operated would guarantee that the 'German Stability Culture would leave its mark on the adjustment programmes' for countries in need of financial help" (Howarth and Rommerskirchen 2013: 764).

Conclusion: Outlining the Agency Slack

Given the nature of the reforms since 2008, their development and their effects on citizens, but also by looking at the political noise around the negotiation process, it is obvious that the European response to the crisis reveals profound agency slack.

European citizens, who are the ultimate principal and owners of European public goods, have witnessed, how their first executive agents, the member states' governments, have excluded or minimized the involvement of their only common representative—the European Parliament. National governments have negotiated and adopted various legislative packages amongst themselves serving partial constituencies, while the task should have been to foster and incorporate the collective preferences of all European citizens (Schwarzer and Wolff 2013). These governments furthermore agreed upon reforms that were based on the conviction that national governments and parliaments cannot be trusted to adopt the kind of policies that meet the functional requirements of the EMU (Habermas 2014; Scharpf 2012). Thus, member states agreed to change the European governance structure in a way that entails a reverse delegation chain, meaning that member states' governments are not only acting as executive agents of their citizens anymore, but also as agents on behalf of the EMU. They do this by subjecting national governments to various monitoring, controlling, and sanctioning mechanisms. Of course, one could argue that these reforms aim to secure the greater common good in the end and are, therefore, legitimate. However, as already pointed out, what matters here is: what counts as the ultimate end?

From the perspective of the citizens, at least in the GIIPS countries, three interrelated aspects have been problematic. First, the political domination of the surplus countries and the way the policy outcomes reflect the successful assertion of their preferences has publicly highlighted the character of these negotiations as zero-sum games. Second, the imposition of austerity measures and supply-side reforms imposed on the GIIPS countries affect the citizens in a way that threatens their livelihoods. Third, the reforms and the imposed policies have been publicly criticized by experts, academics, and the European Parliament as failing to address the underlying causes of the crisis, but also as being economically harmful and even being likely to deepen the economic problems (Habermas 2014; Collignon 2013b; De Grauwe and Ji 2013; Offe 2013; Scharpf 2011, 2012; De Grauwe 2010). Even international organizations such as the World Bank or the International Monetary Fund publicly raised doubts about the likelihood of successful outcomes given such harsh, one-sided austerity measures (Lowrey 2013).[20] This broad public debate about the effectiveness and the usefulness of the severe policy measures has undermine the 'there is no alternative' manner in which the legislative packages were framed.

All three aspects lead to the perception that governments have practically incapacitated their own citizens. While the loss of autonomy seems obvious for the GIIPS countries, it is equally true for the surplus countries. They had to accept large commitments to cover the ever-increasing financial risks covered by the rescue funds. Furthermore, with the adoption of the Fiscal Compact as well as the Six Pack, restrictive European control over national policy-making have become generalised and apply now to all member states, regardless of whether they are in financial difficulties or not (Scharpf 2012). Yet, the fact that citizens of surplus countries are not subject to the same direct interventions by the Commission is likely to mitigate their perception of agency slack. However, the German right-wing populist party 'Alternative für Deutschland' has emerged out of the discussion whether Germany ought to contribute to save Greece from bankruptcy. This suggests that despite the extensive communicative discourse launched by the German government, a growing number of German citizens already perceived Merkel's willingness to back the financial assistance for Greece with national tax revenues as agency slack (Niedermayer 2015).

To sum up, national governments, which are supposed to carry out the "will of the people" and remain their first executive agents, have created a discretionary regime of supranational intervention for the management of national economies and societies without control

---

[20]In April 2013, Christine Lagarde, the director of the IMF, was cited in the New York Times warning that "EU governments may have to ditch austerity policies and switch to fiscal stimulus to kick-start growth and avert lasting damage to the underlying economy" (Lowrey 2013).

mechanisms that would allow the incorporation of the preferences of the *European* rather than national principals. By delegating one of their core competences—deciding economic policy choices and resources— to a European agent that is beyond the citizens' control and only under minimal influence of the member states' governments, member states have incapacitated their citizens and themselves. Such kind of act of delegation goes beyond the competences they have received as the agents of citizens. What needs to be legitimated are not European decisions about European public goods, but European controls over national public goods. Consequently, and less surprisingly, the warning of anti-European political mobilization is omnipresent.

Majone (2012) and Moravcsik (2012) have also criticised the political response to the Euro crisis. Both emphasize that all EMU member states are responsible for the present situation. On the one hand, they all share responsibility for having opted for the EMU project and neglected the various economists who frequently had warned that the economic conditions for a single currency were not yet met. On the other hand, the problem of macroeconomic imbalances implies that deficits and surpluses are two sides of the same coin. Thus, a solution to the Euro crisis requires a European adjustment process, which includes corrections in deficit as well as in surplus countries. In light of the bargaining between deficit and creditor governments, both implicitly acknowledge the weakness of intergovernmentalism as a mode of governance.

Majone (2012), furthermore stresses that, due to the impact on the national welfare state, macroeconomic management cannot be Pareto-improving and does, therefore, not allow a separation of politics and economics. Thus macroeconomic management has to remain in the hands of a majoritarian institution, which takes into account the public opinion. Contrary to his initial reasoning, Majone now highlights the crucial role of the public perception for the effectiveness and efficiency of delegation: "the effectiveness of the EU institutions is increasingly questioned today: rightly or wrongly 'Brussels,' and now also 'Frankfurt,' are perceived less as potential sources of solutions for problems that cannot be solved at the national level, than as causes of many of those very problems" (ibid., 13). He delivers the warning to the defenders of the EMU that solving the debt crisis "by enlarging the democratic deficit of the EU to a point where, given the state of public opinion today, it becomes politically unsustainable" (ibid., 21) may end in a democratic default.

In contrast, Moravcsik, although criticizing the disproportional distribution of political and social costs of the member states' attempt to solve the crisis, still rejects the claim that the crisis has revealed the EU to be undemocratic. He states that the EU is still a form of limited government, which restricts "no one's democratic rights [...] and preserves the same public input and transparency that Europeans expect in domestic policymaking" (Moravcsik 2012: 66). Assuming that a balanced Eurozone is in every member states' interest, he still comes to the conclusion that equal burden sharing is not just a pragmatic necessity, but rather a democratic imperative, and "if the Eurozone collapses, it will be because of an abundance of democracy as much as a lack of it. [Because n]o long-term solution to Europe's woes can be imposed on a member state without the consent of its government, and any government—even the technocratic governments [...]—requires an electoral mandate" (Moravcsik 2012: 67). Thus, Moravcsik continues to assume that the democratic credentials of the member states are, and remain, intact.

Conclusion

Looking at the long lasting discussion on the EU's democratic deficit, this chapter has stressed the question whether the principal-agent theory and its application can provide some valid contribution, which may even help to overcome the discussion deadlock represented by the opposing contributions of Moravcsik, Majone and Hix. We found that the principal-agent theory is indeed turns out as being very useful for the examination of legitimacy and accountability as it enables us to examine delegation, its structure, as well as the various risks, problems and solutions of delegation in more detail.

Contrasting the contributions of the three scholars it has become clear that although they base their argumentation on the logic of delegation, they still come to very different conclusions concerning their assessment of the EU's democratic deficit. It is shown that these diverging conclusions result from different assumptions—in particular who is considered to be the principal—which almost automatically leads to different focuses on certain aspects tied in by delegation. Whereas Majone and Moravcsik consider the member states as principals, they do not see any problem concerning legitimacy, as democratically legitimated governments delegate to supranational agents, which are tightly constrained and controlled by the member states. This ensures that policy outcomes do not conflict with their citizens' preferences. Consequently, they assess the introduction of qualified majority voting in the Council and the increasing politicization as more problematic given that such a development weakens the control and influence of the single member state. Hix, in contrast, focuses on the formation of the citizens' preferences and claims that the EU system requires political contestation. He therefore implicitly considers the citizens as principals, which ties in a greater emphasis on the dependence of legitimacy on the citizens' perception.

The subsequent application of the principal-agent theory not only highlighted that the assumption of member states being the principals may turn out to be problematic for the assessment of democratic legitimacy, but also revealed various critical questions concerning the lasting legitimacy of unanimous decisions. Clearly the legitimacy of delegation crucially depends on the assessment of costs and benefits in relation to the outcome. Apart from that, delegation always entails a trade-off between efficiency and control and, therefore, requires certain flexibility. On the one hand, flexibility is required for the proper calibration of the delegation structure to ensure desirable outcomes and, on the other hand, it must leave room for adjustments in case of a reassessment of costs and benefit—for example due to changed circumstances. Taking all of this into account, the question arises whether unanimous decisions, as they usually tie in relatively high hurdles for revision, can be as legitimate over time as assumed by Majone and Moravcsik.

These findings suggest that whereas effectiveness is primarily instrumental, legitimacy is rather evaluative and, thus, depends on the principal's perception. In light of public opinion polls, all this suggest that a proper assessment of the democratic legitimacy should not be based merely on a single link of the delegation chain, but should rather look at the whole delegation chain. Furthermore, it became clear that from the citizens' perspective the risk of agency slack at the EU level is rather high as long as the Commission is predominantly determined and controlled by the member states. In this regard, the application of the principal-agent theory highlights the potential impact of the Lisbon Treaty, especially the quasi establishment of a new delegation chain between European Parliament and Commission. This development provides not only the citizens with full ownership over European public goods, but it may also change and enhance the communicative components of the EU agents. In this sense, the Lisbon Treaty can indeed increase the EU's democratic legitimacy. However, it remains uncertain whether the European Parliament can fulfil the described communicative function.

In contrast to the Lisbon Treaty, the reforms adopted by the member states' governments in response to the Euro crisis are worrying as they entail a reversed delegation chain leaving many citizens with the perception of being deprived of their right to self-determination. In this sense, the adopted reforms also illustrate the problematic assumption that unanimous decisions among member states' governments are a priori democratically legitimate. Here, the principal-agent theory helps to detect and to stress problematic aspects as well as to generate further questions for an appropriate assessment of legitimacy (see 3.0).

This chapter showed that the principal-agent theory can explain the previous discussion deadlock, and detect certain weaknesses in the different argumentations. It is important to clarify the basic assumptions before starting any discussion. Especially the political response to the Euro crisis illustrates that some long held believes are no longer congruent with European realities. Furthermore, the principal-agent theory turned out to be very useful in assessing the impact of the contractual changes on the EU's democratic legitimacy. Since the political fight over the best possible public order continues every day, such an assessment can only refer to the status quo. Here the principal-agent theory helps to understand delegation in all its complexity, but it also generates further questions, which call for empirical examination. Without further empirical research, the discussion is likely to continue with shaky foundations, but is also likely to cover up serious errors that European citizens ought to discuss publicly.

Appendix

Figure A.1 illustrates a simplified version of the chain of delegation within nation states.[21]

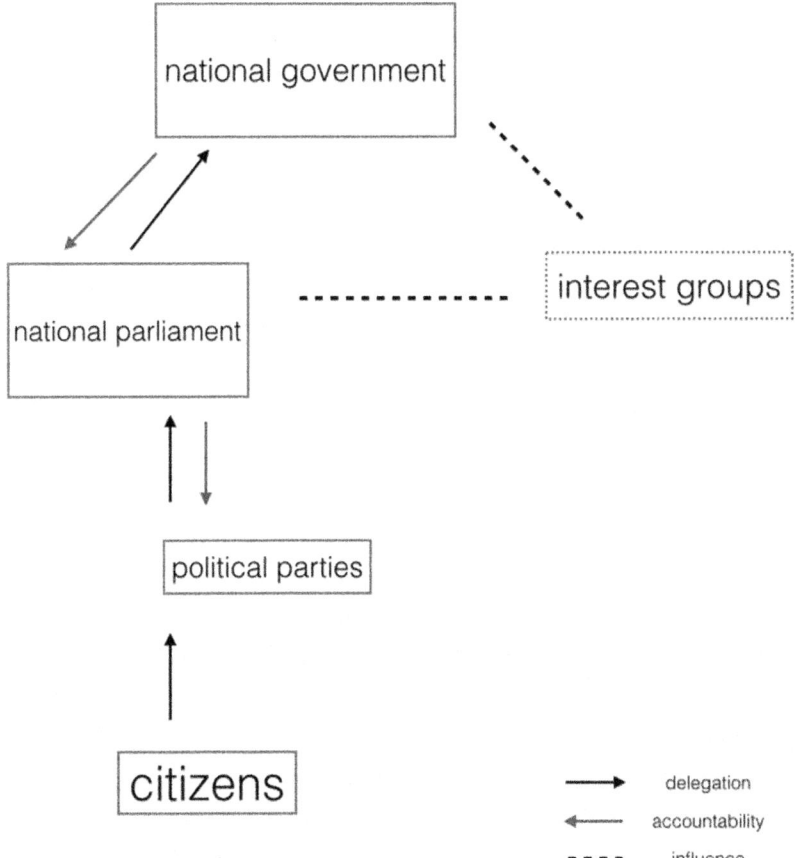

Fig. A.1 Chain of delegation and accountability within parliamentary democracies (own presentation)

---

[21]This presentation obviously applies only to parliamentary democracies. The exclusion of other democratic system shall be justified as this presentation is for explanatory purpose only.

Figure A.2 illustrates a simplified version of the chain of delegation at the European level as it is assumed by Pollack.[22]

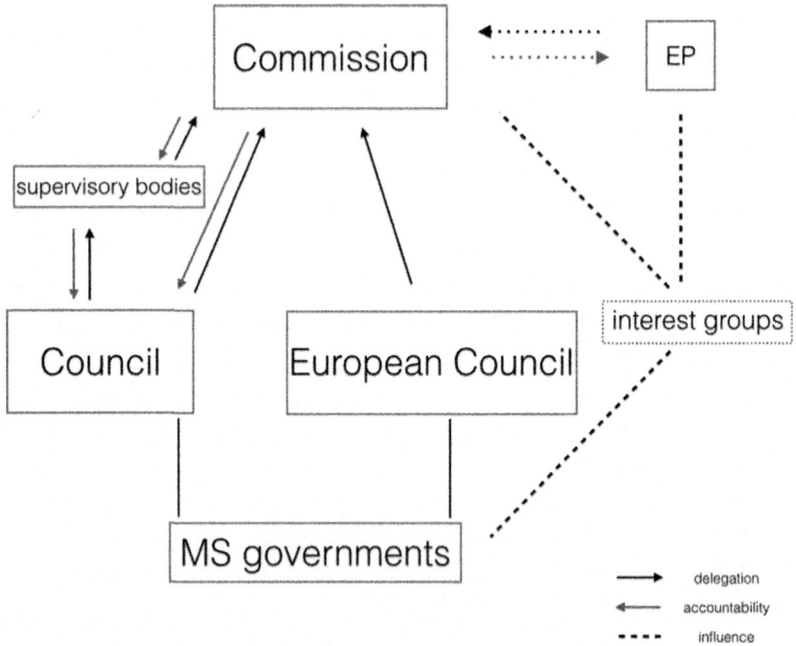

Fig. A.2 Chains of delegation and accountability within the political system of the EU according to Pollack (own presentation)

---

[22]The presentation obviously neglects EU institutions like the ECB or the ECJ. However the exclusion of these institutions is justified insofar as the issue at hand is about the relationship between citizens and governments (member states and EU).

Figure A.3 illustrates a simplified version of the integrated chain of delegation within the political system of the EU and its member states.

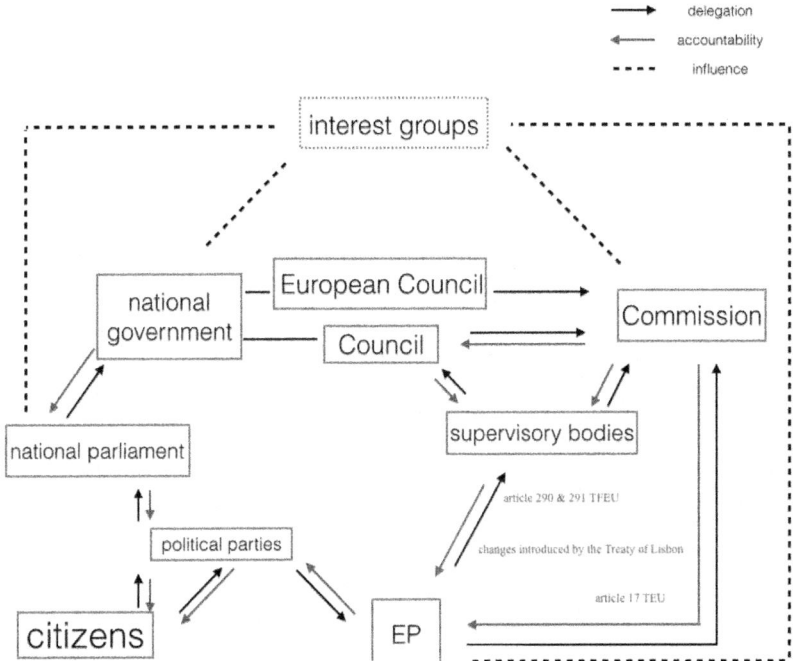

Fig. A.3 Chains of delegation and accountability within the integrated political system of the EU and its member states (own presentation)

References

Andersen, S. S., & Burns, T. R. (1996). The European Union and the erosion of parliamentary democracy: A study of post-parliamentary governance. In S. S. Andersen & K. A. Eliassen (Eds.), *The European Union: How democratic is it?* (pp. 227–252). London.

Auel, K., & Benz, A. (2007). Expanding national parliamentary control: Does it enhance European Democracy? In B. Kohler-Koch & B. Rittberger (Eds.), *Debating the democratic legitimacy of the European Union* (pp. 57–74). Lanham.

Baker, D., Gamble, A., & Seawright, D. (2002). Sovereign nations and global markets: Modern British conservatism and hyperglobalism. *British Journal of Politics and International Relations, 4*(3), 399–428.

Barroso, J. (2011). Speech by the President of the European Commission: Debate on economic governance, European Parliament, Speech 760/11, November, 16. 2011, Strasbourg.

Busch, K., Hermann, C., Hinrichs, K., & Schulten, T. (2013). *Euro crisis, austerity policy and the European social model. How crisis policies in Southern Europe threaten the EU's social dimension*, February 2013. Berlin: Friedrich Ebert Stiftung-International Policy Analysis.

Collignon, S. (2003). *The European republic: Reflections on the political economy of a future constitution.* London: Federal Trust for Education and Research.

Collignon, S. (2012a). *Macroeconomic imbalances and comparative advantages in the Euro Area.* Brussels: European Trade Union Institute.

Collignon, S. (2012b). *Europe's debt crisis, coordination failure, and international effects* (ADBI Working Paper 370). Tokyo: Asian Development Bank Institute.

Collignon, S. (2013a). *The European Union as a Republic.* Paris. http://www.stefancollignon.de/PDF/The%20European%20Union%20as%20a%20Republic.pdf.

Collignon, S. (2013b). How (not) to reform the Euro Area's economic governance. *Global Policy, 4*(1), 50–57.

Collignon, S., Esposito, P., & L ierse, H. (forthcoming). European Sovereign Bailouts, Political Risk and the Economic Consequences of Mrs. Merkel. *Journal of International Commerce, Economics and Policy, 4*(2), April 2013, 1350010-1–1350010-25.

Craig, P. (2010). *The Lisbon Treaty: Law, politics, and treaty reform.* Oxford: Oxford University Press.

De Grauwe, P. (2010). Crisis in the Eurozone and how to deal with it, Centre for European Policy Studies, CEPS-Policy Brief 204.

De Grauwe, P., & Ji, Y. (2013). The Legacy of Austerity in the Eurozone. Centre for European Policy Studies, CEPS Commentaries.

Down, I., & Wilson, C. J. (2008). From 'permissive consensus' to 'constraining dissensus': A polarizing union? *Acta Politica, 43*, 26–49. (11. 2015).

Dür, A., & Elsig, M. (2011). Principals, agents, and the European Union's foreign economic policies. *Journal of European Public Policy, 18*(3), 323–338.

Eurobarometer. (2011). Standard Eurobarometer 76. Public Opinion in the European Union, First Results.

Eurobarometer. (2014). Standard Eurobarometer 82. Public Opinion in the European Union, First Results.

Follesdal, A., & Hix, S. (2006). Why there is a democratic deficit in the EU: A response to Majone and Moravcsik. *Journal of Common Market Studies, 44*(3), 533–562.

Habermas, J. (2014). Für ein starkes Europa - aber was heißt das? *Blätter für deutsche und internationale Politik, 03*, 85–94.

Hassel, A., & Lütz, S. (2010). Durch die Krise aus der Krise? Die neue Stärke des Staates. *Der Moderne Staat - Zeitschrift für Public Policy, Recht und Management, 4*(2), 251–271.

Hawkins, D. G., Lake, D. A., Nielson, D. L., & Tierney, M. J. (2006). Delegation under anarchy: States, international organizations, and principal-agent theory. In D. G. Hawkins, D. A. Lake, D. L. Nielson, & M. J. Tierney (Eds.), *Delegation and agency in international organizations* (pp. 3–38). Cambridge: Cambridge University Press.

Hix, S. (2008). *What's wrong with the Europe Union and How to fix it*. Oxford.

Hobolt, S. B., & Tilley, J. (2014). *Blaming Europe? Responsibility without accountability in the European Union*. Oxford: Oxford University Press.

Hooghe, L., & Marks, G. (2009). A postfunctionalist theory of European integration: From permissive consensus to constraining dissensus. *British Journal of Political Science, 39*(1), 1–23.

Höreth, M. (2010). Die EU-Organe nach dem Vertrag von Lissabon. In A. Marchetti & C. Demesmay (Eds.), *Der Vertrag von Lissabon: Analyse und Bewertung. Schriften des Zentrum für Europäische Integrationsforschung (ZEI) 71* (pp. 167–207). Baden-Baden: Nomos.

Howarth, D., & Rommerskirchen, C. (2013). A panacea for all times? The German stability culture as strategic political resource. *West European Politics, 36*(4), 750–770.

Jones, E. (2009). Output legitimacy and the global financial crisis: Perceptions matter. *Journal of Common Market Studies, 47*(5), 1085–1105.

Klump, R. (2011). *Wirtschaftspolitik, Instrumente, Ziele und Institutionen* (2nd ed.). Munich: Pearson Education Deutschland GmbH.

Lowrey, A. (2013, April 15). Europe split over austerity as a path to growth. *The New York Times.*

Magnette, P. (2001). Appointing and censuring the European Commission: The adaption of parliamentary institutions to the community context. *European Law Journal, 7*(3), 292–310.

Mair, P. (2009). *Representative versus Responsible Government* (MPIfG Discussion Paper 09/8). Max-Planck-Institut für Gesellschaftsforschung.

Mair, P., & Thomassen, J. (2010). Political representation and government in the European Union. *Journal of European Public Policy, 17*(1), 20–35.

Majone, G. (1998). Europe's 'democratic deficit': The question of standards. *European Law Journal, 4*(1), 5–28.

Majone, G. (2002). Delegation of regulatory powers in a mixed polity. *European Law Journal, 8*(3), 319–339.

Majone, G. (2012). *Rethinking European integration after the debt crisis* (Working Paper No. 3/2012). The European Institute.

Milev, M. (2004). *A 'democratic deficit' in the European Union?* Sofia: CIFE (Centre International de Formation Europeenne). http://www.geopolitis. net/EUROPE%20EN%20FORMATION/Democratic%20Deficit%20 in%20the%20European%20Union.pdf.

Moravcsik, A. (1993). Preferences and power in the European Community: A liberal intergovernmentalist approach. *Journal of Common Market Studies, 31*(4), 473–524.

Moravcsik, A. (2002). In defence of the 'democratic deficit': Reassessing legitimacy in the European Union. *Journal of Common Market Studies, 40*(4), 603–624.

Moravcsik, A. (2004). Is there a 'democratic deficit' in world politics? A framework for analysis. *Government and Opposition, 39*(2), 336–363.

Moravcsik, A. (2008). The myth of Europe's 'democratic deficit'. *Intereconomics: Journal of European Public Policy, 43*(6), 331–340.

Moravcsik, A. (2012). Europe after the crisis. How to sustain a common currency. *Foreign Affairs, 91*(3), 54–68.

Neal, L., & Concepción, M. (2013). The economy of Spain in the Euro-zone before and after the crisis of 2008. *The Quarterly Review of Economics and Finance, 53*(4), 336–344.

Niedermayer, O. (2015). Eine neue Konkurrentin im Parteiensystem? Die Alternative für Deutschland. In O. Niedermayer (Ed.), *Die Parteien nach der Bundestagswahl 2013* (pp. 175–207). Wiesbaden: SpringerVS.

Offe, C. (2013). Europa in der Falle. *Blätter für deutsche und internationale Politik, 01,* 67–80.

Pollack, M. A. (1997). Delegation, agency, and agenda setting in the European Community. *International Organization, 51*(1), 99–134.

Pollack, M. A. (2001). International relations theory and European integration. *Journal of Common Market Studies, 39*(2), 221–244.

Pollack, M. A. (2003). *The engines of European integration. Delegation, agency, and agenda setting in the EU.* Oxford: Oxford University Press.

Pratt, J. W., & Zeckhauser, R. J. (1991). *Principals and agents: The structure of business.* Boston: Harvard Business School Press.

Raunio, T. (1999). Always One Step Behind? National Legislatures and the European Union. *Government and Opposition, 34*(2), 180–202.

Rehn, O. (2011). *Eurobonds: Stability and Growth for the Euro Area.* ALDE New Year Seminar, January 10, 2011, Speech 12/1, Brussels.

Saito, J. (2013). *European monetary integration and sovereign debt crisis* (Discussion Paper No. 139). Japan Center for Economic Research.

Scharpf, F. W. (1988). The joint decision-making trap: Lessons from German Federalsim and European integratoin. *Public Administration, 66*(3), 239–278.

Scharpf, F. W. (1997). Economic integration, democracy and the welfare state. *Journal of European Public Policy, 4*(1), 18–36.

Scharpf, F. W. (1999). *Governing in Europe: Effective and democratic.* Oxford: Oxford University Press.

Scharpf, F. W. (2004). *Legitimationskonzepte jenseits des Nationalstaats* (MPIfG Working Paper 04/6). Max-Planck-Institut für Gesellschaftsforschung.

Scharpf, F. W. (2009). *Legitimacy in the multilevel European polity* (MPIfG Working Paper 09/1). Max-Planck-Institut für Gesellschaftsforschung.

Scharpf, F. W. (2011). *Monetary union, fiscal crisis and the preemption of democracy* (MPIfG Discussion Paper 11/11). Max-Planck-Institut für Gesellschaftsforschung.

Scharpf, F. W. (2012). *Legitimacy intermediation in the multilevel European polity and its collapse in the Euro crisis* (MPIfG Discussion Paper 12/6). Max-Planck-Institut für Gesellschaftsforschung.

Scharpf, F. W. (2013). Political legitimacy in a non-optimal currency area (MPIfG Discussion Paper 13/15). Max-Planck-Institut für Gesellschaftsforschung.

Schmidt, V. A. (2010). *Democracy and legitimacy in the European Union revisited. Output, input and throughput* (KFG Working Paper Series No. 21).

Schmidt, V. A., & Radaelli, C. M. (2004). Policy change and discourse in Europe: Conceptual and methodological issues. *West European Politics, 27*(2), 183–210.

Schwarzer, D. (2013). Crisis and reform in the Euro Area. *Current History, 112*(752), 83–87.

Schwarzer, D., & Wolff, G. B. (2013). Neuer Anlauf für die Eurozone. Drei Maßnahmen würden kurzfristige Risiken mildern und die Chance auf eine notwendige Vertragsreform verbessern, SWP-Aktuell 55.

Silva, A. C. (2011). Evolução da crise financeira pode ser o maior determinante para os enormes esforços que Portugal está a fazer, Press release of the president of Portugal, 12.09.2011, Lisbon.

Sonnicksen, J. (2010). Die demokratischen Grundsätze. In A. Marchetti & C. Demesmay (Eds.), *Der Vertrag von Lissabon: Analyse und Bewertung* (pp. 143–158). Baden-Baden: Nomos.

Sonnicksen, J. (2014). *Ein Präsident für Europa. Zur Demokratisierung der Europäischen Union.* Wiesbaden: Springer VS.

Statista. (2015). Unemployment rate in member states of the European Union in November 2014.

Stratulat, C., & Molino, E. (2011). Implementing Lisbon: What's new in comitology? European Policy Center Policy Brief April 2011.

Streeck, W., & Schmitter, P. C. (1991). From national corporatism to transnational pluralism: Organized interests in the Single European Market. *Politics and Society, 19*(2), 133–164.

Strom, K. (2003). Parliamentary democracy and delegation. In K. Strom, W.C. Müller, & T. Bergmann (Eds.), *Delegation and accountability in parliamentary democracies* (pp. 55–106). Oxford: Oxford University Press.

Treaty Establishing the European Stability Mechanism (ESM Treaty). (2012). Brussels: General Secretariat of the Council of the European Union (Depositary).

Treaty on Stability, Coordination and Governance (Fiscal Compact). (2012). Brussels: General Secretariat of the Council of the European Union (Depositary).

Treaty on the Functioning of the European Union. (2012). (Consolidated Version and Protocols). Official Journal of the European Union 55 (C 326).

Vaubel, R. (2006). Principal-agent problems in international organizations. *The Review of International Organizations, 2006*(1), 125–138.

Wallace, W., & Smith, J. (1995). Democracy or technocracy? European integration and the problem of popular consent. *West European Politics, 18*(3), 137–157.

Wimmel, A. (2009). Theorizing the democratic legitimacy of European governance: A labyrinth with no exit? *European Integration, 31*(2), 181–199.

6

Why Does EU Governance Change?

Sebastian Salch

When something is not working, it needs fixing. Europe is in crisis, but it is not fixed. This is what the growing number of Eurosceptics and Europhiles seem to believe. European integration was based on the promise of peace, prosperity, liberty and equality. But Europe's governance finds it increasingly more difficult to respond to the expectations of citizens. The British example shows, the people are withdrawing support for the European project. If we do not develop a common understanding of the Euro and fiscal policies, more and more people will be disappointed and seek to dismantle the European edifice. Europe needs more solidarity. Hence, it is urgent to ask how the European system of governance could change.

How is change possible? I shall argue either with exogenous shocks or endogenous efforts. If you take the pink glasses of exogenous shocks, the strongest actor will impose his stance. For the Euro, this is

S. Salch(✉)
University of Hamburg, Hamburg, Germany
e-mail: Sebastian.Salch@gmx.net

© The Author(s) 2017   **167**
S. Collignon, *The Governance of European Public Goods*,
DOI 10.1007/978-3-319-64012-9_6

Germany, leaving the weaker South unsatisfied behind. If you take the pink glasses of the endogenous effort, change will come slowly and at one point everybody will be happy. In reality both dynamics interact.

The governance of European public goods is a consequence of the gradual process of integration, which is explained by the dominant theories of European integration. Neofunctionalism explains how spill-over effects shape the evolution of integration (Haas 1964, 1968). It explains the ongoing integration well, but it fails to tell us when change actually happens. Liberal intergovernmentalists stress the power of the member states and the importance of economic interests (Moravcsik 1997, 1998). They assume rational choices by governments who respond to social actors. They underemphasize the power of the process and cannot account for externalities and unintended integration. In addition, the more recent and more sophisticated Rational-Choice Institutionalism (Moe 1984; Weingast and Marshall 1988) remains blind to the actors' normative considerations not following purely rational reasons of self-interest. All these theories do not see that the governance flaws in the Euro Area can produce 'economically adequate', i.e. the best common, long-term outcome in terms of aggregated output outcomes. Their common thing is that they prone decentralized decision making by states and other actors who ought to cooperate in pursuit of their interests, but often fail to do so. By failing in cooperation, the states generate unfair distributions of benefits from European integration.

European public goods can only be fairly distributed through governance structures that are binding in every member state. By its very nature, the governance structure of European goods has effects in all member states. In today's Single European Market with equal opportunities and a single set of rules, the rules and regulations of the Union have different implications for different member states. Some carry a larger burden, others are beneficiaries and sometimes non-compliance with the European set of rules–the acquis communautaire–is the member states best choice. Collective decisions create positive and negative externalities. This leads to uncooperative motivation patterns, and partial interests opposing the best for everyone. Then, collective decisions are deadlocked and do not produce optimal outcomes.

Solving conflicts of interests in the EU requires tailor-made solution mechanisms for different types of public goods and situations. I shall discuss two possibilities how changes in the *polity* may occur: endogenous efforts and exogenous shocks.[1] First, with exogenous shocks, the strongest actor will "take over". If a conflict can only be solved by shifting the competences for particular policy fields to the supranational European level, the strategic preference situation will change for the national actors and this may ultimately trigger further exogenous shocks. As a consequence we need a change in competences and in governance. The second possibility for a polity change and further integration results new policy and strategic preference situations. They lead to endogenous efforts by the actors, who do not benefit from the status quo and, therefore, seek to improve distributional positions. However, with both effects, with exogenous shocks and endogenous efforts, there are distributional conflicts.

With this discussion I wish to answer the question whether or not enhanced competences can or will change the governance of the EU. We will discover the correlation between enhanced competences and governance change. However, the evidence of causality depends on the explanatory model one chooses. The theory of public goods provides a good basis for such analysis.

The Frame of Integration

Economic Causes for Governance Problems

Governing Public Goods

Public goods are not just tangible things, but rather, "a good is something from which some utility or benefit is derived" (Collignon 2003: 91), although public goods do not only involve benefits, but also costs. European public goods are institutions which generate net benefits for all Europeans.

---

[1] I distinguish between polity, policy and politics; whereas polity is the given structure or set of institutions within a political system, policies are the output of the latter and politics describe the process in which these policies are decided (Rohe 1994).

As discussed in the first chapter of this book, the possibility of exclusion and the rivalry in supply of benefits differentiates classes of public goods. Exclusion justifies that only so-called insiders are able to "consume" the good, i.e. derive benefits. Rivalry is concerned with the finitude of a good: Will there be enough net benefits for everybody or are additional consumers reducing the benefits for all?

According to these questions, we can differentiate public goods into four groups, which we can further put into two categories: ideal and hybrid types of goods. The two ideal types are private goods and pure public goods. The two hybrid ones are club goods and common resource goods.

Private goods are defined by private property rights. Every owner can claim rights over his private good. If someone else wants it, he needs to compensate the initial owner for giving up property rights, otherwise the rights are not exchanged (Aggarwal and Dupont 1999: 395). This mechanism only functions properly in combination with another aspect of private goods: Excludability. These factors allow their efficient provision by the market mechanism (Musgrave et al. 1994: 72).

If private goods are one end of a scale, we find pure public goods on the other end. Pure public goods are not excludable and supply is not rival. Everybody would be able to consume them without any compensation, if they are cooperatively supplied. However, "the revelation of consumer preferences through the pricing mechanism is no longer assured" (Collignon 2003: 95), which can cause their underprovision. Thus, non-excludability can hinder efficient resource allocation (Collignon 2011a: 43f.; Kaul et al. 1999: 6).

Hybrid goods are more realistic and also more sophisticated to govern. Firstly, club goods are characterized by excludability and cooperation in supply. The restricted consumption may be enforced via special membership criteria and the supply may require cooperation in financial contributions. The club jointly arranges the supply of the goods and every member has access to the consumption of the good. Secondly, club goods are non-rival. All members share the benefits and every additional consumer leads to a better cost/benefit calculation for everybody else, as average costs per member fall. This makes cooperation among club members attractive, although the benefits are subject to capacity limits (Collignon 2003: 92f.).

When the capacity limits are reached, club goods turn into common resource goods: Streets have a capacity limit. Up to a certain limit, space is not rival. However, in traffic jams the space becomes rival. The access of every additional user lowers the marginal benefits and increases the average costs. The attractiveness of the common resource good therefore diminishes as the number of beneficiaries increases and the incentive to cooperate diminishes (Musgrave et al. 1994: 69f, 85). Nevertheless, limiting access through exclusive membership keeps the club functioning and the benefits can be regulated.

If access cannot be restricted, we have proper common resource goods, where the supply of resources but not access to them is limited. As the number of consumers increases, the average and marginal benefits are reduced as well. Without restrictions of access, overconsumption is likely; Hardin (2003) has called this "the tragedy of the commons".

Economically Adequate[2] Governance

If European public goods are institutions which generate net benefits for all Europeans, the governance of these goods determines the extent of these benefits and their distribution. Hence, the characteristics of public goods and their externalities[3] determine the strategic preference situations for their governance. This can be shown by two typical Game Theory situations and their solutions, namely the prisoner dilemma and common aversion games.[4] Table (6.1).

---

[2]I consider 'economically adequate' what is the best common, long-term outcome in terms of aggregated output.

[3]In relation with public goods, "[e]xternalities arise when an individual or firm takes an action but does not bear all the costs (negative externality) or all the benefits (positive externality)[...] of the action.[...] Put differently, externalities are by-products of certain activities – spillovers into the public sphere" (Kaul et al. 1999: 5). For example, global or transnational externalities do not only affect the welfare of one country's citizens, but also the welfare of those citizens in other countries (Aronsson Blomquist 2003).

[4]The selected situations correspond with situations created by the features of the public goods

Table 6.1 *Public goods e.g. Collignon 2003: 92*

		Benefits	
		Excludable/Rival	Non excludable/Non-rival
Costs	Non-Joint/Rival	Private Goods	Common Resource Goods
	Joint/Non-rival	Club Goods	Pure Public Goods

Table 6.2 *Prisoners' Dilemma, own presentation*

Actor A/B	A1 Cooperation	A2 Defection
B1 Cooperation	3/3	1/4
B2 Defection	4/1	2/2

Game Theory: Prisoners' Dilemma

The traditional story is told the following way: Two bandits are caught by the police. They know that both of them would be best off if they denied confessing their crime and cooperate with each other. This would lead to the payoff A1/B1 (3/3) shown in Table 6.2. Therefore, the two actors make a pact to achieve the best common outcome. However, knowing this, the police offers a reward if one of them confesses. If actor A defects from the pact and accuses actor B, while actor B is still cooperating, actor A is individually better off and changes the outcome to payoff A2/B1 (1/4). The same goes for the reverse story, when actor B accuses actor A, while actor A is still cooperating with actor B. This would lead to payoff A1/B2 (4/1). If both of them do not cooperate with each other and accuse the other, they would both end up in payoff A2/B2 (2/2). This strategic preference situation is a suboptimal outcome for both criminals, as both must fear that their companion is not cooperating, and even if he were, they would individually be better off by not cooperating. Thus, they will both end up in payoff A2/B2 (2/2).

The prisoners' dilemma shows clearly the difference between the Nash Equilibrium A2/B2 (2/2) and Pareto Optimum A1/B1 (3/3). Therefore, in this case, the best individual outcome is not the same as the best common outcome. The equilibrium based on pure individual rational choice, and from which no actor has an incentive to depart unilaterally, is suboptimal for both.

If one plays the prisoners' dilemma simultaneously—without any exogenous constraints - the actors' dominant strategy will always be suboptimal. The actors will not cooperate, even if they know that this would lead to the best common payoff (Holler and Illing 2003).

With respect to the governance of European public goods, the prisoners' dilemma shows two underlying problems: free-riding may reduce net benefits (Collignon 2003: 95) and the effects of externalities can generate unfair distributions of net benefits (Snidal 1985). Firstly, because for pure public goods exclusion is not possible, every other actor is able to consume them and free-riding occurs if only one or some actors are providing the good while the other actors do not contribute to its provision. This may result in a situation where one actor understates his interest in the good and waits until the good is provided by someone else, so that the lack of cooperation reduces the supply of the good. Secondly, the prisoners' dilemma shows the problem of externalities, as the actions of each actor has implications for the other actor's payoffs. Consequently, each actor is constrained by the other actors' strategy (ibid.) and, depending on the negotiating power of each actor, the distribution of payoffs may not be equitable.

The standard solution to the prisoners' dilemma consists of two possibilities: Firstly, one may change the outcome for defection in such a manner that it is no longer an attractive option. Secondly, communication between the actors can reduce the problem by overcoming information asymmetries (Holler and Illing 2003: 5f.). The first option—changing the payoffs of the game—can be interpreted as establishing binding rules. In this case, rules give the parties a claimable right to force the other parties to cooperate or to get reimbursed for defection. Such reimbursement changes the outcome: it alters the individual payoffs in such a way that the Pareto optimum is eventually also the Nash equilibrium. The rules of European governance are such game changers, as we shall discuss below.

The second option of overcoming information asymmetries only makes sense for club goods. Here, knowing that the other club member will comply generates the willingness to cooperate. This is the traditional role of the European Commission. The literature calls this a situation of strategic complementarities. However, in the case of common resource goods, information sharing does not change the underlying problem: the Pareto optimum is not a Nash equilibrium. Each actor could improve her payoff by acting against the behaviour of what everybody else does. This is a situation of strategic substitutabilities (Cooper and John 1988; Collignon 2011a: 48).

Game Theory: Common Aversion

Whilst the previous game can be described as a distributive game, the game of common aversion describes the avoidance of negative effects. It can be divided into three different games (Stein 1982), one with a common aversion and common dominant strategies, one with no dominant strategies and one with diverging dominant strategies.

The first is similar to the standard cooperation game, although the payoffs differ slightly. The actors have a similar dominant strategy and they will therefore exhibit similar behavioural patterns that lead to Pareto optimal outcomes and Nash equilibrium (Stein 1982). The second option of the common aversion games entails no dominant strategies, although the two actors mutually prefer one outcome the least. Therefore, they want to eschew it. However, they do not have a dominant strategy for a preferred outcome. At a single-shot game, this leads to the problem that they are not sure whether their courses of action will result in the common aversion. Hence, communication is the solution. Once they mutually know the course of action of their opponent, they can derive their strategy from it (Stein 1982). Again, this situation is characterized by strategic complementarities.

The third option is common aversion with diverging dominant strategies (see Table 6.3). The two actors mutually agree that one outcome is the worst possible outcome for both A2/B2 (1/1). However, they are not sure about how to solve the situation, as actor A prefers the bottom left equilibrium and actor B the top right one. Without communication, both actors ought to choose cooperation, as both of them prefer this equilibrium to mutual defection and both fear the loss of it. Alas, the outcome A1/B1 (3/3) is neither Pareto optimal, nor a Nash equilibrium solution, as this is not the best common output and both

Table 6.3 Common Aversion game with diverging dominant strategies, own presentation

Actor A/B	A1 Cooperation	A2 Defection
B1 Cooperation	3/3	3/4
B2 Defection	4/3	1/1

players have an incentive to unilaterally change their agreed behaviour in order to improve their output. This will generate the worst outcome A2/B2 (1/1) and bring them to the equilibrium of the common aversion, where the actors have substitutable strategies. Therefore, they have strong incentives to do exactly the opposite of what they are supposed to do, which is a situation of strategic substitutabilities (Cooper and John 1988; Collignon 2011a: 48).

Hence, in both games the strategic interests of the players are determined by the nature of public goods. Club goods generate strategic complementarities; common resource goods generate strategic substitutabilities. As a consequence, different institutions are needed for the governance of different public goods.

Explaining Integration

We shall now apply this logic to regional integration. The literature defines integration as rules, regulations, and policies, and also beliefs, which achieve specific outcomes and to foster the required efforts (Mattli 1999: 44; Greif and Laitin 2004: 635). Supranational institutions and regional integration are sets of rules and the institutional environment will affect the actors' preferences and payoffs (Mantzavinos 2001: 248; North 1993: 35).

Integration can be a goal in itself, as it may generate economic pays offs in the form of stability, growth and safer negotiation positions (Fink and Krapohl 2013: 474), but if the governance does not appropriately cope with the strategic interests, these net benefits may fail to materialize. Political actors are assessing the costs and benefits, and if the costs of coordination exceed the benefits, this will obstruct the process of integration (Mattli 1999: 55f.).

Thus, the institutions foster integration, shape preferences and solve conflicts. However, this raises the question, how integration comes into place and how actors decide to make the next integration step and change the polity. I shall argue that integration can be a consequence of exogenous shocks or of endogenous efforts.

Exogenous Shocks

Institutions provide solutions to the dilemma caused by the nature of public goods, but specific institutions serve to solve particular dilemmas. Hence, they have different features, decision-making processes and competences, which are tailor-made for the purposes of particular public goods and strategic preference situations. For example the European Central Bank is an institution that deals with the trade-off between single market and exchange rate fluctuations, while competition policy shapes the pay-offs and distribution of corporate profits. In general, the purpose of European institutions is to build trust and enforce the efforts of regional integration and to avoid insecurities and unnecessary follow-up costs. Hence, we can regard them as enacting the goals of integration, and once they are set up, they reflect a stable Nash equilibrium (Scharpf 1988: 260; Nash 1950).

But if an institution is stable and delivers the desired output, change would only be caused by external events. Hence, exogenous shocks generate the momentum for institutional change: "Institution-building moments occur when a social, economic, or political crisis undermines the current institutional arrangement" (Fligstein and Iona 1996: 3). Economists explain institutional change by changes in relative prices[5] (North 1990: 84; March and Simon 1958: 109). Prices determine the payoff for the actors and, as the cost/benefit calculation and preferences of actors change, new relative prices lead to a different equilibrium. Hence, the equilibrium which was set up to serve as solution for the previous strategic dilemma is no longer stable. The system needs a

---

[5]In this case prices are not only regarded as the pure pecuniary payoff. Prices are seen as all costs which originate from change and influence to the cost/benefit calculation of the actors, may they be monetary, economic, social or every other imaginable costs.

new solution for the new problem and further integration is required. However, under what condition will the need be met?

Motivation is crucial for institutional change (Fligstein and Iona 1996: 12). Actors who initiate change have to be motivated to act. In our case the motivation is caused by the exogenous shock. Once a shock hits the system, it changes the prices and influences the cost/benefit calculation and the preferences of the actors. If the payoff changes but the polity keeps the previous institutional process, the institution may no longer reflect the actors' preferences. For example if the economy is hit by a negative demand shock, a balance budget rule may no longer generate full employment. However, the new net benefits may not be equally distributed among the actors. Hence, not every actor has the same incentives to change the institutional structure and adapt to the new strategic situation. Therefore, the actors who have the highest opportunity cost have the highest motivation for institutional change (Mattli 1999: 19, 44). But these advocates for change do not necessarily have the highest influence on the new integration step and the new equilibrium.

Within the framework of existing institutions, change is more likely to follow the path of previous integration steps (North 1993: 45; Fligstein and Iona 1996: 5). On the one hand, existing institutions make further integration and better cooperation more likely, because they build up trust (March and Olsen 1989). On the other hand, a new institutional framework always bares costs and these costs of re-coordination affect the cost/benefit analysis negatively (Hardin 2003). Most institutions and actors will respond to shocks in a quasi-automatic way, following previously proven good practices, so that institutional paradigms will persist (Mantzavinos 2001: 43). This conservative behaviour is also supported by the established institutional framework (Skocpol 1985). The polity determines the decision-making and voting rules, but these rules are meant to find solutions to old problems in a given strategic preference situation. However, once the situation changes, the old decision-making style does not necessarily lead to an optimal solution. The dominant actor, or coalition, needs to be convinced to take further integration steps (Fligstein and Iona 1996: 3), but will only accept such change if the net benefits make it worth wile. Hence, they can shape the equilibrium to fit their preferences and they will only move if they will be better off.

We conclude that a change in policies can change the strategic preference situations in such a way that the previous mechanism for crisis solution becomes suboptimal and can produce undesired or unfavourable outcomes. This resembles "real" exogenous shocks: a shock to the current system changes the fundamental conditions and the prices for the actors and initiates institutional change.

Endogenous Efforts

External shocks can produce institutional change, but that change is constrained by the framework and the strongest actors within this system. This explanation works if institutions are seen as the equilibrium and institutionalisation as the goal of integration. We now broaden our approach to an enlightened homo sociologicus/oeconomicus model (Mantzavinos 2001: 55f.), since purely rational choice does not reflect every aspect of human relations (North 2005: 5; 23; Mantzavinos et al. 2004: 77). We enrich rational choice with the acquisition of learning skills. This model implies that the preferences are given at the starting point of our analysis, but they can change over time. Nevertheless, the basis for individual decisions is still a cost/benefit calculation and the actors follow their preferences and try to achieve the best, foreseeable outcome.

In this context, actors are themselves affected by the institutions (Greif and Laitin 2004: 633f.). The previous institutions are the starting point which enable cooperation (March and Olsen 1989), but these institutions create new evaluation systems. These new evaluation systems change the cost/benefit calculation and preferences for common goals (Collignon and Schwarzer 2003: 22).

Change Caused by Endogenous Efforts: Motivation

Once again, our starting point for institutional change caused by endogenous efforts is motivation. Without motivation no action is taken. However, the roots of this particular motivation do not stem from something external, but rather from the situation in which the actors sees themselves.

If a given institution does not deliver the desired outcome, frustration will result and the motivation for change will be increased. Likewise, the feeling of being outvoted in collective decision-making might be the cause for frustration (Scharpf 1988: 239). This frustration emerges from the strategic situation described by the Common Aversion game with diverging interests. If this game is solved by preventing the common aversion, while seeking the best outcome for only one actor without other actors being able to change the output, frustration will follow and become a fertile ground for opposing new arrangements (March and Simon 1958: 184; Lechner and Ohr 2011: 360; Mattli 1999: 56).

Change Caused by Endogenous Efforts: Learning

However, to fully grasp the causes of endogenous change, we have to cast light on another key aspect for change: the cognitive aspects that enable it (Mantzavinos 2001: 12).

The institutional framework of European integration does not consist of only one decision mechanism. The relevant decision mechanism, such as voting procedures and required majorities depend on specific policy fields. But when it comes to big integration steps and treaty changes, unanimous voting at the European Council level prevails (Scharpf 1988). We take this as the relevant decision-making procedure. Because any actor can block any decision, coalition building and convincing blocking actors are key to bringing about successful change. If we take this into account, we see that once achieved, equilibriums tend to be strong and stable. Thus, new preferences must be formed and this means we speak about learning and convincing actors.

Before we look at the process of learning, we need to agree on some definitions. Firstly, beliefs "are the subjective ideas that arise in individuals' minds in a given context (background)" (Collignon and Schwarzer 2003: 21). The beliefs might be normative or descriptive. They function as a filter and judge new impressions based upon on their consistency with current beliefs. "Desires are unmitigated normative beliefs"(ibid.). Therefore, desires are not reliable, and only our positive judgment translates them to knowledge or preferences. So, the consistency with our current belief system turns desires into preferences and knowledge.

However, this is not the only way of gaining knowledge and the literature distinguishes between three types of learning: generic, cultural and atomistic (Mantzavinos 2001: 19f.). The first one is based on direct experience, but only the latter two are transmitted as described above. Cultural knowledge is shared and transmitted by the cultural group and atomistic knowledge is gained by individual experiences and learning processes.

In order to analyse learning in the environment of groups or in our case within the European Union, we have to look at the individual (Eisner 2011: 15; Collignon and Schwarzer 2003: 21), as learning first appears at the individual stage and is then reproduced at a larger scale, until a critical mass is reached and the group is convinced as a whole. Learning is based on knowledge and acquiring new knowledge (Mantzavinos 2001: 23ff.). Acquiring new knowledge, in turn, is based on interaction, either with the real world by trial and error (North 1990: 74; Mantzavinos 2001: 23ff.), or interaction with other actors and their validation of the new knowledge (Collignon and Schwarzer 2003: 21ff.; 199ff.). A "stochastic consensus" in terms of the probability of accepting beliefs and preferences emerges when there is a certain degree of trust amongst the interacting partners.[6]

Learning is grounded in the minds of individuals. How it gets there is a flexible and complex process. An individual receives various signals from his or her environment and interprets them along its belief system (Mantzavinos et al. 2004: 76). The process starts with experiences and stimuli from the physical and socio-cultural environment (North 1994: 362f.), which are analyzed through the lens of a person's belief system and knowledge. The actor then connects the new impressions with his goal; in our case the goal is the best possible solution of the strategic situation. This interpretation does not need to be rational or consistent with external standards, as utility is perceived individually and not an external standard for evaluation (Mantzavinos 2001: 13f.).

If these considerations are coherent with an actor's current beliefs, this will confirm and cement his belief system. Alternatively, if they

---

[6]A very strong or stubborn opinion can be treated equally to "no trust in the interaction partners" in this model.

are inconsistent new impressions, learning of new knowledge is possible. However, this depends on other processes, too. In general we grasp knowledge in "if … then" hypotheses and connect them with new and old experiences (Mantzavinos 2001: 23ff.). We can observe a certain hierarchy and competition between hypotheses. Higher ones are the more cemented, they have seen more consistent impressions and therefore need more additional new impressions to be disproved (ibid.). Still, the evaluation system may change and the previously well-established hypothesis may prove to be wrong or no longer functional. This may occur when the actor moves to other socio-cultural environments, in which the sanction/benefit system works differently.

In our case, the European Union with its sanction and benefit system may work as an additional evaluation system. If-then hypotheses and problems cannot merely be viewed in the national context, as one solution might produce the best outcome on the national level, but might be sanctioned at the European level. A good example might be a street toll for foreigners, which has been discussed in Germany for years. In the national context a street toll for foreigners might be perceived as a good thing, as it punishes the "bad foreigners" who destroy national infrastructure. Yet, the German government would also face European sanctions, as a street toll just for foreigners is illegal in Europe.

Hence, in order to cement new knowledge and learn new beliefs, additional, coherent information from other sources is necessary (Searle 1979; Lehrer 1990: 64). Collecting additional information and verification is a communicative process. Actors deliberate and accept new ideas if they are coherent with what they believe and want. The acceptance of the new knowledge does not necessarily depend on its utility, but rather on its reasonability in the context of shared common values and mutual trust (Collignon and Schwarzer 2003: 22f.).

This learning process will shift actors' preferences and will lead after repeated deliberation to a new consensus and a new agreement, because it is irrational to disagree (Lehrer and Wagner 1981). The new outcome is likely to be stable and not to produce long-term losers because all preferences are served. However, the learning process can be complemented by side-payments, supranational institutions with sanctions and/or reimbursement mechanisms.

The Public Goods Approach in a Nutshell

To summarize, our approach here is different from the traditional integration theories such as neofunctionalism, liberal intergovernmentalism, federalism, social constructivism and rational-choice institutionalism. It analyses the public goods generated by the respective policy or policy fields and the required forms of governance. Each public good stands in its own strategic situation, which can be described by preference analysis and Game Theory. Because the strategic situations of different public goods do not necessarily coincide, each strategic situation needs a tailor-maid decision mechanism. If one changes the policy field and therefore the public good, then the strategic preference situation is likely change, too. If the strategic situation changes, then the decision mechanism needs to be adapted. Otherwise, the old mechanism will produce outcomes that the whole group or some actors experience as suboptimal. At this stage, no stable equilibrium will be reached and non-compliance with the common rules might be an option for the actors.

Our first model, exogenous shocks, shows that enhanced competences in a new policy field can lead to distortions in the payoff structure of the strategic situation which change the relative prices for actors. This shock necessitates a change in the polity structure. This change is shaped by the previous institutional arrangement, the power structure between the actors or by the decision-making mechanisms. Our theory predicts that the decision-making structure will change and the strongest actor in the system is likely to steer the change in his direction.

The second model, endogenous efforts, is more concerned with the learning ability of the actors. Actor may advocate change if a Nash Equilibrium with an unfavourable outcome for one actor is achieved and the institutional change cements this outcome. The resulting frustration will start a communicative process. During this learning process, the actors change their preferences and ultimately change the outcome. This outcome is likely to reflect a more stable equilibrium, which does not favour one side and the best solution for all actors will be achieved. We will now apply this theory to explain two major European crises.

Two Crises that Shook the EU

Testing the Theory

I take a Popperian approach to find out whether this public goods theory can explain reality and formulate several falsifiable hypotheses H_1 and build corresponding antitheses H_0. I shall then test them in the case studies. If they fail, it is reasonable to reject the antitheses H_0 and to assume the hypotheses H_1. First, I shall discuss the conjectures based on our theory and then explain why I chose the empty chair crisis and the Euro crisis as the case studies to test the hypothesis.

Hypotheses for the Exogenous Shock Model

From the Exogenous Shock explanation model we can conjecture the falsifiable Hypotheses H_A:

H_{A1}:   If the strategic preference situation changes due to enhanced competences of the European Union in a new policy field, *a change* in the institutional decision-making process is necessary.

H_{A01}:   If the strategic preference situation changes due to enhanced competences of the European Union in a new policy field, *no change* in the institutional decision-making process is necessary.

H_{A2}:   The *strongest actor has the biggest influence* on the change in the institutional decision-making process.

H_{A02}:   The *strongest actor has no or little influence* on the changes of the decision-making process.

Hypotheses for the Endogenous Efforts Model

From the Endogenous efforts explanation model we can derive the falsifiable Hypotheses H_B:

H_{B1}:   The outcome of the communicative process is a *stable equilibrium* that sets up a supranational body which decides about the conflicting preferences case by case.

H_{B01}:   The outcome of the communicative process is an *unstable equilibrium* according to the theory, this may even be a Nash equilibrium) *without setting up a supranational body* that decides about the conflicting preferences.

H_{B2}:   The outcome of the communicative process is a stable equilibrium and *all actors have converging preferences*.

H_{B02}:   The outcome of the communicative process is an unstable equilibrium and the *actors still have diverging preferences*.

This list of hypotheses is not exhaustive. But practically, it is not possible to outline every possible hypothesis. Nevertheless, the selected hypotheses reflect the gist of my approach.

Make the Approach Visible & Selecting Cases

In this section, I start by identifying seven dimensions within the hypotheses that need to be tested and proceed with converting them into variables that can be measured. By dimensions of a hypothesis, I mean individual propositions which are then articulated together to form the hypothesis. The second part deals with the choice of cases.

Dimensions[7] and Variables

1.   *"If the strategic preference situation changes due to enhanced competences of the European Union in a new policy field"* (H_{A1}) - This dimension divides itself into two research matters: firstly, the change of the strategic preference situation and secondly the enhanced competences in a new policy field. In the context of

---

[7]Some of these dimensions are mentioned several times; therefore, they only need to be translated into variables once.

the European Union, the variable is treaty or law change. We can observe this variable in the formal treaties of the European Union or its predecessors. To have a change, there needs to be a new policy field or an extension of that field in the treaty or law which was not or only partly included in a previous agreement. We can assume the variable q_1 is a treaty or law. If q_2 is a second treaty or law, we need to check if in Δq we can identify a new policy field.

The other part of this dimension necessitates a deeper analysis. In order to grasp the change, we need to analyse the underlying good, its special features and the strategic preference situation with the help of Game Theory. This needs to be executed for both situations, i.e. before and after entering the new policy field. A comparison shows if we have a change in the strategic preference situation or not.

2. *"change in the institutional decision-making process"* (H_{A1}) - In order to translate this dimension into a measurable variable, we need to look at the texts that determine the decision-making process before and after. If there is a change, it is fulfilled.
3. *"strongest actor"* (H_{A2}) - Firstly, we need to specify what an actor is. I call an actor every state or institution that has formal or informal decision-making power, e.g. member states of the European Union or the European Commission. In order to observe whether or not an actor is the strongest we have to take into account the economic features, the role the actor plays within the system and other power features which allow the actor to put pressure on other actors.
4. *"influence"* (H_{A2}) - Influence seeks to grasp the effect one has on somebody else. In order to break it down, we need to know the preferences (see below for this dimension) of at least two actors at the beginning of a negotiation process on a topic. We can call the preferences of the first actor x_1 and of the second actor x_2. At the end of the negotiation process, we can subtract x_2 from x_1 and if the result is zero, no actor had an influence on the other. If it is positive, our first actor had an influence on the second and vice versa for a negative result.[8]

---

[8]One has to check if another reasonable preference change might interfere and jeopardize the outcome.

5. *"communicative process"* (H_{B1}) - According to the theory, the communicative process is every action during which the actors exchange their views, learn and/or develop new strategies. Here, the variables are public statements, verbal and written interaction, discussions and formal negotiation rounds. These variables need to be observed over a certain period of time until we can say that the dimension of a communicative process can be observed.[9]

6. *"stable equilibrium,* which sets up a *supranational body to decide about the conflicting preferences in each case"* (H_{B2}) - A stable equilibrium of a negotiation process is not a Nash equilibrium or a Pareto optimum. It is rather an equilibrium which bears no potential frustration for any actor. Therefore, we might observe diverging preferences at the end of the negotiation process and a potentially unfavourable result for one actor (or actor group). Nevertheless, the key factor of this dimension is the supranational body, which decides in each case and therefore allows the outcome to swing to one or another's favour without being manifested in one direction. The supranational body is an agent provided with certain decision-making powers by its principal.[10] These powers need to be particularly relevant when there is the problem of diverging interests within the original principal.

7. *"converging preferences"* (H_{B2}) - This dimension takes into consideration economic, power and moral factors, like trade surpluses, a better negotiation power or the fulfilment of ideas. To measure it, we need to look into the benefit that can be derived from decisions and future outcomes. Observable variables can be monetary benefit, or public and private statements by government officials. Preferences converge if after a change they go in the same direction. A change can be observed, if the Δ of the two variables is not zero before and after the negotiation process.

---

[9]The communicative process is hard to observe, e.g. one condition which needs to be fulfilled is trust among the participators and a certain understanding for each other's position. It is difficult to detect whether a negotiation round or a statement is part of that process.

[10]Benjamin Spörer's chapter Principal and Agents in the European Democracy gives and in-depth analysis of the principal agent theory.

The Choice of Cases

In order to assess the validity of the two explanation models, we need to test them robustly. Therefore, we must be able to observe an overall independent variable of institutional expansion to a new policy field. While the context of European Integration is characterized by innumerable bigger and smaller changes in policy fields, it is impossible to consider them all. "The Empty Chair Crisis" in 1966 is surely a prominent crisis, if not the most prominent. Shortly before, we could observe the first steps towards a common market. The second case, "The Euro Crisis", is the contemporary version of the "The Empty Chair Crisis". Lasting from 2007 and far from being solved, it is interesting to see to what extent the models have explanatory power and at which stage of a process we might be.

Case Studies

The Empty Chair Crisis

In the second half of the 1960s, the Empty Chair Crisis broke out over the financing of the Common Agricultural Policy. The traditional readings trace it back to the geopolitical interests of the French president Charles de Gaulle (Warleigh-Lack 2009: 23). Economic interests can explain most of his actions regarding foreign affairs (Moravcsik 2000a, 2000b), and it was surely no coincidence that the crisis occurred at the time it did (McAllister 2001: 30). In the end, the six member states settled on the so called "Luxembourg compromise". They established a gentlemen's agreement outside of the formal institutions, which guarantees each member state a blocking minority when it comes to the vital interest of this very member state. Therefore, the crisis circumvented the Treaty of Rome, but the crisis did neither suspend it completely or formally. The Luxembourg compromise never became legally binding. Nevertheless, this informal agreement was considered as "in force" until the first revision of the treaty of Rome in 1986, with the Single European Act.

This case shows the underlying factors and reasons for the crisis, it connects the crisis to the approach outlined above and provides an answer for the timing of the crisis.[11]

Case Analysis: CAP as a Public Good

The empty chair crisis was caused when President de Gaulle withdrew his representatives from negotiations within the European Commission because of a disagreement with the other five nations on how to integrate Europe. In this part is dedicated I look at the Common Agricultural Policy (CAP) as a public good and its strategic features. Thereafter, I deal with the strategic preference situation stemming from these features.

In order to classify the CAP as one of Europe's public goods, we have to classify its characteristics of rivalry and exclusion from consumption. Firstly, we look at its objectives laid down in Article 33 of the Treaty of Rome which can be subsumed to food security (Jovanovic 2005: 213).

The public good food security describes that everybody is able to nourish himself. On the one side, if more people consume, a higher output needs to be achieved. Hence, it is rival, as at a certain point of time, an additional consumer figuratively partly eats up the benefit of the others. On the other side, every additional member state is able to contribute to the food security and provides a market for agricultural goods. Therefore, it can be considered as non-rival. Nevertheless, if we connect the food security to the Community wide funding for the CAP, it is fairly reasonable to conclude that this funding is finite. Therefore, the consumption of this good can be classified as rival with a certain capacity limit.

The question of the possibility of exclusion can be answered from two sides: on the micro level, it can be considered that there is no possibility of exclusion for citizens of a Community member state. This would mean no exclusion is possible, as the number of citizens of the

---

[11]For a detailed description of the Empty Chair Crisis c.f. Ludlow 1999; Gilbert 2003; Lambert 1966; Moravcsik 2000a, b.

European community exceed hundreds of millions. On the macro level, it is possible to exclude other consumers, as member states need to fulfil the acquis communautaire. Hence, you need to be a member state of the European Community, in order to benefit from the CAP. Given that we analyse at the macro level and consider member states as actors, it is fair to conclude that the Common Agricultural Policy is a Club Good with capacity limits.

Case Analysis: The Strategic Preference Situation

For the analysis of the strategic preference situation, I start with analysing the particular interest of the six member states of the Community and of the European Commission in the Empty Chair Crisis. Afterwards, I move to a Game theoretic analysis. The preference analysis starts with France as the major actor in this crisis.

As we can see in the historical events part, France was against the qualified majority voting and the CAP funding by Community resources. France largely benefited from the first stages of CAP, it had huge surpluses in the intra-community trade and its intra-community exports grow over 350% from 1958 until 1963 (Ludlow 1999: 238). Without the CAP and French access to the Community markets, the French economy and the French budget would have suffered (Moravcsik 2000a: 23). Its agricultural interest groups pressured for a tariff liberalisation and export opportunities, but insisted on safeguard options (Moravcsik 2000a: 15). Once the CAP was achieved, France insisted on a secure funding (McAllister 2001: 32). However, France opposed the Commission plan, as it connected the secure funding with qualified majority voting. France would have risked to be outvoted (Gilbert 2003: 108). The economic circumstances were not in France's favor: French farmers were relative productive compared to the European Community, but not on the world stage. If one pairs this fact with the consequences of the enhanced Community competences in the field of trade and transport and possible future free trade agreements or global agreements like the GATT (General Agreement on Tariffs and Trade), the French agricultural sector was vulnerable (Moravcisk 2000a; 16; 19;

Moravcsik 2000b: 37). If France had said yes to the qualified majority voting, it would have exposed itself to a potential threat for French farmers. This was the worst-case scenario and the De Gaulle regarded it as France's main interest to overcome the qualified majority voting (Moravcsik 2000b: 40ff.). Additionally, his government was in a relatively strong negotiation position: the basic CAP as it was set up benefited France economically, the British accession was vetoed by France, and the government of the Federal Republic of Germany was considered as relatively weak. Therefore, de Gaulle was confident to win this battle (Moravcsik 2000b: 40).

The second big player during the Empty Chair Crisis showed a different set of interests. German diplomats pushed into the opposite direction of France and favoured deeper integration. They pushed for a synchronised progress in European integration (Bajon 2011: 255). The German government made concessions during the coordination phase of the agricultural harmonisation (Gilbert 2003: 105). In return for their farmers' exposure to international competition pressure (Moravcisk 2000a: 31) and the relatively high cost of the contribution fund financing scheme (Ludlow 1999: 237), they wanted further integration. Germany aimed for deeper integration in order to gain market access for their very competitive industry sector and to secure a profitable development in the GATT round (Ludlow 1999: 241). The German government joined forces with the Dutch and Italians and tried to exploit the French interest for a permanent settlement of the agricultural financing scheme, in order to institutionalise further political integration (Gilbert 2003: 109).

Italy was generally in favour of the Commission's proposal and the qualified majority. Accompanied by the Germans and the Dutch, the Italians pushed several times to deal with the Commission's proposal as a whole and to take the next integration step (Lambert 1966). Economically, Italy was the biggest loser of the contribution fund financing scheme. This fund was based on contributions proportionate to the non-community imports and Italy did contribute the most (Ludlow 1999: 237). Previously Italy had made a political choice in favour of the European Integration and under the ongoing financing scheme it paid a high price for it (ibid.). Therefore, Italy needed an agreement on the revenue based financing scheme and on the qualified majority voting, in order to ensure potential gains in the future.

The Netherlands had no special interest in agriculture and were rather more concerned about the development in the trade sector. On the one side, they were heavily affected by European Integration in the trade sector, as a large part of the European external trade was conducted via the Dutch harbour in Rotterdam and the Dutch government gained a large amount of revenues from the resultant economic activity (Gilbert 2003: 107). On the other side, they benefited from agricultural liberalisation, as their agricultural exports had risen by about 66% from 1958 until 1963 (Ludlow 1999: 238). The Dutch government and parliament, generally in favour of European integration, made a concession towards deeper integration but demanded more power for the European Parliament (Ludlow 1999: 246; Lambert 1966: 197). Consequently, together with Germany and Italy, they tried to isolate France and get their approval for the qualified majority voting and deeper political integration (Lambert 1966).

The Belgium Foreign Minister, Paul-Henri Spaak, as "Père de l'Europe", was personally involved and committed to deeper integration (Bajon 2011: 260). Nevertheless, Belgium, traditionally was a close ally of the French, sided with France in the later stages of the crisis (Lambert 1966: 209) and constantly sustained bilateral negotiations with the French government throughout the crisis (Genin 2013: 274f.).

The sixth member of the European Community, Luxembourg was essentially too small to have a huge impact on the decision and sided with Italy, Germany and the Netherlands against France (Bajon 2011: 260; Lambert 1966: 209).

The last important player in the Empty Chair Crisis is the European Commission itself. The Commission was far from united and the different Commissioners did more or less secretly express concerns alongside with their national governments (Bajon 2009). However, the Commission and its President, Hallenstein, tried to achieve a balance of power between the different member states and pushed for a supranational decision mechanism, like qualified majority voting (Gilbert 2003: 106).

Table 6.4 Strategic preference situation before the Empty Chair Crisis, own presentation

Actor A (Germany and others)/ B (France)	A1 Cooperation	A2 Defection
B1 Cooperation	2/3	2/1
B2 Defection	2/1	2/1

Let us now look at the Game theoretic analysis of the strategic preference situation with the contribution fund financing scheme and without qualified majority voting in several sectors (see Table 6.4) as well as for the situation that would have been created by the Commission proposal based on the Community's own revenue based financing scheme and qualified majority voting (see Table 6.5). The values of each country are derived from the preference analysis above. In order to simplify the presentation, I group Germany, the Netherlands and Italy as actor A and France as actor B. As we have seen above, Germany, the Netherlands and Italy all made concessions in order to complete the European market for agricultural goods and all called for the qualified majority voting, in order to achieve potential gains in the future against the opposition of France. The Commission, Belgium and Luxembourg are too small, too weak or had too little interest in the subject matter, in order to be included in this simplified analysis. Furthermore, they joined sides with either France or the three bigger member states anyway.

In Table 6.4, Cooperation stands for a participation in the common market for agricultural goods without a qualified majority voting and with a contribution fund financing scheme. Defection means the fall back option: no common market, no financing scheme and no decision-making on the supranational level.

Table 6.4 shows that France is the major winner of this situation and the others are more or less indifferent about the situation. On the one side, if actor A (Germany and others) cooperates and provides the Club Good food security with the Common Agricultural Policy, they suffer from harmonisation costs or in the case of Italy from high financial contributions, but gains from market access and a higher food security. On the other side, if they defect, everything would stay national, they

Table 6.5 Strategic preference situation of the Empty Chair Crisis, own presentation

Actor A (Germany and others)/ B (France)	A1 Cooperation	A2 Defection
B1 Cooperation	4/1	2/4
B2 Defection	2/4	2/4

had no increased food security, no gains from market access and needed to finance food security and their farmers on their own, but had no harmonisation or financing costs. For France the situation presents itself differently; they had huge domestic agricultural surpluses, thus market access was key for them. Cooperating and a Community-wide CAP means for them that they can export their surpluses and finance their agricultural sector. The only negative implication while cooperating is that the financing scheme, at that time, was not permanent and needed to be revised. Defecting would mean everything stays national and the French needed to finance their surpluses by themselves. In line with this figure, the outcome A1/B2 could either mean that the actor group A (Germany and others) would establish their own Club Good CAP, although without France, or that there is no establishment of the Club Good CAP and in turn no harmonisation or financing costs that accrue.

The strategic preference situation is very similar to the cooperation game, as the actor group A is more or less indifferent and B can steer the way. In this case, the Nash equilibrium and the Pareto Optimum coincide.

In Table 6.5, Cooperation stands for participation in the common market with a Community own revenue funded financing scheme and with qualified majority voting in the policy sectors of trade, agriculture and transport. Defection in this case means the fall back option: participation in the common market for agricultural goods without a qualified majority voting and with a Community own revenue funded financing scheme. In order to achieve the qualified majority voting, both actors need to cooperate.

In Table 6.5, we can see high potential gains for each actor. However, these outcomes do not coincide. At A2/B2, both actors defect and each actor has a payoff of 2. The actor A (Germany and others) is not able to synchronise the integration and future gains in other fields are put on hold. The actor group gets the same output as in Table 6.4 and they have no securities for their previous concessions. To some degree, they are better off than with the previous scheme, as none of them would be a major contributor to the financing scheme, but e.g. the Netherlands are worse off, as they lose the income which they generated with the duties from Rotterdam harbour. France, actor B, on contrary, generates its highest outcome, as they prevent qualified majority voting and therefore secure possible future losses, are assured against future capacity limits of the Club Good CAP and at the same time, maintain the common market which allows them to export their domestic surpluses without domestic funding. The same counts for the outcomes A1/B2 and A2/B1 or precisely every time that someone defects and the qualified majority voting is prevented. The outcome A1/A2, both actors cooperating, generates the highest possible output for the actor group A (Germany and others). They gain securities for their previous concessions and are able to synchronise the integration for future gains. However, for France this is the worst output, as they fear potential future losses due to the capacity limit of the Club Good CAP and future concessions in trade liberalisations. This strategic preference situation reminds of the Common Aversion Game with diverging interests. The Pareto Optimum and the Nash equilibrium do not coincide. The dominant strategy of the actor group A is cooperation, as it would be the only way for them to achieve all possible gains. However, France's dominant strategy is defection, as this is the only possibility to avoid their worst outcome and achieve their best possible outcome. Additionally, they are in the powerful position to steer the outcome in the direction they want.

Case Analysis: Hypothesis Test

We are now equipped to test the selected hypothesis. I start with the hypothesis of the Exogenous Shock Model and use the antithesis $H_{A/B0n}$ by relating the connecting facts and considerations to it. Thereafter, I am able to accept the antithesis or if it is reasonable to reject it I accept the hypothesis.

In connection with the first antithesis, H_{A01} (If the strategic preference situation changes due to enhanced competences of the European Union in a new policy field, no change in the institutional decision-making process is necessary), we need to check first, if there were any enhanced competences shifted to the European level. Before the crisis and during it, we can observe enhanced competence. As we have seen, the Treaty of Rome paved ways for the Club Good CAP and competences on the European level. The six member states harmonised their agriculture, trade and transport sectors. They were not able to decide alone on how much they would subsidise, how they would set the price levels and which duties and levies would apply. The variable q_1, treaties or laws, in this case it is 0, as the previous European treaty, the Treaty of Paris, the Treaty establishing the European Coal and Steel Community had no chapter on agriculture, trade or transport (Chamlers et al. 2010: 9). The second variable q_2, in this case the Treaty of Rome and the following legislation in the agricultural sector, is not 0, since it deals with the financing and harmonising of the agricultural sector and trade. Therefore the Δq is not 0 and the first condition is fulfilled.

The analysis of the Club Good Common Agricultural Policy and the Game theoretic analysis have shown that the Club Good has a capacity limit, and the strategic preference situation leads the member states into conflict. France on the one side and Germany, Italy and the Netherlands on the other side could not continue with their policy making approach alone and achieve their aims. The system of European Integration got hit by the exogenous shock "enhanced competences" and the former decision-making system produced unfavourable outcomes for the actors. Germany, the Netherlands and Italy pushed for qualified majority voting, but France advocated a secure financing scheme and no qualified majority voting. So we can observe that the initially enhanced competences necessitated a change of the decision-making process, which was finally executed with the Luxembourg compromise. *De jure*, qualified majority voting was in place for the community policies of agriculture, trade and transport. De facto, one country could veto the decisions with an argumentation based on their vital interests. Therefore, we conclude that there was a change in the decision-making process, but as previously there was no coordination at all. Hence, we can reject H_{A01} and adopt the hypothesis H_{A1}: If the strategic preference situation changes due to enhanced competences of the European Union in a new policy field, a change in the institutional decision-making process is necessary.

The next hypothesis to test is H_{A02} (The strongest actor has no or little influence on the change in the institutional decision-making process). In order to adopt or reasonably reject this hypothesis, we need to look for the strongest actor and influence. In the case of the Empty Chair Crisis, this is France. Because France was the Chair of the Council Meetings in the first half of 1966, it had the agenda-setting power, the power to close meetings and to move from one discussion item to the next. The French used this procedural power during the first stage of the crisis. Besides that, France can be considered as a powerful negotiation player. Just before the crisis, they vetoed British accession and had a big influence on the European position in the GATT negotiations (Moravcsik 2000a, b). Additionally, France was the actor who had the best fall back option. If the negotiations on the issue of qualified majority voting were unsuccessful, France already had what they needed from the CAP: market access. For a further integration with qualified majority, the French vote was needed. In comparison to this, the opposing member states were more dependent on the further integration with qualified majority voting. These three points make France the strongest actor in the case of the Empty Chair Crisis. Now we have to see if they had influence on the final outcome. Therefore, we look at the preferences when it came to the Luxembourg compromise. We can take the preferences from Table 6.5. The final outcome after the Luxembourg compromise was A1/B2. A secure financing scheme of the CAP with de facto no qualified majority voting. x_1, the preference of the actor group A, is 2 and x_2, the preference of France, is 4. If we subtract this, we get -2. This negative result shows that France had a positive influence on the outcome after the Luxembourg compromise.

Therefore, we can reasonably reject the hypothesis H_{A02} and adopt the hypothesis H_{A2}: The strongest actor has a strong influence on the change in the institutional decision-making process.

Now we can turn to the Endogenous Efforts Model and its first hypothesis H_{B01} (The outcome of the communicative process is an unstable equilibrium and it does not set up a supranational body to decide about the conflicting preferences in each case). The first dimension of this hypothesis requires us to look at is the communicative process. During the first stages of the crisis there were many interactions, both formal and informal ones. However, after the Luxembourg compromise, we hardly find any exchange about the topic of qualified majority voting, except for some progress reports and unbinding resolutions concerned with the strengthening of the Union e.g. the Tidemanns Report in 1976 and the Solemn Declaration on the European Union in 1983 (Urwin 2010: 28). However, we can expect that there was some kind of exchange, as the member states frequently interacted. For the next dimension, the unstable equilibrium with a supranational body deciding about conflicting preferences, there is no evidence. With the Luxembourg compromise, the member states undermined the power of supranational institutions. Only the Single European Act, twenty years later, re-established qualified majority voting and power shifted towards supranational institutions. However, in this case, the conditions for supranational institutions - as conceived of in my theory - were not completely fulfilled. The qualified majority voting proposal did intend to shift power away from the states and towards the parliament in the case of disunity. If there was no qualified majority within the Council, it was left to the Commission to overrule or accept a bill. The Commission can now prevent the institutionalisation of one member state's preferences. Hence, by discarding the Luxembourg compromise, the Single European Act created a supranational body able to decide case by case. However, we cannot reasonably reject our hypothesis H_{B01}. The last dimension might be fulfilled, but the first - the communicative process - merely shows limited empirical evidence.

The last hypothesis tested is H_{B02} (The outcome of the communicative process is an unstable equilibrium and the actors still have diverging preferences). As already shown above, we can neither reject nor assume that a communicative process took place after the Luxembourg compromise.

The second dimension, diverging preferences, can only be observed via the secondary variable, the completion of the Single European Act and the introduction of qualified majority voting. However, we do not have enough governmental statements and academic research on the topic of CAP and qualified majority voting after the Luxembourg compromise for a profound preference analysis. Therefore, we cannot reject the hypothesis H_{B02}.

The Euro Crisis

We now deal with the European Monetary Union, the establishment of a single currency, and the current Euro crisis. There are many discussions about what caused the crisis, for example, if there were the flaws in the system or if some actors simply misbehaved. Besides the institutional innovations, the ECB has contributed in many other ways to the survival of the Euro, although before 2011 none of them overcame the confidence and solvency crisis. When Mario Draghi became ECB president in late 2011, the strategy changed and eventually he announced the unlimited purchase of government bonds on the secondary market in the second half of 2012 (Krampf 2014: 307; Holinski et al. 2014: 6).

Article 4a and Title VI of the Maastricht Treaty[12] laid the foundations for the Euro and established the European Central Bank (ECB), the European System of Central Banks and a common Economic and Monetary Policy. The treaty centralized competences in the field of monetary and economic policies and set price stability as the primary objective. The ECB became the only institution that conducts policies and it began its work in 1999 (Wrase 2001: 179).

The member states also set up the Stability and Growth Pact (SGP)[13] to guarantee the stability of the Eurozone. Its rules were broken several times and by almost every member state, except by Finland and Luxembourg.

---

[12]For a detailed history of the previous monetary integration steps c.f. Dyson and Featherstone (1999).

[13]C.f. Benjamin Spörer's chapter Principal and Agents in the European Democracy for a detailed analysis of the Stability and Growth Pact.

Greece and Portugal broke the rules consistently since 1998, as did Spain and Ireland after 2008. Even Germany did not comply in almost every year since 2008. Most member states broke the SGP in the early 2000s and then again after 2008. However, the ratios of how severe the SGP was broken are quite different (European Commission 2012b: 154ff.). Despite the strict approach in the beginning and the centralised monetary policy in the hands of the ECB, governments settled for a compromise: The economic policy-making was left to the member states and common decisions were undertaken in an intergovernmental fashion (Collignon 2012a: 5 and Fabbrini 2013: 1004). Some aspects of the Maastricht Treaty were changed in the Treaty of Lisbon - most notably the how to change the provisions of the European System of Central Banks (ESCB) statute.

During the years before and after the introduction of the Euro, all countries experienced high growth. Due to low interest rates, credit fuelled consumption and corporate investment, the economic performance of the housing and the construction sector increased. During these early years, the inflation rate was relatively low, and even Germany experienced a lower inflation rate than in the years before the introduction of the Euro. The European Union witnessed a strong increase in intra-union trade. Only Germany and France got into difficulties during the early 2000s after the burst of the high tech stock market bubble and a short phase of reluctance due to the uncertainty stemming from global terrorism. All states benefited from the single currency in two ways: because the risk on sovereign debt was rated very low interest rates for government bonds were low. Additionally, all governments benefited from increased tax revenues (Heise 2013).

In 2008, the Euro experienced its first strong external shock. In the US, creditors of low-quality mortgage loans could not service their debt anymore and a bubble in the housing and the construction sectors burst. The global financial markets were getting more and more risk averse, a crisis of confidence spread and capital flows dried up. This led in turn to even more loan defaults and more distrust in the market, resulting in even less willingness to provide credits. With the sudden stop of external capital flows, commercial banks came under stress. Governments needed to bail out their banks and thereby they increased their debt levels and violated the SGP. Especially Greece, Spain, Italy, Portugal and Ireland[14] were severely hit. The previously booming southern member states were no longer able to generate budget surpluses and to tackle structural problems. With the slowdown of capital productivity, their locational advantage of capital productivity vanished and the labour productivity[15] gap was still high in comparison with the northern states of the Eurozone. (Sanchis i Marco 2014: 77ff.; Collignon 2013: 1f; Collignon 2012a: 4f.; Hall 2012: 360).

With this vulnerability and no real crisis mechanisms in place, the GIIPS were left to the vagaries of markets, which had previously been under-priced the risk of default and were now over-pricing the risk of default (Collignon 2012a: 6; Krampf 2014: 304). The European Union and the ECB needed to adapt to the new situation and introduced measures to minimise the damage.

In May 2010, the Council reacted and established the European Financial Stability Mechanism (EFSM), followed in June by the European Financial Stability Facility (EFSF). The EFSM allowed the Commission to borrow up to 60 billion Euros from the financial markets, guaranteed by the EU budget, and lend it to member states. The EFSF mandate is wider and permits buying government bonds on the primary and secondary market[16] in order to recapitalise commercial banks. It had initially a capacity of 440 billion Euros and was extended to 780 billion Euros in December 2010. In December 2010, the European Council agreed to a permanent crisis mechanism, the European Stability Mechanism (ESM). It allows member states to borrow on the secondary and eventually even on the primary market. The capacity of this mechanism is 700 billion Euros. Thereof, 80 billion were paid directly to the ESM, the rest are callable reserves and the ESM can access them, if needed. The Board of Governors where the Finance Ministers of the Eurozone are represented have decision-making power and the Commissioner for economic and financial affairs and the President of

---

[14]I refer to these countries as GIIPS (Greece, Italy, Ireland, Portugal and Spain).

[15]Labour and capital productivity contribute to the concept of competitiveness. For a detailed description of this concept, see Spörer et al. 2014: 55ff.

[16]On the primary market, a country directly issues its bond, on the secondary market the initial buyer resells the bond.

the ECB have observatory status. All of these financial institutions and mechanisms lend money to the member states only conditionally and their major aim is to cut the public debt and set the member states on track for reaching the Maastricht Criteria. During March 2011, the Council also adopted the Euro Plus Pact, basically reemphasising the SGP, but it also includes automatic sanctions for violations and calls for labour productivity convergence among member states. In July 2011, a revised structure was established that ensured cheaper finance costs and longer maturity (Collignon 2011b, Sanchis i Marco 2014).

Every one of the GIIPS got financial assistance, except for Spain. In the Spanish case, only the commercial banks were directly recapitalised (Krampf 2014: 312; Collignon 2011b). After December 2011, the crisis became less acute. The situation in most of the GIIPS countries did improve and moderate economic growth did return. Still, the deeper roots of the crisis are not tackled and the situation in Greece remains unchanged. The lending conditions following an austerity dogma did not bring growth back to the country (Collignon 2011b: 14ff.; 2012b: 3f.).

Case Analysis: The Euro as a Public Good

I shall now consider the euro as a public good.

It is the task of the ECB to ensure an efficient resource allocation in the real economy by creating money and keeping it scarce. Money is the hard budget constraint in a monetary economy, and this implies preserving price stability. The ECB is an independent central bank. Hence, it is free from governmental interventions and no member state has direct access to ECB money; only banks have, and governments must get credit from banks and financial markets. What defines monetary union is that all banks have unrestricted access to central bank money, and because the ECB controls aggregate money supply, the interest rate reflects the scarcity price that competing banks are willing to pay to get central bank money. Therefore, the euro is a typical common resource good: no bank can be excluded from the benefit of having access to liquidity, but the cost of money makes it rival for supply (Collignon 2011a: 50f., 2012b: 8).

Classifying the Euro as a Common Pool Resources highlights possible strategic substitutabilities. Governments are subject to the hard budget constraint, which means the cost of credit is low for everyone if they cooperate and keep net borrowing down. However, for individual member states, the incentive is to do the opposite of everyone else, because the cost of borrowing is so low. An individual member can increase national welfare by over-borrowing – which is ultimately unsustainable. Such behaviour drives interest rates up and will ultimately threaten financial and price stability and thus placing the whole system is at risk (Spörer et al. 2014: 46f.). Besides inflation due to over-borrowing, the price stability may also be jeopardised by deflation. If the Eurozone is hit by a shock and the markets are getting more and more risk-averse, too low inflation or even deflation may result.

Case Analysis: The Strategic Preference Situation

The decision to adopt the single currency coincides with German reunification. The German government agreed to the single currency as a trade-off for a general consent to German reunification and pushed for deeper European Integration within a privileged framework for Germany (Mazzucelli 2014: 46ff.; Kenen 1995: 20). From the macro perspective, Germany, as an export-oriented economy benefited from the single currency, as a potent and stable market was protected against exchange rate fluctuations. Furthermore, the external exchange rate of the Euro is determined for the Eurozone as a whole and the export-oriented Germany economy benefits from a single currency with import-oriented countries, since 'German surpluses are compensated by other members' trade deficits, thereby keeping the exchange rate down relative to the rest of the world (Heise 2013: 32f.). The German government pushed for closer political cooperation, but only obtained the Stability and Growth Pact as a rigid fiscal framework without close political cooperation (Krampf 2014: 303). Once the Euro was established, monetary union functioned as a fully integrated market economy: money is invested, where it yields the best return (Collignon 2013: 3). Germany gained competitive advantages by improving its labour productivity which sustained its export-orientation (Bonatt and Fracasso 2013: 1027ff.). Hence, Germany has a general interest in maintaining the Euro. However, the Euro faces pressure from economic shocks and the cost/benefit calculation of the German government changed when potential losses came into play.

In a fully integrated economy with a single currency, the bankruptcy of one country affects the confidence of the capital markets and the interest rates for future debt of the other participating member states (Sanchis i Marco 2014: 20). Therefore, every country has an interest that none of the others defaults. The German position on a direct bail-out for other countries was clear: no bailout. The German government saw the problem of the crisis as a problem of "fiscal fecklessness" (Hall 2012: 367) and the Bundesbank, a major opinion leader in this topic, argued that direct bailout would lead to a collectivization of public debt and an ever growing desire for debt-funded demand (Collignon 2012a: 32f.). In the end, conditional bailout funds were adopted at the European level, financed by capital markets but guaranteed by the whole Eurozone. Germany agreed to this on condition of tight austerity policies, but insisted on keeping control by national governments. It kept liabilities low, but thereby externalized potential default risk costs[17] for member states, which faced pressure from capital markets (ibid. Collignon 2013: 15ff.).

The strategic preference situation in the GIIPS states was very different. These countries were in favour of the single currency, too, as the exchange rate system and the early stages of the EMU put them into a position in which they were dominated by the German Bundesbank (Jovanovic 2005: 89). Furthermore, low interest rates generated a domestic demand-led boom. Thus, the traditional constrains for macroeconomic policy were loosened. Additionally, in a single currency and payment union, an import country does not need to earn foreign exchange reserves as they have free access to the ECB liquidity (Collignon 2012a: 23 Hall 2012: 360).

---

[17]This only externalises the potential default risk costs, not the actual ones: i.a. the guarantees, the bailout funds can capitalise with low interest rates and the debt is actually held by the bailed-out state. In this way the risk premium or the default risk costs are minimised. However, if the bailed-out state eventually defaults, Germany and the other guarantors are directly liable.

In the early years of EMU, the expected benefits from the Euro materialized. The GIIPS states experienced low inflation and low interest rates, which translated into demand-led economic growth. However, these countries had no institutional obligations or market incentives to implement structural reforms (Claeys 2008; Bonatti and Fracasso 2013: 1026). When capital productivity slowed down, capital markets questioned their ability to service their debt, and a massive outflow of money occurred, depressing demand, and GDP shrunk (Collignon 2013). Therefore, the policy objective in the Euro crisis was to restore growth of the GIIPS states, softening or ultimately reversing the demand shock. Moreover, they had to rebuild financial stability, in order to have access to money with low interest rates. In the long-term, they need to implement structural reforms, in order to increase their capital and labour competitiveness without unduly high social costs.

During the crisis, France's position can be viewed as standing between the GIIPS states and Germany. She was reluctant in terms of financial help, but similar to the GIIPS states, France borrowed massively - about the same amount as Germany and Italy together. In order to reduce pressure from the capital markets, French governments would like to make bailouts by the ESM and the EFSF a permanent practice of the ECB and avoid conditional lending (Collignon 2011b: 17).

We can now look at the strategic interest of these actors from a Game theoretic perspective. In Table 6.6, I only analyse Germany and the GIIPS states, since it is these two actor groups which had the biggest clash of interests. The preferences of the other states of the EMU can either be placed in the middle of them or are mostly sided with Germany, good examples being the Netherlands and Finland.

In Table 6.6, Actor A stands for Germany, and B stands for the GIIPS states. We analyse the situation after the creation of the single currency, characterized by the clash of interest and the underlying problem of the Euro as a Common Pool Resource. Therefore, Cooperation stands for the compliance with the Stability and Growth Pact and maintaining the country-specific competitiveness equilibrium.[18] As a deviation from that

---

[18]For a comprehensive discussion on the general competitiveness equilibrium and the country-specific ones c.f. Collignon 2012b, Collignon and Esposito 2014.

Table 6.6 *Strategic preference situation of the Euro up to the year 2008, own presentation*

Actor A (Germany)/ B (GIIPS)	A1 Cooperation	A2 Defection
B1 Cooperation	3/3	4/2
B2 Defection	2/4	1/1

equilibrium can attract investment or lead to an outflow of investment (Spörer et al. 2014: 55ff.). Defection stands for not complying with the SGP or not maintaining the general competitiveness equilibrium. In this case, as a defection with compliance to the SGP, but without maintaining the general competitiveness equilibrium, might not lead to macroeconomic distortion. For example, if Germany lowers its relative labour cost and therefore increases its labour competitiveness and the GIIPS states do the same, no distortion would occur. However, if Germany violates the SGP and the GIIPS states increase their labour competitiveness, one can expect money flowing out of Germany towards the GIIPS states. Hence, in the present case the characteristic of defection is important. According to the macroeconomic stances, Defection for the GIIPS is a violation of the SGP and Defection for Germany means increasing their labour competitiveness against the general competitiveness equilibrium.

Table 6.6 is very similar to the Prisoners' Dilemma. Nevertheless, it shows three Pareto Optima and no Nash equilibrium. The first Pareto Optimum is A1/B1 where both actors cooperate. In this case, all member states of the Eurozone keep up the equilibrium competitiveness and comply with the SGP. All member states get the benefits of a single currency, but have to deal with the cost of losing monetary independence, needing to comply with the SGP and getting less investment than they would if they would increase their competitiveness against the general equilibrium. In the scenario of the second Pareto Optimum, A2/B1, Germany as actor A, defects, while the GIIPS states as actor B cooperates. Germany increases its competitiveness against the general competitiveness equilibrium and the GIIPS states stick to the general competitiveness equilibrium and the SGP. In turn, Germany attracts more investment, as they get more competitive in comparison to the rest of the Eurozone. With the nature of the Euro as a Common Resource good, there will be less investment in the rest of the Eurozone.

Therefore, Germany turns out to get the outcome four and the GIIPS states the outcome two. The third Pareto Optimum, A1/B2, shows the scenario that Germany cooperates and sticks to the SGP and the general competitiveness equilibrium, while the GIIPS states violate the SGP.[19] In the last equilibrium A2/B2, both actors defect and get the outcome one. Germany on the one side increases its competitiveness against the general competitive equilibrium and the GIIPS states violate the SGP. Thus, the Euro is put under pressure when market confidence vanishes and the creditworthiness of the GIIPS states is questioned. For the GIIPS, the new money is too expensive and Germany appears to be a safe haven for investment, while the capital flows out of the GIIPS states and the demand breaks down. If no further actions are undertaken, the GIIPS states might default. Due to the fact that they cannot devaluate their currency, the burden of the Euro might become too heavy and the GIIPS states might be forced to leave the Eurozone. This in turn results in an even higher demand shock, which actually affects the exports of Germany and of the other Euro states.

The last equilibrium is likely to be the overall outcome, as we do not have a Nash equilibrium. Hence, every actor can move from the intended cooperation to a higher output via a unilateral change of behaviour. Therefore, the dominant strategy of both actors is Defection. The reason for that equilibrium lies in the Maastricht Treaty and its institutional framework. The treaty enshrines the monetary stance of Germany, but leaves fiscal policies to the member states and the decision-making method is intergovernmental. We find no mechanisms to safeguard the fiscal stance with executive powers. Hence, on the one side, the GIIPS states get frustrated and break the SGP, on the other side every member state is able to attract investment. A stronger central authority and a more balanced fiscal stance could have prevented that problem.

---

[19]It is only fair to say, that only three of the GIIPS states did in fact break the SGP and Germany, as most of the other states, did break it, too.

Table 6.7 Strategic preference situation of the Euro after the year 2008, own presentation

Actor A (Germany)/ B (GIIPS)	A1 Cooperation	A2 Defection
B1 Cooperation	2/4	4/1
B2 Defection	2/3	2/2

Table 6.7[20] displays the strategic preference situation during the crisis. Here, Cooperation means European solidarity and compliance with the rules. Defection stands for pursuing the individual nation state's interest. Only if both actors cooperate a burden sharing instrument will be implemented. If one state defects, they move to the fall-back option, the ESM. If both actors defect, all GIIPS states or at least some leave the Eurozone and re-introduce their own currency.

In Table 6.7, there is no Nash equilibrium, but one Pareto Optimum. The Pareto Optimum, A1/B1, shows the outcome, if both actors cooperate. In the real world this would mean convergence efforts from the GIIPS states, while Germany contributes and shares the burden e.g. via Eurobonds. The GIIPS states get the payoff A2/B2, as they can cooperate without paying the price alone. Germany sees its fiscal stance violated and is directly liable for the debt, which the GIIPS states incur. Hence, they get payoff A2/B1. This outcome shows the situation where Germany is not willing to share the burden and shows no solidarity, while the GIIPS states undertake convergence efforts and comply with conditional provisions of the ESM. The GIIPS states get assistance from the ESM, but need to comply with the austerity rules and do not create spillovers to the other Eurozone member states. Germany externalises the cost of convergence to the GIIPS states, minimizes its own risk of liability and gets the benefits from a stable Eurozone. Thus, they get payoff A2/B2.

---

[20]Table 6.7 does not display all options that are subject of the current discussion. However, for argument's sake, it shows the tendency.

But the GIIPS states carry the burden of the convergence measures alone and are obliged to have another fiscal stance than their preferred. This leads to the Payoff A1/B1. In this situation, the GIIPS states do not comply with the austerity rules and do not undertake measures to achieve further convergence with the rest of the Eurozone, but receive assistance from the ESM, as Germany cooperates. The GIIPS states suffer in this point, as they carry the burden of the new debt all by themselves, but get a lower interest rate due to the ESM and the guarantee from the rest of the Eurozone. Therefore, they get payoff A1/B2. Germany on the other hand, gets the payoff A2/B1, since their preferences on the fiscal stance are not fulfilled. Furthermore, the GIIPS states might eventually default and Germany would be partially liable for their debt. The outcome A2/B2 describes the situation, in which both actors defect. In this case the GIIPS states leave the Eurozone and implement their own currencies. With this step, they get their monetary independence back, are likely to get a haircut on their debt and are able to adjust the exchange rate. Therefore, they are able to decrease the social cost, but they do not enjoy the stability and low interest rate of a well working single currency. Hence, they get the payoff A2/B1. Germany suffers from GIIPS default write-offs and financial stability is jeopardised. However, Germany can impose its fiscal stance to the rest of the Eurozone and prevent taking on future burdens. This leads to payoff A2/B1.

The dominant strategy of Germany, as actor A, is Defection, as this is their only way to achieve their highest outcome. Even the second best outcome with this dominant strategy leads to the same output as the strategy Defection would. The dominant strategy of the GIIPS states, as actor group B, is Cooperation. This is the only possibility to achieve their best outcome. However, Defection might be an option, if this game is repeated and they experience that their dominant strategy leads to the worst outcome for them. If we combine the dominant strategies of the two actors, we can see that they end up at the equilibrium A2/B1. Table 6.7 is similar to the Common Aversion game with diverging dominant strategies. The current approach seems to manifest the best outcome for Germany; the GIIPS states carry the burden and are likely to be frustrated in the long-term.

Case Analysis: Hypothesis Test

In order to test the first antithesis, H_{A01} (If the strategic preference situation changes due to enhanced competences of the European Union in a new policy field, no change in the institutional decision-making process is necessary), we start by looking at a competence change on the European level. As we have seen, the Maastricht Treaty sequentially led to the Euro as the single currency for all members of the Eurozone. With the implementation of the Euro, the member states shifted monetary policy to the European level. Hence, we observe enhanced competences at the EU level. As we have seen, the euro is a European common resource good, and with this shift the strategic preference situation changed, too. This was a gradual process. The Single European Act included only minor provisions and rules concerning the monetary or economic policy mix at the European level. The Maastricht Treaty dealt with these policies in a more detailed manner in Title VI. Subsequently, the Treaty of Lisbon changed some decision-making rules concerning the statute of the ECSB. Furthermore, we can observe that the Treaty of Amsterdam, the Nice Treaty and the Treaty of Lisbon substantially change the decision-making process for decisions that are taken under qualified majority. The Lisbon Treaty implemented a system in which at least 55% of the member states, that represent at least 65% of the people of Europe, need to vote in favour of a proposal, in order to be adopted in the Council. This change is also relevant for Title VII of the Lisbon Treaty and therefore changes the decision-making process. Thus, Δq is not zero, as the Single European Act is q_1, the Maastricht Treaty q_2 and the Treaty of Lisbon q_3.

We conclude that a new decision-making process was adopted when the European Union first enhanced its competences in the field of monetary and economic policies. Thus we can reject H_{A01} and adopt the hypothesis H_{A1}: If the strategic preference situation changes due to enhanced competences of the European Union in a new policy field, a change in the institutional decision-making process is necessary.

For a profound analysis of the second antithesis H_{A02} (The strongest actor has no or little influence on the change in the institutional decision-making process) we need to identify the strongest actor first. As we have seen, Germany is and was the anchor of the single currency. Its credit trustworthiness and its economic strength were essentially influencing the exchange rate during the early times of monetary cooperation and, later on, they were the main factors that determined the interest rate for the whole Eurozone. However, Germany's negotiation position was weakened as German unification became a major issue before the Maastricht Treaty. In the first stages after the implementation of the Euro, Germany was among the first member states that violated the SGP when it faced an economic slowdown in the early 2000s. This undermined the German negotiation power. In this case, it is only fair to conclude, that while Germany had the best exit option, it was still not the outstandingly strongest actor.

Now we can move to the second part of this hypothesis. Traditionally, Germany's position on monetary issues was very strict. The German government favoured the Euro and wanted it to be designed as the deutschmark: with a strong and independent central bank and a fiscal stance which contributes to a low inflation and political cooperation. The early design of the Euro did follow this concept, except for a strong political cooperation. The subsequent weakening of the SGP under Chancellor Schröder was also intended. Hence, we can see that Germany did shape the Euro, but it did not have the power to shape the greater regulatory stance entirely according to their preferences. Nevertheless, it did shape the Euro and EU's fiscal stance.

Therefore, we can reject the antithesis H_{A02} and adopt the hypothesis H_{A2}. Germany as the strongest actor had essential influence on the overall outcome, since the SGP ensures their fiscal stance and inflation preference, even after it was changed. However, Germany could not ensure political cooperation.

We now test the hypothesis H_{B01} (The outcome of the communicative process is an unstable equilibrium and it does not set up a supranational body to decide about the conflicting preferences in each case). The first dimension, the communicative process, is relatively easy to observe. Before and especially during the Euro crisis, scholars, newspapers and politicians had intense debates on the best fiscal stance and monetary policy for the Eurozone.

Concerning the unstable equilibrium without setting up a supranational body deciding about conflicting preferences, we observe the ECB as a supranational body which decides monetary policy. It is independent and no country has an unduly high influence. However, the second piece of the institutional framework of a single currency, economic policy, was left mainly in the national sphere of influence. The policies are coordinated and the Stability and Growth Pact guides the national budgetary stances.

With these findings, we should reject the first of the twin antitheses (H_{B01}) and adopt the hypothesis H_{B1}. The outcome of the communicative process is a stable equilibrium, which sets up a supranational body, which is, however, limited to monetary policy. The empirical findings show that we cannot reject this antithesis for the economic policy. Therefore we need to take the second of the twin hypotheses into consideration.

The last antithesis to test is H_{B02} (The outcome of the communicative process is an unstable equilibrium and the actors still have diverging preferences). Previously, we have seen that the dimension of communicative process is fulfilled. As we have seen in Tables 6.6 and 6.7, the actors still have diverging interests. Therefore, the antithesis H_{B02} cannot be rejected.

Synthesis

The empirical part and the two case studies "The Empty Chair Crisis" and "The Euro Crisis" have produced informative insights on the theory developed in the first part of this chapter. Both cases have different explanatory power. Contrary to the Endogenous Efforts Model, the antithesis of the Exogenous Shock Model should be rejected and we can reasonably adopt the hypothesis and this model. Therefore, we conclude that the baseline assumptions of the theory are valid and that an *extension of competences leads to a shift in the decision-making process*. This agrees with common sense.

Unfortunately, the more sophisticated part of the approach, the Endogenous Efforts Model, could not be tested to full satisfaction. Only once was the selected hypothesis reasonably acceptable, as we could observe a supranational body and heavy debates in the case of "The Euro Crisis". This leads us to conclude that the communicative process has produced a stable equilibrium, in which diverging interests are bridged by a supranational institution deciding with discretion. In the case of "The Empty Chair Crisis", we can neither reject nor adopt the antitheses of the Endogenous Efforts Model. On the one side, we observed the outcome of one of the twin hypotheses, the supranational body. The European Commission seriously gained decision-making powers and we can view it as a supranational decision-making body in the case of the CAP. Nevertheless, one essential part of the hypothesis, namely the communicative process, remains still undetermined due to the long period of time between the competence change and the change in the decision-making procedure.

In order to draw significant conclusions from the two case studies, we need to put the empirical part into a bigger picture. As I have outlined above, there are numerous cases in the history of European Integration which could be considered and I just selected merely four hypotheses out of many possible. A comprehensive study of every case and all hypotheses is not possible within the limits of this chapter. Especially the methods of testing the second explanation model with more sophisticated variables would be time consuming, but doing so is possible and the tools are available. Hence, the indecisive result of whether or not to adopt the hypotheses of the Endogenous Efforts Model, should not imply that it should be rejected as a whole, but the current findings should be taken as revealing information that lead to a deeper study of this explanation model. Furthermore, if the Endogenous Efforts Models proves its explanatory power, we can expect a conciliatory outcome for the Euro crisis.

Conclusion

The present study deals with European integration in general and the time frame of decision-making procedural changes in particular. Consequently, it answers the overall research question as to whether or not enhanced competences change governance in the EU. This question can be answered positively. The causality one adopts depends on the explanation model one chooses. The two explanation models differ in their empirical support.

This study connects several theoretical approaches and combines them to provide a new approach on European Integration. The two explanation models differ in their significance. The Exogenous Shock Model is similar to most other rational choice approaches and does not deliver innovative insights. However, it sharpens the view on the actors, the dependency on the policy field, as well as the governance and the respective decision-making procedure. In comparison, the Endogenous Efforts Model is in line with some assumptions of the Social Constructivists. It deploys an enlightened form of rational choice and can lead to new insights on how European Integration works. The approach of this paper can be used in a broader framework and lead to a new, broad integration theory.

The Game Theory and public approach in European Integration gives us more insights how integration functions. Basically, we need to look at the resource conflict which is created by the new public good and according to that, the conflict is solved and the integration steps can be observed. The Exogenous Shock and Endogenous Efforts approach explain in which direction the integration is going.

The lessons we can draw from the Exogenous Shock approach for the governance of public goods is: Tailor the governance system to the new situation in order to avoid inefficient resource allocation. The Endogenous Efforts approach can neither be neglected, nor adopted. Therefore, we have limited lessons. However, if we adopt it, it gives hope for the governance of European goods. There needs to be a public discourse and at the end, there will be a stable equilibrium and a common way to govern the public good.

References

Aggarwal, V. K., & Dupont, C. (1999). Goods, games, and institutions. *International Political Science Review, 19*(20), 393–409.

Aronsson, T, & Blomquist, S. (2003). Optimal taxation, global externalities and labor mobility. *Journal of Public Economics, 87*(12), 2749–2764.

Bajon, P. (2011). De Gaulle Finds His "Master" Gerhard Schröder's "Fairly Audacious Politics" The European Crisis Of 1965–1966. *Journal Of European Integration History, 17*(2), 253–270.

Bajon, P. (2009): The European commisioners and the empty chair crisis of 1965-66. *Journal of European Integration History*, 15 (2), 105–124.

Bonatti, L., & Fracasso, A. (2013). The German model and the European Crisis. *Journal of Common Market Studies, 51*, 1023–1039.

Chalmers, D. Davies, G, & Monti, G. (2010). *European Union Law*. Cambridge: Cambridge University Press.

Claeys, Peter (2008). Budgetary Spillovers And Long-Term Interest Rates. In B.van Aarle & K. Weyerstrass. (Eds.). Economic Spillovers, Structural Reforms And Policy Coordination In The Euro Area. (pp. 55-106). Heidelberg: Physica-Verlag.

Collignon, S. (2003). *The European Republic: Reflections on the Political Economy of a Future Constitution*. London: Federal Trust for Education and Research.

Collignon, S. (2011a). The Governance of European Public Goods. In D. Tarschys (Ed.), *The EU budget: What should go in? What should go out?* (pp. 42–57). Stockholm: SIEPS.

Collignon, S. (2012). *Macroeconomic imbalances and comparative advantages in the Euro area*. Brussels: European Trade Union Institute.

Collignon, S., & Esposito, P. (2014). Unit labour costs and capital efficiency in the Euro Area: A new competitiveness indicator. In Stefan Collignon & Piero Esposito (Eds.), *Competitiveness in the European Economy* (pp. 46–71). London: Routledge.

Collignon, S., & Schwarzer, D. (2003). *Private sector involvement in the Euro: The power of ideas*. London: Routledge.

Collignon, S. (2011b). The ECB, The ESM And Stability Bonds: A Way Out Of The Crisis European Parliament. Accessible online at http://www.stefan-collignon.de/PDF/EP_Dec2011.pdf, last access April 9, 2015.

Collignon, S. (2012b). 'Europe's Debt Crisis, Coordination Failure, and International Effects', ADBI Working Paper 370, Tokyo: Asian Development Bank Institute.

Collignon, S. (2013). Taking European Integration Seriously: Competitiveness, Imbalances, And Economic Stability In The Euro Area, S.Collignon and P. Esposito (Eds.), Competitiveness in the european economy. london: Routledge, 2013. Accessible online at http://www.stefancol-lignon.de/PDF/Taking%20euro%20seriously.pdf, last access 9 April, 2015.

Cooper, R., & John, A. (1988). Coordinating coordination failures in a Keynesian model. *The Quarterly Journal of Economics, 103*(3), 441–463.

Dyson, K, & Featherstone, K. (1999). *The road to Maastricht: Negotiating Economic and Monetary Union.* New York and Oxford: Oxford University Press.

Eisner, M. A. (2011). *The American Political Economy.* New York: Routledge.

European Commission (2012b). General Government Data: General Government Revenue, Expenditure, Balances and Gross Debt Part II: Tables by series Spring 2012. Accessible online at http://ec.europa.eu/economy_finance/db_indicators/gen_gov_data/documents/2012/spring2012_series_en.pdf, last access April 9, 2015.

Fabbrini, S. (2013). Intergovernmentalism and its limits: Assessing the European Union's answer to The Euro Crisis. *Comparative Political Studies, 46*(9), 1003–1029.

Fligstein, N., & Iona, Mara-Drita. (1996). How to Make a Market: Reflections on the Attempt to Create a Single Market in the European Union. *American Journal of Sociology, 102*(1), 1–33.

Genin, V. (2013). La Politique Etrangère De La Belgique Face A La France Lors De La Crise De La Chaise Vide (1965–1966). Rôle D'Un "Petit Pays", Poids D'Une Relation Bilatérale. *Journal of European Integration History, 19*(2), 259–276.

Gilbert, M. (2003). *Surpassing realism: The politics of integration since 1945.* Oxford: Rowmann & Littlefield Publishers.

Greif, A, & Laitin, D. D. (2004). A Theory of Endogenous institutional change. *American Political Science Review, 98*(4), 633–652.

Haas, E. B. (1964). *Beyond the Nation State: Functionalist and international organization.* Stanford: Stanford University Press.

Haas, E. B. (1968). *The Uniting of Europe: Political, Social and Economic Forces 1950–1957.* Stanford: Stanford University Press.

Hall, P. A. (2012). The Economics and politics of the Euro crisis. *German Politics, 21*(4), 355–371.

Hardin, R. (2003). *Liberalism, constitutionalism, and democracy.* Oxford: Oxford University Press.

Heise, M. (2013). *Emerging from the Euro Debt Crisis: Making a single currency work.* Heidelberg: Springer.

Holinski, N. Kool, C. Piplack. Jan (2014). After The Fall: Euro Area Adjustment. Accessible online at http://dspace.library.uu.nl/handle/1874/293958, last access 9 April, 2015.

Holler, M. J., & Illing, Gerhard. (2003). *Einführung in die Spieltheorie.* Berlin: Springer Verlag.

Jovanovic, M. (2005). *The Economics of European Integration: Limits and prospects.* Cheltenham: Edward Elgar Publishing Inc.

Kaul, I. Grunberg, I. Stern, Marc A. (1999). 'Defining Global Public Goods', In: Kaul, Inge. Grunberg, Isabelle. Stern, Marc A. (Eds.), *Global Public Goods: International Cooperation in the 21st Century*, (pp 2–19). New York: Oxford University Press.

Kenen, P. (1995). *'Economic And monetary Union In Europe: Moving beyond Maastricht'.* Cambridge: Cambridge University Press.

Krampf, A. (2014). From the Maastricht treaty to post-crisis EMU: The ECB and Germany as drivers of change. *Journal of Contemporary European Studies, 22*(3), 303–3017.

Krapohl, S, & Fink, S. (2013). Different paths of regional integration: Trade networks and regional integration building In Europe, Southeast Asia and South Africa. *Journal Of Common Market Studies, 51*(3), 472–488.

Lambert, J. (1966). The constitutional crisis 1965–1966. *Journal of Common Market Studies, 4*(3), 195–228.

Lechner, S, & Ohr, R. (2011). The right of withdrawal in the treaty of lisbon: A game theoretic reflection on different decision making processes in the EU. *European Journal of Law and Economics, 32*(3), 357–375.

Lehrer, K. (1990). *The theory of knowledge.* London: Routledge.

Lehrer, K., & Wagner, C. (1981). *Rational consensus in science and society.* Dordrecht/Boston/London: D. Reidel Publishing Co.

Ludlow, P. N. (1999). Challenging French leadership in Europe: Germany, Italy, the Netherlands and the outbreak of the empty chair crisis of 1965–1966. *Contemporary European History, 8*(2), 231–248.

Mantzavinos, C. (2001). *Individuals, institutions, and markets.* Cambridge: Cambridge University Press.

Mantzavinos, Chrysostomos. North, Douglass, & Shariq, Seyd. (2004). Learning, institutions and economic performance. *Perspectives on Politics, 2*(1), 75–84.

March, J. G., & Olsen, J. P. (1989). *Rediscovering institutions: The organizational basis of politics.* New York: Free Press.

March, James G., & Simon, Herbert A. (1958). *Organizations.* New York: Wiley.

Marco, S, & Manuel. (2014). *The Economics of the Monetary Union and the Eurozone crisis.* Heidelberg: Springer.

Mattli, W. (1999). *The logic of regional integration: Europe and beyond*. Cambridge: Cambridge University Press.

Mazzucelli, C. (2014). *France and Germany at Maastricht: Politics and negotiations to create The European Union*. London: Routledge.

McAllister, R. (2001). From EC to EU: A historical and political survey. New York: Routledge.

Moe, T. M. (1984). The new economics of organization. *American Journal of Political Science, 28*(4), 739–777.

Moravcsik, A. (1997). Taking preferences seriously: A liberal theory of international politics. *International Organization, 51*(4), 513–553.

Moravcsik, A. (1998). *The choice for Europe: Social purpose and state power from Messina to Maastricht*. Ithaca, NY: Cornell University Press.

Moravcsik, A. (2000a). De Gaulle between grain and grandeur: The political economy of French EC policy, 1958–1970 (Part1). *Journal of Cold War Studies, 2*(2), 3–43.

Moravcsik, A. (2000b). De Gaulle between grain and grandeur: The political economy of French EC Policy, 1958–1970 (Part2). *Journal Of Cold War Studies, 2*(3), 4–68.

Musgrave, R. A., Musgrave, P. B., & Kullmer, L. (1994). *Die öffentlichen finanzen in theorie und praxis*. Tübingen: Mohr.

Nash, J. F. (1950). The bargaining problem. *Econometrica, 18*(2), 155–162.

North, D. C. (1990). *Institutions, institutional change, and economic performance*. Cambridge: Cambridge University Press.

North, D. C. (1993). Institutional change: A framework of analysis. In Sven-Erik Sjöstrand (Ed.), *Institutional change: Theory and empirical findings* (pp. 35–46). London: M.E. Sharpe Inc.

North, D. C. (1994). Economic performance through time. *American Economic Review, 84*(3), 359–368.

North, D. C. (2005). *Understanding the process of economic change*. Princeton: Princeton University Press.

Rohe, K. (1994). *Politik - Begriffe und Wirklichkeiten*. Stuttgart: Kohlhammer.

Scharpf, F. W. (1988). The joint decision-making trap: lessons from German Federalsim And European Integration. *Public Administration, 66*(3), 239–278.

Searle, J. (1979). *Expression and meaning: Studies in the theory of speech acts*. Cambridge: Cambridge University Press.

Skocpol, T. (1985). Bringing the State back. in: Strategy of analysis in current research. In P. Evans, D. Rueschmeyer, & T. Skocpol (Eds.), *Bringing the State back in* (pp. 3–43). Cambridge: Cambridge University Press.

Snidal, D. (1985). The game theory of international politics. *World Politics,* *38*(1), 25–57.

Spörer, B. Diessner, S. Hislop, S. Kephart, A. & Salch, S. (2014). *Governing Europe efficiently: An analysis into the theory of public goods and democratic legitimation for the Eurozone, with examples from the USA and Canada.* Hamburg: Anchor Academic Publishing.

Stein, A. A. (1982). Coordination and collaboration: Regimes in an anarchic world. *International Organization, 36*(2), 299–324.

Urwin, D. W. (2010). The European Community: From 1945–1985. In Cini, Michelle and Pérez-Solórzano Borragán, Nieves (Eds.), *European Union Politics,* (pp. 15–31) Oxford: Oxford University Press.

Warleigh-Lack, A. (2009). *European Union: The basics.* New York: Routledge.

Weingast, B. R., & Marshall, W. J. (1988). The industrial organization of Congress; or, why legislators, like firms, are not organized like markets. *Journal of Political Economy, 96*(1), 132–163.

Wrase, J. M. (2001). Organization and policy procedures in the European system of central banks. In Jeffrey M. Wrase & Jongmoo J. Choi (Eds.), *European monetary union and capital markets* (pp. 179–194). Bingley: Emerald Group Publishing Limited.

7

The ASEAN Economic Community (AEC) as a Public Good

A. Han

In 2007, the leaders from the Association of Southeast Asian Nations (ASEAN) proudly announced to the world the decision to set up the ASEAN Economic Community (AEC)[1] by 31st December 2015. The AEC will be the creation of a single market and production base which will allow the free flow of goods, services, investments and skilled labour, and the freer movement of capital across the region. Despite its origin as a loose and modest intergovernmental regional organisation aimed at preventing political conflict among its members, this decision marks ASEAN's evolution into a regional grouping with a more ambitious agenda of regional integration and cooperation. The AEC

---

[1]The ASEAN Economic Community (AEC) is one of three pillars of the broader ASEAN Community, announced in the Declaration of ASEAN Concord II, Bali, 7 October 2003. The other two pillars are: the ASEAN Political-Security Community (APSC) and the ASEAN Socio-Cultural Community (ASCC).

A. Han(✉)
Lowy Institute for International Policy, Sydney, Australia
e-mail: hanshiyunangela@gmail.com

© The Author(s) 2017
S. Collignon, *The Governance of European Public Goods*,
DOI 10.1007/978-3-319-64012-9_7

219

would make ASEAN one of the largest economies in the world (Asian Development Bank [ADB] 2015) which has indeed generated huge expectations as well as anxiety internationally.

Yet, the process of constructing the AEC has been no easy feat. Throughout the process of constructing the AEC, there have been many instances in which the dilemma of reconciling the need for strong and effective regional institutions on the one hand, and overriding concerns to maintain national autonomy and preserve regional diversity on the other, has come to the fore. At the heart of this dilemma lies a pertinent question regarding economic integration: at what stage must the decision-making locus be shifted from the national to regional domain? What are the factors that influence this shift? These questions are especially relevant to ASEAN states, whose actions are guided by the principles of the 'ASEAN Way', a group of underlying norms that emphasises the principles of sovereignty, non-intervention in domestic affairs, aversion to legalism and decisions made by mutual consultation and consensus to maintain unity amid regional diversity. Many observers have attributed the 'ASEAN Way' as the cause for inaction and an impediment to the integration process. With the ASEAN Way, inter-state problems and diverging interests that are natural by-products of any international process, are not being solved but simply avoided. Regional institutions like the ASEAN Secretariat are still constrained by member states' unwillingness to provide more resources and thus do not have the ability to enforce compliance.

Yet, despite the hiccups and slow progress, ASEAN does not intend to stop its integration efforts at the AEC. In its 2030 Vision, the organisation states that it views the AEC only as a "stepping stone to deeper integration" and that by 2030, ASEAN should evolve into a "truly borderless economic community" (ADBI 2014: xxi). Why do ASEAN members engage in the rhetoric of greater centralisation and a more 'rules-based' organisation to keep it in the 'driver's seat' of Asian regionalism, but yet face so much problems in cooperation problems as evidenced in the construction of the AEC?

It is within this context of greater rhetorical commitment to deepen integration yet retaining an incessant commitment to the 'ASEAN Way' that this chapter seeks to explore the current stage of ASEAN economic integration and determine whether it requires a shift of some authority to a regional institution. Is it possible for ASEAN countries to deepen economic integration whilst still holding onto the norms of the 'ASEAN Way' which prides the national over the regional? In order to do so, two questions need to be answered. First, why has the progress of AEC been so slow? The answer to this question is important to ascertain whether the very broad-stroke argument of the 'ASEAN Way' is to blame for the slow progress. If not, how can greater and deeper institutionalisation address these problems and improve the process for further integration? In answering these two main questions, this chapter draws upon the theories of public goods, collective action and fiscal federalism. In so doing, this chapter analyses the AEC as an ASEAN public good and concludes that further integration would only increase the number of ASEAN public goods and it is thus necessary for ASEAN to examine its underlying norms and structure in order to achieve its goals.

Background of ASEAN Integration

From Political to Economic Cooperation

ASEAN was formed in 1967 with the main political-security goal to create a "prosperous and peaceful community of Southeast Asian Nations" (ASEAN, 1967). In a period where these young, newly-independent states were undergoing a series of disputes[2] and locked in the politics of the Cold War, the 5 founding members—Indonesia, Malaysia, the Philippines, Thailand and Singapore—saw ASEAN integration as a means to unite against communist threat and achieve political stability.

---

[2]The most notable of ASEAN conflicts was *Konfrontasi* (Confrontation), a coercive strategy adopted by Indonesia's President Sukarno against the newly independent Malaysian state between 1963 and 1966. Other bilateral tensions which threatened to escalate into war during the 1960s existed between Malaysia and the Philippines, Singapore and Malaysia, and Singapore and Indonesia.

From 1960s till the early 1990s, ASEAN's main focus was to stabilize the region and prevent the "Balkanization of Southeast Asia" (Smith 1999: 238). Half a century later, the regional organisation can proudly say that it has fulfilled its aspiration of bringing about an era of peace and stability in a region of fledging nation states with a history rife with conflict. Moreover, the success of ASEAN has attracted 5 new members—Brunei (1984), Vietnam (1995), Myanmar (1997), Laos (1997) and Cambodia (1999). Against this backdrop of relative political stability, ASEAN has been exploring new ways of corporation and deepening integration through economic means.

The start of economic cooperation emerged in the late 1970s, through the establishment of a Preferential Trading Agreement (PTA) in 1977 (Winanti 2012). Efforts intensified in the mid-1980s with a new wave of regionalism spreading throughout the world, such as the US-Canada Free Trade Area agreement (the predecessor of NAFTA), the Asia-Pacific Economic Cooperation (APEC), MERCOSUR in Latin America and the European Union (EU). But it was not until 1992 when the ASEAN Free Trade Area (AFTA) was established. AFTA was a sign of a new political purpose for Southeast Asia after the end of the Cold War and the Cambodian crisis (Buszynski 1997) and was seen as a "quantum leap in the history of ASEAN economic cooperation" (Abad 1996: 245). The implementation of AFTA was then brought forward from 2008 to 2003, and subsequently to 2002 for ASEAN-6 members,[3] due to three reasons. First, ASEAN members were increasing in confidence and commitment to the process of economic integration. Second, ASEAN members felt the urgency to enhance regional competitiveness in the face of competition from China and India as they reintegrated into global markets and third, the 1997–1998 Asian Financial Crisis revealed the interdependency of East Asian economies and the weakness of international institutions like the IMF.

---

[3]ASEAN-6 refers to the original 5 members of ASEAN (Indonesia, Malaysia, the Philippines, Singapore, Thailand) and Brunei Darussalam.

The ASEAN Economic Community

After the implementation of AFTA in 2003, leaders of ASEAN took yet another noteworthy step in deepening ASEAN economic declaration by signing the Declaration of ASEAN (Bali) Concord II, which would essentially transform AFTA into a single market by 2020 and establish the ASEAN Economic Community (AEC). The AEC was definitely a step further than the AFTA as the agreement was for a "single market and production base where there is a free flow of goods, services, foreign direct investment, freer capital and skilled labour".[4] The shift from a 'free trade area' to an 'economic community' led some observers (such as Pablo-Baviera 2007, 229–230) to argue that AEC indicated ASEAN members' intentions to move from intergovernmentalism toward supranationalism. The positive impacts of constructing the AEC were felt so strongly that by 2007, ASEAN leaders agreed to push forward the deadline for completion to 2015, with a longer timeline of 2018 to 2020 for CLMV countries.[5] ASEAN leaders believed that an integrated market and production base would clearly boost intra-regional trade and investment flows, and an ASEAN consumer market of over half a billion would be attractive for investors.

The AEC was a highly ambitious effort at deeper integration and was bolstered by legal tools such as a dispute settlement mechanism. Compared to AFTA which focused on tariff liberalization the AEC also includes the removal of Non-Tariff Barriers (NTBs) and beyond the border measures affecting goods trade, as well as liberalization of service and investment. The AEC is based on four pillars and its core elements are shown in Table 7.1.

---

[4]Article 1, Paragraph 5 of the Charter of the Association of Southeast Asian Nations (ASEAN) [not sure if this is in the biblio].

[5]CLMV refers to Cambodia, Laos, Myanmar and Vietnam, countries who joined ASEAN at a later date and were less developed than the other 6 members.

Table 7.1 AEC Blueprint—Four pillars and core elements

Pillars	Core elements
A. Single market and production base	A1. Free flow of goods A2. Free flow of services A3. Free flow of investment A4. Freer flow of capital A5. Free flow of skilled labour A6. Priority integration sectors A7. Food, agriculture, and forestry
B. Competitive economic region	B1. Competition policy B2. Consumer protection B3. Intellectual property rights B4. Infrastructure development: 10 strategic approaches B5. Taxation B6. E-commerce
C. Equitable economic development	C1. SME development C2. Initiative for ASEAN Integration
D. Integration into global economy	D1. Coherent approach toward external economic relations D2. Enhanced participation in global supply networks

Source ASEAN economic community (AEC) Blueprint (2007)

The potential gain from AEC is immense. Petri et al. (2012)[6] found that ASEAN economic welfare under the AEC should rise by 5.3% relative to the baseline. All ASEAN countries stand to benefit, ranging from 2.7 to 9.7% increase in welfare gains. The projections from the study also suggested that competition policy alone could raise per capita GDP by 26–38% in ASEAN6. And by creating opportunities for production networks and spreading best practices that boost productivity, AEC should help CLMV converge with ASEAN6. Moreover, the

---

[6]Based on a Computable General Equilibrium (CGE) model of the AEC which incorporates assumptions on the complete elimination of tariffs and NTBs, the liberalization of five service sectors, AEC-induced changes in FDI, and a 5% reduction in trade costs.

paper also argued that the net benefits of the AEC would be larger than the estimated 5.3% increase in ASEAN economic welfare, due to gains that have not been quantified by their model. These include lower cost of capital due to freer movement of capital and improved financial systems; efficiency gains from freer movement of skilled labor; and greater macroeconomic stability due to the conservative macroeconomic policies necessary to support the AEC. The creation of a single market and production base should allow ASEAN to benefit from economies of scale and efficiency in production network processes.

Despite the great economic benefits that ASEAN members stand to gain from AEC, progress has been slow. In fact, as at August 2014, the AEC is said to have achieved only 82.1% of the stipulated targets mentioned in the 2007 Blueprint (ASEAN Secretariat, 2014). The slow progress in domestic reforms have also resulted in a lack of incentive for the private sector to fully utilize regional preferential measures at only around 22% in the region (Basu Das, 2015).

Many have observed that the depth and speed of ASEAN economic integration, when compared with other regions of the world, has been relatively slow. Criticisms of ASEAN have been primarily directed at deficiencies in the organisational structures and the slow pace of institutionalisation of the Association (Sukma 2014). Some have even labelled the AEC a 'failure', and ASEAN a mere 'talk shop', a largely rhetorical forum where process takes precedence over progress (Jones 2016). Yet, we also cannot ignore the fact that economic integration is an incremental process with each path being unique and contingent on each region's peculiarities. Proponents of this view believe that not accomplishing the AEC by 2015 is not an admission of failure of ASEAN's integration effort. Instead, it has started many important initiatives. For example, the data indicates that the AEC has contributed to a sharp growth in intra-ASEAN investment (Razak 2015).

Yet, much of the literature that surrounds the AEC expounds on the possible reasons for ASEAN's slow progress in implementing AEC measures. These include disparities in good governance and the rule of law, large developmental gaps that spurs cross-border illegal migration, too much dependence on open regionalism, weak links between ASEAN and strong distrust between ASEAN members due to political-security conflicts in the region arising from unresolved intra- and extra-regional territorial disputes. The most commonly cited reason for the slow progress of ASEAN integration, though, has been attributed to the 'ASEAN Way', a set of norms and principles that has resulted in the lack of political will for deepening regional integration. ASEAN members are very reluctant to pool sovereignty over some policy areas and delegate it to a regional institution.

ASEAN Way

The ASEAN Way is a set of long-standing norms that have driven the integration process since its founding. From the very beginning, the organisation's modus operandi has revolved around the concepts of musjawarah (consultation) and mufakat (consensus) in dealing with one another. Since its founding, its leaders and institutions have adhered to and internalised the principles of non-interference in domestic affairs, respect for national sovereignty and independence, non-commitments and the avoidance of controversial issues. The ASEAN Way is so important for the organization that its values are enshrined in many official documents including the 1976 Treaty of Amity and Cooperation (TAC), the Bali Concord II and the ASEAN Charter.

Poole (2011) have grouped these the 'ASEAN Way' values into constitutive norms and procedural norms. Constitutive norms include "mutual respect for independence, sovereignty, equality, territorial integrity and national identity of all nations; the right of every State to lead its national existence free from external interference, subversion or coercion and non-interference in the internal affairs of one another" (ASEAN 1976, Art 2). Procedural norms include an informal style of decision-making by consensus, informality and non-binding commitments, pragmatism, and moving at 'a pace comfortable to all'.[7]

---

[7]"At a pace comfortable to all" is a favourite phrase in ASEAN documents, which means advancing as fast, or as slowly, as the most reluctant or least confident member allows'. (Severino 2006).

The ASEAN Way can be credited for being a useful political tool in bringing and keeping countries together in the most diverse neighbourhood in the world. Countries in Southeast Asia are at varying stages of development with developed Singapore's GDP per capita at 47 times that of Cambodia's. Myanmar is still coming to terms with the modern economy. Southeast Asia holds the largest Muslim population, the second largest Christian population and third largest Buddhist population in the world. Moreover, most ASEAN members are not liberal democracies, consisting of a myriad of political systems: democracies, military juntas, socialists, communist states and sultanates. Combined with the diverse colonial legacy left by the Spanish, Dutch, British, Portuguese and Americans and such diversity in the region, it is no wonder that strategic preferences concerning regional integration count more on sovereignty costs and their effects of political stability and economic growth, both of which are central to regime security (Kim 2011). As relatively new independent states,[8] ASEAN came together in 1967 with the recognition of the potential from cooperation but still very keen to the 'norm of equality' as Poole (2011) puts it. It is precisely because of ASEAN's diverse population and their status as young nations that the norm of equal status of members becomes all the more essential. This has resulted in what former Secretary-General Rodolfo Severino (2006) as the 'scrupulous observance of the sovereign equality of the member-states' (p. 32).

Politically, the ASEAN Way has been indispensable in enabling ASEAN to become an effective platform in resolving political issues such as bilateral border disputes between member states. Economically, however, the ASEAN Way is often used as a criticism to explain why processes regarding economic integration move slowly or do not get done. The need for consensus building means that even when contentious issues are not circumvented or avoided altogether, the process of decision-making is slow and drawn out. Advisory committees that do not threaten national sovereignty are also preferred instead of autonomous bodies with sanctioning capacities. It is no surprise then why the ASEAN Way has caused the slow implementation of AEC commitments and is often criticized for hampering collective efforts to address regional problems.

---

[8]With the exception of Thailand, which was never colonized.

Any integration theory would tell you that subscription to any regional organization means that nations do, to some extent, have to surrender some sovereignty and defer it to a decision-making body for the greater good. However, somewhat parodoxically, ASEAN leaders see being part of a regional organization as a means to securing (as opposed to pooling) national sovereignty. This is because many less-than-democratic regimes in Southeast Asia maintain their regime legitimacy through what Ferguson (2004) terms "output effects" of economic growth, political stability, and containment of ethnic or minority tensions. In the eyes of ASEAN states, being more competitive economically in an increasingly interdependent world is a necessary condition for political power and a means to defend and preserve their independence and existing ways. Yet, deeper integration through the creation of a single market can threaten the survival of authoritarian ASEAN regimes by locking them into radically liberal economic reforms that incumbent ruling elites cannot afford. The ASEAN Way was a regional order that allowed member states to focus on, and devote their resources for the more pressing task of nation-building (Sukma 2014). As such, securing sovereignty through regional cooperation and effective nation building has almost always been ASEAN members' top priority when it comes to the issue of regional integration. In practice, this means that even when ASEAN members expect great national benefits through closer economic cooperation, they often sacrifice them if it is perceived to threaten their sovereignty.

One symptom of the ASEAN Way is its aversion to empower the ASEAN Secretariat, the regional bureaucracy. In 2015, when the AEC is scheduled to launch, the ASEAN secretariat has remained largely as it has been since 15 years ago. It has a budget of US$17 million, which comes from an equal contribution of US$1.7 million from each country, and 300 staff. Comparatively, the EU has a budget of US$181 billion and 30,000 staff. This is not to say that such an excessive amount spent in the EU model is right, but the vast disparity in both model certainly highlights the lack of funding for the ASEAN Secretariat. On top of the numbers, the Secretariat has little discretion as even the most menial issues are being decided by the Council or ambassadors. The ASEAN Secretary General also does not have much room to make his own decisions as heads of states or foreign ministers still hold the decision-making powers. The former Secretary General, Dr. Surin Pistuwan, has once half-jokingly said that the ASEAN Secretary-General is more 'Secretary' than 'General' (Razak 2015).

ASEAN's Potential

Indeed, the economic potential of ASEAN today is undeniable. 60% of the region's population of over 600 million are under 35 and its middle class is expected to double from 190 million to 400 million in 2020 (Razak 2015). As a whole, it would be the 7th largest economy in the world with a combined gross domestic product of US$2.4 trillion (ADB 2015). ASEAN's average growth rate of 5.1% makes it the third highest in the world, only behind China and India. With current trajectories, ASEAN's GDP is set to reach US$10 trillion by 2030, which would make it the 4th largest economy. International investors are also recognizing the economic prospects of ASEAN. Consistent strong emphasis on education over the years has put ASEAN ahead of many emerging markets in meeting the needs of international businesses and in 2013, FDI inflows to ASEAN reached US$125 billion, exceeding even that of China's (Razak 2015). Indeed, ASEAN's future looks bright, especially when one observes the forecasted growth rate of ASEAN compared to the rest of the world in Table 7.2.

It is worth emphasizing here that ASEAN often looks toward the EU model and experience and this paper will also make certain comparisons between the processes of ASEAN Integration and the European Integration. This is not to say that the EU 'model' is the mould in which all forms of regionalism should seek to replicate lock stock and barrel. In fact, ASEAN has continually emphasized that its intent not to embark on the exact same path that the EU has, vowing not to

Table 7.2   GDP growth (in %) of ASEAN vs rest of the World (2013–2018)

ASEAN	World	United States	EU	Japan	China	India
5.8	4.2	3.0	1.4	1.3	8.4	6.6

Source IMF World economic outlook, April 2013

"transform itself into a highly bureaucratic organization, or a structure similar to the European Union" (ADBI 2014: xxi). Many scholars have also cautioned against comparing the two integration processes due to their different circumstances (Murray 2010; Kim 2011). For example, the EU model is largely dependent on intra-regional trade and investment among wealthy industrialized democracies with highly developed market structures. Contrastingly, ASEAN is more reliant on strong extra-regional trade and investment and features underdeveloped market structures.

Instead, this chapter adopts the position that there are many paths to development and regional integration, of which the EU's approach is one of them. However, we adopt as an implicit assumption that in the field of regionalism, the EU is at present the only reference from which to judge and measure the pace and degree of regionalism in the world. It is only through this inevitable comparison with Europe that the remarkable differences between the two regions seem to stand out.

The AEC as a Public Good

The theory of public goods can be useful in examining why the progress of the AEC has been slower than expected and give reasons for the collective action problems that ASEAN members face. In fact, the concept of ASEAN public goods is not recent. The Asia Regional Integration Centre (ARIC) categorizes some ASEAN regional public goods as: climate change, clean energy and environmental protection, anti-corruption and good governance (ARIC 2015). ASEAN was itself formed in 1967 based on the idea of 'regional security' as a public good. Due to the threat of political unrest from Indochina, the founding ASEAN states felt unable to guarantee national security by relying exclusively on their own resources and thus saw cooperation as instrumental in ensuring regional security and cohesion by guaranteeing a stronger collective identity (Langhammer 1991).

The concept of the economic ASEAN public good was far more recent. More specifically, it became only evident in the Asian Financial Crisis which highlighted the importance of the public good of regional economic stability (Naya 2005). The crisis demonstrated that ASEAN economies are jointly affected by economic shocks and that policies in one ASEAN country could affect the entire region, as evidenced by the contagion effect. It was since then that ASEAN leaders sought to internalize these externalities through the production of a new public good—ASEAN economic cooperation. The closer integration of ASEAN economies meant that their markets became more symmetrical over time and their business cycles increasingly correlated. The more integrated the economies of different nations are, the more fiscal and monetary policy decisions made in one country can influence economic activities and stability in other countries, thus limiting a nation's autonomy over its own stabilization policies. In turn, the 'public good' nature of appropriate policies in the region becomes more salient. In other words, economic cooperation is akin to a continuous cycle where integration begets more integration and the production of public goods begets more public goods.

If we say that an economic good is "a reproducible thing or event that affects individuals' needs, desires and preferences positively or negatively" (Collignon 2011: 4) and "something from which some utility or benefit is derived" (Collignon 2003: 91), then we can adopt the view that good governance or effective policies are public goods. Just like the global governance of environmental protection is a widely-accepted global public good, so is regional governance over economic integration. As such, even ASEAN economic integration policies such as the AEC, which is inherently a policy for the "creation of a single market and production base", would be considered a public good. Moreover, the AEC embodies the characteristics of public goods mentioned in the second chapter of this book. First, the benefits of the AEC are available to all members and these benefits are non-rivalrous—one country's welfare benefits gained from integration does not subtract from another. The policies of the AEC also produce externalities and are thus unlikely to be provided by private actors and justifies state intervention. Without government action, such goods are liable to under-provision.

If one looks at the 4 pillars of the AEC, it is undeniable that they all share the same properties of public goods as explained above—(1) the creation of a single market and production base; (2) the construction of a competitive economic region; (3) equitable economic development and (4) integration into the global economy. Within these four pillars, there are yet other ASEAN public goods under each umbrella such as the Common Effective Preferential Tariff (CEPT) Scheme, the Single Window, the free movement of resources, competition policy etc. As we can see, the AEC is a public good which has in turn also caused the production of many other public goods, all of which with its own externalities that affect the whole of ASEAN.

However, the AEC is not a pure public good. Its benefits are excludable as it is available for all ASEAN citizens, but exclude non-ASEANs. This makes it a club good whereby a toll or membership fee applies in order for governments to be part of the 'club' and reap the benefits of the regional organization. These fees are then used to expand and maintain the shared good.

Robert Berith in Chap. 2 has also explained how club goods are inclusive in that ever additional consumer in the 'club' causes additional benefits for other consumers as average costs per member fall or average benefits increase and members subsequently have an interest in including more potential consumers.

The level of economic integration that ASEAN is going through is very much similar to the early stages of European Integration. During the early years, the EU was characterized by the provision of inclusive club goods such as the customs union, the single market and the Schengen Agreement. Such policies are European club goods as only those who fulfil certain criteria are admitted as members. My co-author, Stefan Collignon (2003), has argued that these European club goods are inclusive in the sense that such goods generated incentives to cooperate—any one state's decision generates externalities which cause everyone else to move in the same direction. In other words, the creation of a customs union, up to the single market, could be justified in terms of welfare gains from cooperation. As such, they can be provided on a voluntary and cooperative basis in the form of voluntary intergovernmental policy coordination. Only when it comes to exclusive common property resources is when the Union requires a political process beyond mere coordination to achieve an efficient resource allocation. In short, Collignon's (2003) argument was that although the early phases of EU integration were influenced by inclusive club goods that produced win-win situations and community interests, the later stages of integration involved the creation of exclusive collective goods which required harder forms of coordination.

When you compare this with ASEAN, it is very much still at the 'inclusive club good' phase, where positive externalities should force everyone to voluntary coordinate policies for the greater good of the entire region. Yet, the progress of the AEC has been slower than expected and collective action problems have arisen. By classifying the AEC as a public good, we can further examine and better understand the collective action problems of the regional grouping. For example, a frequently mentioned reason for the under-provision of public goods has become known as the prisoner's dilemma. It characterizes a situation in which the independent pursuit of self-interest makes both worse off than they would be, if they had cooperated. There are also increasing amounts of externalities in the AEC, both positive and negative, and markets cannot alone satisfactorily manage the externalities of the creation of the AEC. A central authority is needed. Increased cross-border flows brought about by the AEC requires international coordination if resources are to be allocated efficiently to their most valued use. The following section examine these factors in greater detail and understand why ASEAN is facing various collective action problems.

Obstacles to ASEAN Economic Integration

Increasing Externalities

Externalities or 'spillovers' are external and indirect effects that confer appreciable costs or benefits to parties that are not fully consenting in reaching the decisions that led to the event in in question (Meade 1973). Externalities occur whenever an individual or firm undertakes an action that has an effect on another individual, for which the latter is not compensated for. As Robert Berith in the first chapter has explained, today's interconnected world means that decisions made in one state have repercussions or spillovers in the jurisdictions of other states. Collignon (2011) argues that it is the nature of externalities that is the crucial criterion for the definition and scope of public goods. Different categories of public goods produce different externalities and thus offer contrasting incentives for coordinated action. Even government intervention in the provision of public goods can itself create externalities.

This section argues that one of the main obstacles to fulfilling the commitments of the AEC is that the shift from AFTA to AEC produces increasing externalities. Indeed, to understand the significant leap that ASEAN leaders have taken by committing to the AEC, we first need to understand the four levels of economic integration or regionalism based on the depth of integration and the institutional framework of the region (Panagariya 1999; Cuyvers 2002)

1. *Free Trade Area (FTA):* The lowest level of economic integration is reached when members agree to remove trade barriers of goods and services, such as tariffs and quotas. Each member, however, retains its independent system of tariff duties on products from non-member countries.
2. *Customs Union*: The second level of economic integration is a Customs Union whereby member states agree to not only reduce trade barriers against each other, but also implement common trade regulations with respect to non-members through the implementation of Common External Tariff (CET).
3. *Common Market*: On top of the free movement of goods and services and the implementation of a CET, the third level also consists of the removal of all barriers to movement for labour and capital. This scheme is also often combined with a broader common policy aiming at policy harmonization in the region.
4. *Economic Union*: The highest level of regional economic integration is reached when an Economic Union is established. On top of a common market, an Economic Union also brings about the unification of formal economic institutions. Members also agree on broader and deeper coordination of economic policies to maintain free movement of goods, services, persons, capital, including common currency and monetary policy.

As a Free Trade Area, AFTA is an example of the first level of economic integration. The AEC, however, does not fit neatly into any of the above categories. Despite the use of the term 'economic community', the AEC is most certainly not at the fourth level of 'Economic Union'. It is also neither at the 'Customs Union' stage since it does not adopt a common external tariff system, nor at the 'Common Market' stage as it only aims for the 'freer' flow (as opposed to completely 'free') of capital and skilled labour.

Yet, despite the ambiguity, it is undeniable that the AEC is a significant step above a Free Trade Area. Unlike in a free trade agreement like AFTA, the AEC requires that all barriers to trade in goods and services as well as investment be fully removed. Transitioning from the first level of economic integration (AFTA) to the next level of economic integration is certainly no small feat.

At the FTA stage of economic integration, although member states recognize the need for collaboration to reap benefits, they are still competitors, each with its own economic and political systems with different economic philosophies (Langhammer 1991). The primary goal at this stage is to lower or eliminate tariffs and quotas. As such, economic cooperation relied mostly on national measures and any policies needed to facilitate cooperation remained in the domain of the nation state. Policies such as "home country rule", "country-of-origin principle" and "mutual recognition of national policies" are predominantly policies that are implemented by the nation state. While striving for AFTA, ASEAN states saw no need to shift responsibility from the national to the regional level and negotiate a common regional policy such as competition or intellectual property policies.

As tariff rates became almost non-existent within ASEAN and a free trade regime has been established, the AEC goes one step further and aims to tackle the more difficult issues of Non-Tariff Barriers (NTBs), trade in services, financial services integration, customs harmonization and the movement of labour and talent. The removal of NTBs, in particular, have been a persistent obstacle which impedes ASEAN integration and are still notoriously prevalent among member states (Kawai and Wignaraja 2011a, b; Hu 2013). The ASEAN Trade in Goods Agreement (ATIGA) defines NTBs as "measures other than tariffs which effectively prohibit or restrict imports or exports of goods within Member States" (ASEAN 2009). As of March 2016, the WTO listed ASEAN as having over 2000 NTBs, an increase of almost 30% compared to 2010 (WTO 2016).[9] Compared to tariffs and quotas which are 'at the border' measures, NTBs are usually 'beyond the border' measures such as industrial standards, regulations and domestic laws of each member country that prevent the free movement and access of goods and services across the region and consequently the competitiveness of goods after they cross borders. Some examples of NTBs include high business registration costs or poor domestic infrastructure which increase firms' production costs, technical barriers to trade or sanitary standards which translates into higher domestic and export prices, restricting trade.

Thus, we observe that the move from AFTA to AEC equates to moving from at the border measures such as tariffs and quotas to beyond the border measures such as NTBs. In order to internalise these externalities, it requires a move from national to regional policy making where there is a unified policy on issues like competition, government procurement, subsidies and other issues. As integration deepens, there is a greater need for policy coordination as the externalities or 'spillovers' that one country's actions would have on another increases. The more likely that the degree of effectiveness of one state's policies can be hampered by policies of another state, the more there is a need to coordinate national policies and shift decision-making from the national to the regional level. In turn, the policies that result have greater externalities still on other states. As integration deepens, the less control each member state has over their own domestic policies, as they are unable to callously amend laws without first consulting and agreeing with other member states who would be impacted by the change in laws.

---

[9]Data calculated by author. Based on information from WTO, Integrated Trade Intelligence Portal. Retrieved 2 March, 2016 from https://i-tip.wto.org/goods/Forms/MemberView.aspx?data=default.

Information Asymmetries

Externalities are also very much related to information asymmetries. By nature, externalities are not always known by every party and information is asymmetric when one side of a transaction is knowledgeable while the other is not. Uncertainty must be resolved before nations are prepared to act and collective action can be achieved. For example, what are the distribution of costs and benefits involved in the transaction? What are the consequences of inactivity? Uncertainty regarding the net benefits and costs from action is anticipated to inhibit decisiveness especially when actions require huge expenditures or costs. Countries cannot be expected to make costly investments unless the associated payoffs are known. As such, when it comes to collective action, information is therefore a valued commodity.

Akin to the Prisoners' Dilemma, which Sebastian Salch discussed in the Chap. 6, if information is absent, a party is only able to see how he can benefit and does not realize how he is affecting the common good. Going back to the case of Non-Tariff Barriers, for example, the reason why they have been increasing might well be because ASEAN member states want to protect their domestic (and often infant or underdeveloped) industries from external competition as tariff rates go down. In this scenario, every state has an interest in acting in his own interest because all the benefits will accrue to him. But by doing so, negative externalities would be felt by all other parties. The tragedy is that because individual incentives deviate from collective incentives, and there is no external enforcement, everyone is bound to suffer. To solve the Prisoners' Dilemma, Salch has elaborated on how informational asymmetries can be overcome by having an external body ensure compliance and minimise the possibility of free-riding. In fact, once sufficiently credible information is available, Sandler (1997) argues, most transnational problems can be resolved in one way or another. Institutions could play a role in reducing information asymmetries regarding (1) expectations of agents' intentions, that is, whether others will behave in a certain way and (2) that their cooperative behaviour would benefit themselves. Only when information of the above two factors are fulfilled can negotiations start and cooperation follow (Sandler 1997).

It is thus necessary that actors have information and knowledge about how others will behave. If agents expect others to behave in a certain way and expect that their cooperative behavior generates benefits for themselves, they will choose to cooperate. Otherwise, they will not. Asymmetric information about agents' intentions can generate expectations of non-cooperation and therefore, yield suboptimal welfare equilibria. The removal of uncertainty is in itself a transnational public good whose provision may require collective action.

But even when there is an external body to provide information, it has to be transparent and efficient. In the case of ASEAN, decision-making and implementation of commitments suffer from a lack of transparency due to the 'ASEAN Way'. Member states have traditionally rejected the 'legalistic', formal style of Western institutional structures, and instead favour a private and informal political culture embodied by small elite networks. The ASEAN Way norm of non-interference in internal affairs entails that domestic governance is excluded as a criterion of membership of ASEAN, and as a topic of official dialogue. They are spared the embarrassment of dissent, through closed-door dialogue that precedes formal meetings with final decisions officially made by 'consensus' (Acharya 2014). Each member also refrains from criticizing the policies of others in public" and this subdues bilateral tensions (Katsumata 2003: 107). Regional institutions in ASEAN often lack transparency and accountability, key anti-corruption laws are absent and civil society engagement is restricted (Transparency International 2015). Although ASEAN has made progress in publicizing its many initiatives, it has a rather poor record in informing the public about the implementation and outcomes of these initiatives. Many observers have complained about ASEAN's lack of transparency. One of the key manifestations of a lack of transparency in the AEC is the fact that the AEC Scorecards, the tool for monitoring and reporting on the progress of AEC implementation, is based entirely on member states' self-reporting, academic and business observers are highly skeptical of even this limited progress report. The Secretariat has subsequently discontinued its scorecards, relying instead on secret ERIA reports, suggesting that these criticisms are accurate (Jones 2016).

Different Marginal Benefits and Costs

One of the factors that affect successful collective action outcomes in determining the provision of transnational public goods is the balance between nation-specific and group benefits. For a transnational public good to be provided, the marginal benefits for the entire group must be equal to or exceed the group marginal costs of the public good. Collective action is easier to achieve if there are mutual net gains for all participating countries. Although this is a necessary condition in order for the public good to be provided voluntarily by the group, it is not a sufficient condition. Even though total group marginal benefits might equal or exceed total group marginal costs, the public good would not be provided for if the nation-specific marginal benefits do not equal or exceed the nation-specific costs. If the benefits for one government are less than the total cost of providing the good, there is a rational incentive to this government not to participate in the collective good and to free ride. These benefits and costs cannot be measured only in economic terms but must also encompass political and social factors as well.

Another necessary condition is the proportion of nation-specific marginal benefits to group benefits. Even if a country has nation-specific marginal benefits that equal or exceed the nation-specific costs, if they feel as if the net gains from collective action is not equitably distributed, they might still choose not to participate in the collective action. If some nations gain more relative to others, then those that gain the least may resist supporting the action. For nations that gain the least, an action on their part does not provide any nation-specific benefits that bolster the states' share of group gains. Instead, the nation-specific costs may dwarf the nation's share of the resulting benefits. Therefore, as the proportion of nation-specific benefits to total benefits increases, the likelihood of national action increases (Sandler and Forbes 1980; Sandler 1992).

To illustrate the above point in the context of the EU, Collignon (2003) provides a European example:

> The benefit of the Common Agricultural Policy, the single market or EMU would depend on the size of the market in terms of euros, GDP

etc. Yet, the benefit to an individual member of the group would depend upon the fraction or share of the group gain he or she would be able to appropriate. How much of the collective good will be optimal depends on the calculation of marginal benefits and costs of individual group members with respect to quantity.

To summarise, the conditions that must be fulfilled in order for a transnational public good to be provided is as follows:

1. The *sum* of marginal benefit must exceed or equal the *sum* of marginal cost.
2. The *sum* of every actor's individual contributions must cover the *sum* of marginal cost of producing the transnational public good.
3. *Nation-specific* benefit must exceed or equal *nation-specific* cost.
4. Proportion of *national-specific* benefit to *group benefit* must be equitable.

Regarding conditions 2 to 4, we can see that the individual nation plays a big part in determining whether the public good is provided. In other words, whether the individual decides to contribute to the collective good depends largely on the rate or level at which the good is obtained and on the value assigned to it.

Different Individual Marginal Benefits from the AEC

Table 7.3 by Petri et al. (2012) depicts the welfare gains from the AEC in 2015. The table shows that although the AEC will result in overall aggregate gains, each country stands to benefit differently.

From Table 7.3, we see that the full implementation of the AEC would increase ASEAN real incomes by US$69.4 billion, or 5.3% over 2004 baseline income. The amount of benefits that would be derived from the AEC are indeed substantial due to the comprehensive ambitions of the AEC project and are larger than those compared to other studies of free trade areas. In fact, they are similar in magnitude to the estimates for the European Single Market. Also, we notice that all

Table 7.3   Welfare gains of the AEC in 2015

	$ billion, 2004 price	Percentage of baseline GDP*
Brunei Darussalam	0.5	7.0
Cambodia	0.6	6.3
Indonesia	27.6	6.2
Lao PDR	0.2	3.6
Malaysia	5.7	3.0
Myanmar	0.6	4.4
Philippines	4.5	3.2
Singapore	15.1	9.7
Thailand	12.2	4.9
Vietnam	2.4	2.8
ASEAN Total	69.4	5.3

Source Petri, Plummer and Zhai 2012
The percentage figures are used instead of aggregate amounts as it takes into
account real ASEAN incomes.

ASEAN members stand to benefit from the AEC, although some benefit more than others. For example, Singapore will achieve welfare gains of 9.7% in terms of an increase in GDP due to its nature as an open economy that has very intensive trade relations with the region. It thus stands to gain most from the removal of regional trade barriers. The benefits are also relatively large in percentage terms for economies that are relatively heavily protected by tariffs and NTBs, such as Cambodia and Indonesia.

Instead, Vietnam would only achieve a welfare gain of 2.8% increase in GDP. In other words, Singapore stands to gain more than 3 times that of Vietnam. In fact, other evidence has shown that ASEAN members have themselves felt this difference in individual marginal benefits. For example, larger economies like Indonesia has been more averse to deeper integration due to their status as the biggest economy in ASEAN, thus they have less of a need to achieve economies of scale through trade openness. Other ASEAN leaders have also openly voiced their views that the more competitive smaller ASEAN economies (particularly Singapore) would gain more from an integrated regional market (Razak 2015).

Thus, we can see from the ASEAN case that one of the factors that might hinder cooperation in ASEAN is the fact that individual marginal benefits are different. Net benefits are not the only thing that matters when it comes to cooperation between states, but also the proportion of benefits that are nation-specific. Even when the benefits of cooperation are large, cooperation is harder to achieve if these benefits are concentrated in a state besides your own.

Not Only Different Benefits, but Different Costs

The problem of cooperation is exacerbated by the fact that many countries have different levels of 'costs' when it comes to deepening integration. Firstly, there is significant variation among ASEAN members in the level of external tariffs against non-members. For example, this ranges from 0.1% for Singapore to 43.2% for Thailand (Kim 2011). Moreover, tariffs are also a major source of government revenues for most ASEAN members. Cambodia, for instance, derives about 70% of its government income from import-related taxes. CLMV countries are reluctant to reduce tariffs because it will not only mean losing substantial amount of customs revenue from ASEAN imports but will also generate huge social costs for structural adjustments (Tongzon and Khan 2005).

Domestic factors also present a huge cost to some member states. For example, Indonesia's ruling elites have feared that lower (or no) tariffs through AEC could result in a flood of cheaper regional products into the country, generating electoral pressures and hurting its competitiveness both regionally and globally (Smith 1999). Politically important industries like agriculture in Thailand and Indonesia, automobiles in Malaysia, petrochemicals in Philippines and Thailand, textiles in Cambodia and the Philippines is also feared not to be able to withstand regional competition. This could explain Indonesia's and Malaysia's backtracking in 2005 on their trade liberalization commitments in the automobiles, petrochemicals and agriculture sectors (Nesadurai 2006).

Pressures from state-owned firms and private businesses intimately connected to political elites for protection against regional competition are also very strong (Jayasuriya 2004). The military-linked businesses and small inner circle of ethnic Chinese konglomerat in Indonesia, the clientelist business networks and a group of Malay entrepreneurs in

Malaysia and the business tycoons backed by bureaucrats and the military in Thailand, are all examples of individuals with 'vested interests' that prevent ASEAN economic integration. There are definitely factors involving cronyism at play—given the critical role of these groups' support for political survival, authoritarian ASEAN leaders had vigorously pursued economic policies that protected and maximized these groups interests.

In this way, we can see that ASEAN member state governments, although have lots to gain from economic integration, also face many 'costs' that might affect their decision to contribute to the public good. As we have explained above, if the benefits for one government are less than the total cost of providing the collective good, there is a rational incentive for this government not to participate in the ASEAN's provision of the collective good and to free ride. There are two problems here. Firstly, since there is no effective enforcement mechanism and a credible dispute settlement institution, states fear that other member states might not fulfil their commitments to a single market and essentially free ride on the effects of others. Secondly, the benefits and costs experienced by each government might not be aligned to the citizens of that state. Without a monitoring or enforcing mechanism, governments are free to do as they desire, thereby pursuing a path that brings most benefits to themselves.

Developmental Gaps and the Lack of Leadership or a Redistributive Mechanism

However, economic integration will almost always result in different individual marginal benefits in any kind of grouping. This is especially true when the grouping is composed of actors with largely different preferences. This is the case for ASEAN, which is composed of a large developmental gap between ASEAN-6 and CLMV countries. Since expanding membership to Cambodia, Laos, Myanmar and Vietnam from 1995–1999, the developmental gap within ASEAN has widened dramatically. In 2013, the biggest gap in terms of GDP per capita within ASEAN was 46 times, between Singapore (US\$ 54,648) and

Myanmar (US\$ 1183.5) (UNSD 2013). By contrast, the ratio in the EU of its highest GDP per capita member, Luxembourg, and that of its lowest, Bulgaria, is only approximate 7 times. Some see ASEAN's vastly different levels of development between and within members in income, human capital, institutions and infrastructure as an advantage as the region can leverage on economies at different levels of economic development to provide complementary locations for production networks. Yet, because of the vast developmental gap, CLMV countries lack the capacity to implement the commitments of the AEC and are understandably reluctant to open up their domestic markets due to the need to protect their infant industries. They also have less open political systems, lower levels for economic development and little experience in participating in regional institutions (Wesley 1999). Needless to say, the costs and benefits of regional integration experienced by CLMV countries are vastly different from those experienced by ASEAN-6 states.

However, despite different individual marginal benefits, the provision of a public good can still be optimal if those who derive more net benefits from the collective good should then pay for the production costs of the collective good. For example, the provision of a public good could still be optimal if the group is privileged—i.e. if it contains members who derive sufficient net benefits from belonging to the Union so that they are willing to pay for the cost of the collective good. The European integration process, for instance, has been driven largely by France and Germany. Because both countries derived considerable benefits from European Economic integration, they cooperated to be the motors of European integration and covered the costs of providing European collective goods.

Unlike the EU before the Euro Crisis, ASEAN lacks leadership in the drive for integration. Acharya (2014) has written about collective action in Asia suffering from a "capability-legitimacy gap". Successful collective action requires leadership with both capability (in terms of material resources) and political legitimacy. Although Singapore fulfils the role of the most developed country in ASEAN and could therefore fulfil the material capability requirement, it lacks legitimacy. Contrastingly, it could be said that Indonesia has the most legitimacy if one considers that it is the largest ASEAN state with the highest overall GDP, but it lacks capability. Similarly, Mattli (1999) emphasizes the importance of undisputed regional leadership in the regional integration process. He believes that such a state would serve "as a focal point in the coordination of rules, regulations, and policies; it may also help to ease distributional tensions by acting as regional paymaster". ASEAN's lack of a regional leader means that it not only lacks a 'driver for integration' but also a 'paymaster' that is willing to supply the costs of the public good.

Regional economic integration can therefore only be as successful as its 'weakest link' state. The accelerated process of market liberalisation for regional integration brings along with it the risk of provoking further distributional problems due to intensified competition. Hence, when different countries of various development levels agree to integrate their economies, institutional mechanisms need to be designed in order to cope with the divergence between countries involved. There are many reasons that support the establishment of redistributive mechanisms. Firstly, there is evidence that regional economic integration intensifies present regional disparities (Venables 2005). Secondly, it is also argued that side-payments are necessary to ease the concern held by less developed members toward regional integration. For example, the EU Cohesion Fund[10] only came into existence when Italy and Ireland threatened to boycott the 1974 Paris Summit due to disagreement over how best to deal with regional disparities.

In fact, redistribution policies can itself be considered a regional public good. It has non-rival and non-excludable benefits as it reduces regional disparities and increases regional solidarity for all its members. It also cannot be adequately provided by individual member countries and thus intervention by a regional entity is required to ensure optimal provision. The importance of redistributive policies is apparent in the EU. Reducing income disparity (between and within countries) by redistributing funds from richer to poorer member states is achieved through the Cohesion Policy, a compensatory regional transfer

---

[10]Or the European Regional Development Fund, as it was known at that time.

mechanism that is used to tackle regional income gaps. It is essentially a transfer from richer parts of the EU to poorer ones, aiming to achieve higher growth in poorer regions. In the case of the EU, redistribution is necessary to achieve positive externalities as "the interdependence of EU economies means that the stimulation of economic development in one area will have positive knock-on effects on others" (Zuleeg 2009: 5). Previous EU Commissioner for Regional Policy, Danuta Hübner has stated that the main aim of cohesion policy is to provide public goods aimed at "improving skills, innovation capacity, entrepreneurship, sustainability, employment and accessibility, to enable all European territories to realise their full potential" (Hübner 2008).

Even other South-South regional integration projects have various forms of regional redistribution schemes. In Africa for example, tax transfers are used to reduce regional disparities. In the French-speaking West African monetary union and Central African equivalent, so called community solidarity tax is collected to pay compensation for landlocked Sahel countries which lose tariff revenues due to the removal of internal tariff (Masujima 2013). ASEAN's main program for dealing specifically with the CLMV countries is the Initiative for ASEAN Integration, a programme established in 2000, whose objective is "Narrowing the Development Gap" (Severino 2006). However, it is not a direct transfer system and only emphasizes technical assistance and partnership with dialogue partners.

No Mechanism for Preference Revelation

As Robert Berith explained in Chap. 2, one of the main problems with the provision of public goods is that a provider cannot keep a non-payer from consuming the good's benefits. Even if users have a strong desire for a good, they have no incentive to reveal their preference for the good via bidding for it with a price. They understate or hide their true preferences, hoping to free ride and enjoy the good for nothing. It is thus difficult to induce individuals to truthfully reveal their preferences concerning public goods and efforts to judge the true demand of pure public goods by asking respondents to reveal what benefits they derive are doomed to failure. Instead, Berith has shown how the optimal provision of public goods is dependent on other preference revelation mechanisms such as voting on policies or contributions to a regional fund. For example, EU member states make contributions to the Union based on their respective GDPs and so does the Organisation of American States (OAS) and the African Union (AU).

ASEAN, however, remains the only major regional organization that maintains a system of equal contributions (Poole 2011) and has no voting mechanism when making decisions. Unlike other major regional intergovernmental organisations, ASEAN member states make equal contributions, which are kept low enough for the less-developed states to manage. Moreover, annual increments to the budget is agreed by consensus and therefore kept hostage to what the least willing member could pay. This does not only mean that they have no means to reveal their preferences through their contributions, but also means that ASEAN is constantly having its hands tied its back by a lack of resources. This is the same with voting. The EU has frequently revised their treaties to increase the efficiency of policymaking in a larger Union (e.g. majority vote to Qualified Majority Voting). But despite the expansion of membership to CLMV countries, the voting mechanism in ASEAN has always stayed the same—through consensus. The problem with consensus is that it ensures that cooperation is only achieved on the lowest common denominator policies. Although Article 20.2 of the ASEAN Charter allows the ASEAN Summit to decide how a decision can be made in the absence of consensus, it has never been used.

As such, ASEAN has no existing mechanism to reveal preferences regarding integration. Given the large differences in resource endowment, size, per capita income level and political heritage, ASEAN countries would rarely have identical preferences. Nor had there been a hegemonic power within ASEAN which enforced its preferences. ASEAN needs some form of mechanism for honest accurate revelation of individual preferences.

Strengthening ASEAN Institutions for the Better Governance of ASEAN Public Goods

Central Level or Voluntary Cooperation?

We have now analysed, using the theory of public goods, why ASEAN is facing difficulties with the AEC. Now, we will seek to address the how. Specifically, how can ASEAN solve the problems that have been mentioned in the previous section? This section would argue that ASEAN needs to strengthen its institutions in order to overcome the problems illustrated in the previous chapter.

We are confronted with two solutions when it comes to overcoming ASEAN's collective action problems: ASEAN states can either delegate part of their sovereignty to a central regional entity, or voluntarily co-ordinate their policies. As previously mentioned, Collignon (2003) argues that for inclusive club goods, marginal net benefits might increase whilst for exclusive collective and pure public goods benefits will fall (p. 109). The implication of this is that only inclusive club goods might be provided efficiently by voluntary intergovernmental policy co-ordination. In fact, this is what we have seen happening in ASEAN. Since 1967, much has been achieved in ASEAN without a decision-making mechanism or a supranational entity. All parties involved understood that further integration would bring about benefits that outweigh the costs.

However, we have shown that despite being at the inclusive club good stage, voluntary cooperation has not worked when it comes to the AEC due to (1) increasing externalities and information asymmetries (2) different marginal benefits and costs (3) developmental gaps and the lack of leadership or a redistributive mechanism and (4) the lack of a preference revelation mechanism. The appropriate conclusion then, is to strengthen institutional arrangements to better govern the ASEAN public good of economic integration. If not, the regional organization risks losing its momentum of economic integration.

As such, ASEAN states has to redouble its commitment in undertaking greater institutionalisation efforts. ASEAN needs an 'agent of integration' that is not necessarily supranational in structure, much like the European Commission, but an independent institution that acts as an honest broker in coordinating policies, monitoring commitments and driving integration. After all, to leave the efforts of integration to governments is to leave it in the hands of agents that "have much to lose and little to gain from giving powers away and this fact may distort an efficient assignment" (Collignon 2003: 95).

Unlike the EU, ASEAN does not have strong regional institutions to deal with economic integration. Nor does ASEAN have detailed legal agreements and robust dispute settlement procedures like NAFTA. The current principal coordinating mechanism of the integration effort is the ASEAN Secretariat, which has often been accused of being weak and ineffectual. The ASEAN Secretariat has virtually no powers over the ASEAN member states to cajole or compel compliance with AEC measures. Unlike the European Commission, the ASEAN Secretariat cannot initiate legal action against a member state; dispute resolution can only be initiated by another member state. Moreover, the ASEAN Secretariat cannot, like the EU Commission, impose sanctions on a non-compliant member state. Instead, the ASEAN Secretariat's one and only tool is the potential to name and shame non-compliant member states in its AEC Scorecard.[11] The annual operating budget of the ASEAN Secretariat is about US$ 18 million annually and currently has around 300 personnel. It is restricted by ASEAN's policy of funding common expenditures with equal contributions by all members regardless of population size or economic development. Ostensibly this is to encourage consensus among the ASEAN member states, as equal contributions mean equal consideration during the policy making process. Although leaders recognize the implications of these constraints, they have yet to agree on relaxing them (Petri et al. 2012).

It is not that the Jakarta-based ASEAN Secretariat is weak per se but its weakness resides in the functions it has legitimately been assigned. The ASEAN Secretariat is also neither mandated nor positioned to

---

[11]To track progress towards the AEC 2015, a scorecard mechanism has been developed to monitor the implementation of measures listed in the AEC Blueprint.

assess the progress of AEC implementation independently. Unlike the European Commission, the ASEAN Secretariat cannot investigate the behaviour of member states and Instead, it must rely on self-reporting by the member states to prepare the AEC scorecard. Consequently, the current approach to monitoring and disseminating data on regional economic integration is largely driven by political motives and incentives (Dosch 2015). For example, the need for national governments, and ASEAN collectively, to demonstrate substantial progress toward the implementation of the AEC. Therefore, there is a need to augment the ASEAN Secretariat because it is the only ASEAN institution which can be counted upon to act on behalf of the common goals of the AEC. If given the choice, ASEAN national governments will almost always act to serve their self-interest and free ride on the efforts of other members.

The Case for Increased Institutionalisation

The theory of public goods was initially statist in nature—nation states with general taxing powers and a monopoly of the legitimate use of force facilitated the production of national public goods. When it comes to global public goods, however, the more salient challenge internationally is that there is a lack of legitimate, centralized institutions with general taxing and regulatory powers. In the case of ASEAN, and many other instances of international cooperation, states have thus traditionally depended on cooperation which involved decentralized forms of implementation and enforcement domestically to advance collective goals. International law is one tool that facilitates cooperation by creating international institutions and common norms and rules, thereby reducing transaction, monitoring, and enforcement costs and building shared understandings. States created institutions such as the UN and its Security Council to help to ensure the global public good of international peace and security; the World Health Organization (WHO) to protect public health from the spread of infectious diseases; the World Trade Organization (WTO) to address trade liberalization and the International Monetary Fund (IMF) to stabilize currency and sovereign debt crises. Concerns addressed by these institutions are over global public goods. Yet, none of these institutions have a general taxing power to address them. Instead, all of them depend on negotiations between states over the amount of 'contributions' (Shaffer 2012).

Before, we have elaborated on how the transition from a free trade area to an 'economic community' means addressing 'beyond the border' issues which lead to an increase in externalities in the region. In such a case, Oates' decentralization theorem does not hold, since there is a violation of the principle of fiscal equivalence due to the presence of externalities. Collignon (2003) explains the associated inefficiencies that would occur if decisions were indeed taken at local level: "The more jurisdictions take decisions independently from each other in a given policy domain, the greater is the likelihood that the outcome of their policies will conflict or create externalities for each other" (p. 107). Put differently, the decentralization theorem, or the principle of subsidiarity, would likely create policy coordination failures over a wide range of collective goods. This is the case with ASEAN, where deepening economic integration has enlarged the policy domain, thus producing more spillovers and externalities.

Thus, the appropriate conclusion is that when it comes to the AEC, economic policy-making can no longer remain fragmentized between different member states, who rely on the formulation of policy preferences based on what emerges from their domestic epistemic constituencies. For example, substantial NTBs remain whose perceived aim is to protect or assist domestic industry. When one government takes the decision not to abide by its commitment to lower NTBs because of its own key domestic players, this slows down the integration process and affects the economies of all other states in ASEAN. When countries back out and not respect their prior commitments in an agreement, there are undoubtedly externalities, other states might have already spent huge investment in changing their systems. Institutions are therefore key in this aspect in order to monitor and enforce the commitment of states that do not contribute and 'free ride' on the commitment of others. As the Eminent Persons Group (EPG) has noted, the main problem with ASEAN is not the lack of vision, but the lack of responsibility to implement (ASEAN 2006: 21). Where decisions over implementation can have negative externalities, international legal obligations and institutions that constrain unilateral action can better ensure fairness and manage conflicts, and possibly produce public goods more efficiently. There is a greater need for centralized institutions to produce public goods, which means that some relinquishment of national sovereignty is inevitable.

Institutions are also needed to overcome informational asymmetries and the problems of the Tragedy of Commons. Reducing information asymmetries can be achieved by appointing an impartial adjudicator that ensures that the information circulates freely and completely. In the EU, this was one of the principle functions of the European Commission, which reassured member state governments that they had good reasons to expect their contributions to yield benefits that would increase general welfare. Such institutions could reduce information asymmetries when one does not understand how his individual action would affect the common good. A centralized authority could overcome such informational asymmetries by having the means to monitor and enforce compliance.

If ASEAN views the AEC as a collective or public good that affects all citizens of ASEAN and wants to continue doing more in its post-2015 agenda, it needs to increase the capabilities and resources for the governance of this public good. With neither strong regional institutions nor robust dispute resolution, there is nothing in the AEC to hold ASEAN member states accountable to their AEC responsibilities, particularly on issues related to market access and competition after goods, services, capital and people cross the national borders. ASEAN is essentially transitioning to a common market, which means that it has increasing number of public goods, widening the policy domain and increasing externalities in the region. The incidences whereby citizens of another state would become affected by a decision made in a state would only increase. A certain degree of centralized decisions, operations and human and financial resources to govern the newly created markets is needed. Eventually, ASEAN members must agree on the adoption of common rules and regulations, the provision of a proper feedback system, the introduction of sanctions, and the use of compensating mechanisms for those who are negatively affected by regional economic integration.

Institutions can also serve as the 'redistribution' mechanism in fiscal federalism theory and solve the large development gap between ASEAN6 and the CLMV countries. As mentioned before, ASEAN suffers from a problem of developmental gaps and lacks not only leadership in the drive for integration but also a redistributive mechanism. As such, when different countries of various development levels agree to integrate their economies, institutional mechanisms need to be designed in order to cope with divergence between, as well as within the countries. Centralized governance can help to address distributive concerns. Centralized institutions, operating under a constitutional frame of checks and balances, can help to keep national decision-makers accountable (Shaffer 2012). Institutions can help facilitate interaction that can produce shared understandings and common purposes. Unilateral action is problematic because it can be self-serving and fail to take account of the values and perspectives of affected others (Shaffer 2012).

New Procedural Rules for ASEAN?

We have already discussed the need for stronger institutionalism in ASEAN. Yet this cannot be achieved if the underlying norms and values of the 'ASEAN Way' remain. Different forms of institutional processes may encompass different biases of participation and present alternative decision-making processes that define priorities and goals (Shaffer 2012). International institutions can assume a wide variety of forms, ranging from very loosely integrated linkages (for example, NATO alliance) to tightly linked structures where participating countries act like a single decision-making unit. Greater tightness can take the form of a smaller decision-making majority, a larger share of common funding of the collective action, more frequent meetings, less lee-way for binding decisions and stricter sanctions for non-compliance (Sandler and Forbes 1980). As such, before the choice of institution, ASEAN needs to first reexamine its underlying norms and its 'rules of the game'.

Collignon (2003) argues that the issue with cooperative action in regional groupings are less about "distribution" issues and more about "constitutional arrangements"; conflict about distributional outcomes can be overcome by procedural rules. This is certainly no easy feat when it comes to regional groupings. While nations can internalize negative externalities by mechanisms such as taxes, tradable permits, or direct control, these methods cannot work in an international organization such as ASEAN. Citizens within a state have already agreed on the direction they would like their country to take via voting. Likewise, ASEAN members need to do the same through negotiations or an agreement to decide on the rules of the game. What is important, therefore, is not whether members of a group will cooperate, but how they can be compelled to do so. The conditions under which they bind themselves to participate have to be specified. As such, it is less about tangible measures that aid enforcement but rather the initial commitment to do so.

In fact, ASEAN has in the past made some attempt to change its constitutive norms in order to fulfil its ambitious goal of the ASEAN Community. In 2007, the same year that ASEAN members decided on the construction of the AEC, the ASEAN Charter was adopted and ASEAN leaders declared it as "a historic milestone for ASEAN, representing our common vision and commitment to the development of an ASEAN Community" (ASEAN 2007a). The Charter, which came into force in 2008, purports to strengthen the Secretariat and Secretary-General, through measures such as appointing two additional Deputy Secretaries-General (Art 11.4) and providing the Secretariat with the "necessary financial resources to perform its functions effectively" (Art 30.1). It also promises to transform ASEAN into a more rules-based organization rather than a loosely organized association, the ASEAN Charter serves as an important step towards, and a confirmation of ASEAN's commitment to the realization of the AEC. However, many observers maintain that the willingness of member states to rely on regional institutions is still circumscribed by member states' attachment to the principle of sovereignty and overriding preference for maintaining unity amid regional diversity (Sukma 2014). For example, the Charter makes no changes to the formula for member state contributions. Thus, the ASEAN Secretariat remains underfunded and understaffed.

Indeed, the ASEAN Way has worked for ASEAN member states. When objectives and commitments are driven by a consensus process, it is more accommodative of the development differences of the member countries, thus providing flexibility and adjusting mechanisms in reaching the common end-goals. The ASEAN Way, purported to achieve equality amongst young, diverse and therefore fragile states, could perhaps be a mask over a more fundamental dynamic—that some members do not want an Association with increased capacity. They prefer to limit the capacity of ASEAN and for the locus of decision-making to remain within the national secretariats based in each member state's foreign ministry. Now, however, ASEAN faces a critical juncture where a real change has to occur.

This is not to say, however, that ASEAN should follow the path of Europe and establish an EU-style supranational government. In order to achieve the goals that ASEAN has set for itself, this paper argues that regional organization needs to realize that it needs a transformation of its constitutive norms and procedural rules away from the 'ASEAN Way'. ASEAN has already created a post-2015 vision, which lays down the economic initiatives for the near future. Instead, a reassessment of ASEAN norms and values should be examined first. Resources should be spent on rethinking and redeveloping a new ASEAN Way that will aid the integration process instead of impeding it. ASEAN members may have to re-examine its negotiating principles and recognize the obstacles their minimalist and reactive approach (Ferguson 2004) presents for deeper integration and institution building.

We cannot forget that the ASEAN Community has vowed to be a "people-centered" or people-oriented community. In fact, ASEAN decision makers have downgraded the vision of this community from a people-centered to a people-oriented ASEAN community, perhaps an indication of the continuing resistance among the region's leadership to a future where the state-centric security paradigm would be less dominant.

References

Abad, M. C. J. (1996). Re-engineering ASEAN. *Contemporary Southeast Asia, 18*(3), 237–253.

Acharya, A. (2014). *Foundations of collective action in Asia: Theory and practice of regional cooperation* (pp. 19–38). Japan: Springer.

ASEAN. (August 8, 1967). *The ASEAN Declaration (Bangkok Declaration).* Bangkok, Thailand. Retrieved December 11, 2015, from http://www.asean.org/the-asean-declaration-bangkok-declaration-bangkok-8-august-1967/.

ASEAN. (1976, February 24). Treaty of Amity and cooperation in Southeast Asia. *Bali, Indonesia.*

ASEAN. (2006). *Report of the eminent persons group on the ASEAN charter.* December, 2006, p. 21. Retrieved February 28, 2015, from http://www.asean.org/storage/images/archive/19247.pdf.

ASEAN. (November 20, 2007a). *Chairman's statement of the 13th ASEAN Summit, One ASEAN at the heart of dynamic Asia, Singapore.* Retrieved February 2, 2016, from http://www.asean.org/?static_post=chairman-s-statement-of-the-13th-asean-summit-one-asean-at-the-heart-of-dynamic-asia-singapore-20-november-2007.

ASEAN. (November 20, 2007b). *Charter of the association of Southeast Asian nations, Singapore.* Retrieved January 29, 2016, from http://www.asean.org/storage/images/ASEAN_RTK_2014/ASEAN_Charter.pdf.

ASEAN. (November 20, 2007c). *ASEAN economic community (AEC) blueprint.* Retrieved December 19, 2015, from http://www.asean.org/archive/5187-10.pdf.

ASEAN. (February 26, 2009). *ASEAN trade in goods agreement (ATIGA).* Retrieved January 7, 2016, from http://fta.miti.gov.my/miti-fta/resources/2.ASEAN_Trade_in_Goods_Agreement_.pdf.

Asia Regional Integration Center (ARIC). (2015). *Regional public goods.* Retrieved February 11, 2016, from https://aric.adb.org/regional_public_goods_beta.

Asian Development Bank (ADB). (2015, December 29). *ASEAN economic community: 12 things to know.* Retrieved January 4, 2016, from http://www.adb.org/features/asean-economic-community-12-things-know.

Asian Development Bank Institute (ADBI). (2014). ASEAN 2030: Toward a borderless economic community.

Basu Das, S. (2015). *The ASEAN Economic Community and Beyond.* ISEAS – Yusof Ishak Institute.

Buszynski, L. (1997). ASEAN's new challenges. *Pacific affairs*, 555–577.

Collignon, S. (2003). *The European republic: Reflections on the political economy of a future constitution.* London: Federal Trust for Education and Research.

Collignon, S. (2011). The governance of European public goods. In D. Tarschys (Ed.), *The EU budget: What should go in? What should go out?* (pp. 42–57). Stockholm: SIEPS.

Cuyvers, L. (2002). Contrasting the European Union and ASEAN integration and solidarity. Fourth EU-ASEAN think tank dialogue, European Parliament, Brussels.

Dosch, J. (2015). The ASEAN Economic Community: What stands in the way?

Ferguson, J. R. (2004). ASEAN Concord II: Policy prospects for participant regional development. *Contemporary Southeast Asia, 26*(3), 393–415.

Hu, A. G. (2013). ASEAN Economic Community business survey. In S. B. Das, J. Menon, R. C. Severino, & O. L. Shrestha (Eds.), *The ASEAN Economic Community: A work in progress* (Vol. 14). Institute of Southeast Asian studies.

Hübner, D. (2008). *EU regional policy post-2013: more of the same or a new beginning? European policy centre breakfast briefing* Available at: http://neurope.eu/article/europe-s-future-safe-cohesion-policy/.

Jayasuriya, K. (2004). *Asian regional governance: Crisis and change.* London: Routledge.

Jones, L. (2016). Explaining the failure of the ASEAN Economic Community: The primacy of domestic political economy. *The Pacific Review, 29*(5), 647–670.

Katsumata, H. (2003). Reconstruction of diplomatic norms in Southeast Asia: The case of strict adherence to the ASEAN way, *contemporary Southeast Asia, 25*(1).

Kawai, M. & Wignaraja, G. (2011a). Main findings and policy recommendations. In M. & G. W. Kawai (Eds.), *Asia's free trade agreements: How is business responding?* Cheltenham and Northampton: Asian development bank institute and Edward Elgar Publishing.

Kawai, M., & Wignaraja, G. (2011b). Asian FTAs: Trends, prospects and challenges. *Journal of Asian Economics, 22*(1), 1–22.

Kim, M. H. (2011). Theorizing ASEAN integration. *Asian Perspective, 35*(3), 407–435.

Langhammer, R. J. (1991). ASEAN economic co-operation: A stock-taking from a political economy point of view. *ASEAN Economic Bulletin*, 137–150.

Masujima, K. (2013). Is the "EU Model" relevant to other regions? MERCOSUR, ASEAN and adoption of regional policy. *Kobe University Law Review, 47*, 1–13.

Mattli, W. (1999). *The logic of regional integration: Europe and beyond*. Cambridge: Cambridge University Press.

Meade, J. E. (1973). *The theory of economic externalities*. Leiden: Sijthoff.

Murray, P. (2010). Comparative regional integration in the EU and East Asia: Moving beyond integration snobbery. *International Politics, 47*(3–4), 308–323.

Naya, S., & Plummer, M. G. (2005). *The economics of the enterprise for ASEAN initiative*. Institute of Southeast Asian studies.

Nesadurai, H. S. (2006). Southeast Asia's new institutional architecture for cooperation in economics and finance. *Berkeley APEC Study Center Working Paper*.

Pablo-Baviera, A. S. (2007). Regionalism and community building in East Asia: Challenges and opportunities. In M. Curley, & N. Thomas (Eds.), *Advancing East Asian regionalism*. London, New York: Taylor and Francis.

Panagariya, A. (1999). The regionalism debate: An overview. *The World Economy, 22*(4), 455–476.

Petri, P. A., Plummer, M. G., & Zhai, F. (2012). ASEAN economic community: A general equilibrium analysis. *Asian Economic Journal, 26*(2), 93–118.

Poole, A. (2011). *The state versus the secretariat: Capacity and the norm of equality in ASEAN, International Studies Association (ISA) Asia Pacific regional section inaugural conference, September, The University of Queensland*. Available at http://www.uq.edu.au/isaasiapacific/content/AveryPoole1-3.pdf.

Razak, N. A. (2015, January 28). *AEC 2015: A perspective from business*. Retrieved January 29, from http://www.lse.ac.uk/newsAndMedia/videoAndAudio/channels/publicLecturesAndEvents/player.aspx?id=2847.

Sandler, T. (1992). *Collective action: Theory and applications* (Vol. 4). Ann Arbor: University of Michigan Press.

Sandler, T. (1997). *Global challenges: An approach to environmental, political, and economic problems*. Cambridge: Cambridge University Press.

Sandler, T., & Forbes, J. F. (1980). Burden sharing, strategy, and the design of NATO. *Economic Inquiry, 18*(3), 425–444.

Severino R. (2006). *Southeast Asia in search of an ASEAN community: Insights from the former ASEAN Secretary-General*. Singapore: Institute of Southeast Asian Studies.

Shaffer, G. (2012). International law and global public goods in a legal pluralist world. *European Journal of International Law, 23*(3), 669–693.

Smith, A. (1999). Indonesia's role in ASEAN: The end of leadership? *Contemporary Southeast Asia, 21*(2), 238–261.

Sukma, R. (2014). ASEAN beyond 2015: The imperatives for further institutional changes. *ERIA Discussion Paper*. Jakarta: Economic Research Institute for ASEAN and East Asia.

Tongzon, J. L., & Khan, H. (2005). The challenge of economic integration for transitional economies of Southeast Asia: Coping with revenue losses. *ASEAN Economic Bulletin, 22*(3), 266–283.

Transparency International. (2015). *ASEAN integrity community: A vision for transparent and accountable integration*. Retrieved from http://files.transparency.org/content/download/1911/12654/file/Transparency+International+ASEAN+Integrity+Community_web.pdf.

United Nations Statistics Division (UNSD). (2013). *Country data services*. Retrieved March 3, 2016, from http://data.un.org/Default.aspx.

Venables, A. J. (2005). *Regional disparities in regional blocs: Theory and policy* (No. 24658). Washington, DC: Inter-American Development Bank.

Wesley, M. (1999). The Asian crisis and the adequacy of regional institutions. *Contemporary Southeast Asia, 21*(1), 54–73.

Winanti, P. S. (2012). Towards an ASEAN Community: The Challenges Ahead. *the 6th International Turkish – Asian Congress "Asian Union? Parameters of Politics, Security, Economy and Culture", Turkish Asian Center for Strategic Studies (TASAM),* Istanbul, 7 June 2012.

World Trade Organisation (WTO). (2016). *Integrated trade intelligence portal*. Retrieved March 2, 2016 from https://i-tip.wto.org/goods/Forms/MemberView.aspx?data=default.

Zuleeg, F. (2009, February). The rationale for EU action: What are European public goods?. In *workshop the political economy of EU public finances: Designing governance for change organized by the Bureau of European policy advisers,* European Commission. Brussels.

Index

© The Editor(s) (if applicable) and The Author(s) 2017
S. Collignon, *The Governance of European Public Goods*,
DOI 10.1007/978-3-319-64012-9

Printed by Printforce, the Netherlands